Passion and Paradox

Passion and Paradox

Intellectuals Confront The National Question

JOAN COCKS

PRINCETON UNIVERSITY PRESS

PRINCETON AND OXFORD

Library of Congress Cataloging-in-Publication Data

Cocks, Joan, 1947–
Passion and paradox : intellectuals confront the
national question / Joan Cocks.
p.   cm.
Includes bibliographical references and index.
ISBN 0-691-07467-4 (cloth : alk. paper) —
ISBN 0-691-07468-2 (pbk. : alk. paper)
1. Nationalism–Philosophy.   I. Title.
JC311 .C6135 2002
320.54′01 — dc21
2001038755

British Library Cataloging-in-Publication Data is available

This book has been composed in Sabon and Bernhard

Printed on acid-free paper. ∞

www.pup.princeton.edu

Printed in the United States of America

1   2   3   4   5   6   7   8   9   10

1   2   3   4   5   6   7   8   9   10
(Pbk.)

FOR PETER

MARK MAZOWER
Dark Continent:
Europe's Twentieth
Century

The First World War and the collapse of Europe's old continental empires signalled the triumph not only of democracy but also—and far more enduringly—of nationalism. With the extension of the principle of national self-determination from western to central and eastern Europe, the Paris peace treaties created a pattern of borders and territories which has lasted more or less up to the present. Yet the triumph of nationalism brought bloodshed, war and civil war in its train, since the spread of the nation-state to the ethnic patchwork of eastern Europe also meant the rise of the minority as a contemporary political problem. Where a state derived its sovereignty from the "people," and the "people" were defined as a specific nation, the presence of other ethnic groups inside its borders could not but seem a reproach, threat or challenge to those who believed in the principle of national self-determination.

ZYGMUNT BAUMAN
"Exit Visas and Entry
Tickets: Paradoxes of
Jewish Assimilation"

Universality is the war-cry of the underprivileged . . . [and] Jews were underprivileged . . . *universally* . . . The Jews, in [Isaac] Deutscher's poignant words, "dwelt on the borderlines of various civilizations, religions and national cultures . . . they lived on the margins . . . of their respective nations." As for the great Jewish prophets of universality, like Spinoza, Heine, Marx, or Rosa Luxemburg, "each of them was in society and yet not in it. It was this that enabled them to rise in thought above their societies, above their nations, above their times and generations, and to strike out mentally into wide new horizons and far into the future." The idea of redemption through universality was . . . at home in Jewish history. . . . [But it] was the most perverse paradox of emancipation that, under the banner of universality, it promoted a new particularization. In practice, it meant the renunciation of a specific *Jewish* particularity . . . at the price of embracing a new one, be it of a religious, national, or cultural kind.

AIJAZ AHMAD

Partitions make it seem as if liberation comes in the form of a series of surgical invasions.

Contents

Acknowledgments

When I was a child, my father told me to extend to strangers the same fair treatment I wanted for myself. My mother told me, "Take care of your own first, because no one else will." This book can be read as reflections at the friction point of these two principles, between which the whole world seems to sway. Even though beleaguered minorities have a special reason to believe that particularistic solidarity is for realists and universal justice is for dreamers, my own inclinations tilt strongly toward the dream. One result of that tilt is that many members of my own minority may be disturbed by critical comments on Jewish nationalism made between the covers of this book. I hope they will come to realize that my criticisms apply to all ethnonationalisms equally. That is, they concern not Jews or Judaism per se but the deformations that occur whenever any ethnic or religious or racial identity becomes the basis of a political community. Such deformations are inevitable even when historical events close off to an oppressed people all political paths except the ethnonational path.

Passion and Paradox owes a special debt to Bonnie Honig, who has been writing in her own, unique vein on foreignness and national identity. If my sympathies lie with a "new cosmopolitanism," my habits of life are rooted in one place, and Bonnie has been indefatigable in trying to push me out of my western Massachusetts shell. She bears some responsibility for this book, although not of course for its point of view, both because she was an unstinting reader of so many of its pages and because it was she who first insisted that I undertake it as a project.

The book's greatest debt is to Peter Cocks, who has kept up a running argument with me on the national question for more than a decade, turning every dinner conversation into a seminar and sometimes into a battle of clashing political positions. Out of the combustible material of our debates have come many of the lines of inquiry I pursue here. My favorite memory is of us each lying on our own bale of straw one sunny afternoon at Peter's brother's farm in Devon, looking out over the English countryside — so much still something out of Constable — and swapping views for hours on Tom Nairn. An irrepressible bibliophile and library lover, Peter was always on the lookout for material on nationalism while pursuing his own different research interests. He discovered many of the reviews and articles on which I draw here and at least one obscure book. I could not have had a more vociferous, stimulating, or generous intellectual companion.

Other people also deserve more than a word of thanks. Paul James and an anonymous second reader for Princeton University Press submitted well-considered and well-crafted comments on my manuscript. Ian Malcolm, my editor at Princeton, was warmly encouraging about the manuscript's destiny and, in his own suggestions for revision, applied just the right light but astute editor's touch. Jenn Backer was a sensitive copy-editor with a spartan approach to the comma. My dedicated friends Amrita Basu in political science at Amherst College, and Debbora Battaglia in anthropology and Karen Remmler in German studies at Mount Holyoke College, paid close attention to earlier versions of several of these chapters, which eased my task of improving them. Conversations at two faculty seminars were especially pivotal for me. The first was a Pew Foundation–funded Faculty Seminar on Ethnicity and Nationalism organized by Stephen Jones at Mount Holyoke College; the second, a Ford Foundation–funded Five College Faculty Symposium at Hampshire College titled "Rethinking Secularism and Human Rights," organized by Amrita Basu and Ali Mirsepassi. At that symposium, I was fortunate to have Pavel Machala as the commentator for my paper on nationalism and cosmopolitanism. His brilliant thoughts on the significance of exile deserve an essay of their own. It was at the same conference that the charismatic human rights activist, lawyer, and intellectual Abdullahi Ahmed An-Na'im made his unforgettable appearance. The words of this humane man convinced me that a "new universalism" is not simply an academic's fantasy but is already practiced in local settings all over the world.

I express my gratitude to Mount Holyoke College for awarding me several faculty fellowship and grants to fund my research.

Finally, although I may speak sharply of a number of thinkers in the pages that follow, almost every one of them has a favored place on my bookshelf.

Earlier versions of portions of the introduction, chapter 1, and chapter 2 appeared in "From Politics to Paralysis: Critical Intellectuals Answer the National Question," *Political Theory* 24, no. 3 (August

1996): 518–37. A briefer version of chapter 1 appeared as "Touché: Marx on Nations and Nationalism," *Socialism and Democracy* 11, no. 2 (Fall 1997): 47–70. A briefer version of chapter 2 appeared as "On Nationalism: Frantz Fanon, 1925–1961; Rosa Luxemburg, 1871–1919; and Hannah Arendt, 1906–1975," in *Feminist Interpretations of Hannah Arendt*, ed. Bonnie Honig (University Park: Pennsylvania State University Press, 1995), 221–45. A portion of chapter 2 appeared in "On Commonality, Nationalism, and Violence: Hannah Arendt, Rosa Luxemburg, and Frantz Fanon," *Women in German Yearbook: Feminist Studies in German Literature & Culture* 12, ed. Sara Friedrichsmeyer and Patricia Herminghouse (Lincoln: University of Nebraska Press, 1996), 39–51. A briefer version of chapter 3 appeared as "Individuality, Nationality, and the Jewish Question," *Social Research* 66, no. 4 (Winter 1999): 1191–1216. A briefer version of chapter 5 appeared as "Fetishizing Ethnicity, Locality, Nationality: The Curious Case of Tom Nairn," *Theory & Event* 1, no. 3 (Fall 1997): 1–20; and in *Arena Journal*, no. 10 (Spring 1998): 129–50. A briefer version of chapter 6 appeared as "A New Cosmopolitanism? V. S. Naipaul and Edward Said," *Constellations* 7, no. 1 (March 2000): 46–63.

Introduction

THE POLITICAL CONTEXT

Nationalism began to outweigh all other political problems for me in 1991, when a large segment of the American people backed the U.S. offensive against Iraq in retaliation for Iraq's invasion of Kuwait. Inevitably, the Gulf War flagged that enduring question in the modern age of how a first state is able to whip up popular feeling against a second, often for its intrusions in a more distant third. Why do the citizens of any one state see themselves as violated by violations of the sovereignty and borders of another state they may know or care little about? How is the identification of a people not only with its own state but also with the entire state system accomplished, and to what ends?

In common with the whole post–cold war period, however, the war raised knottier questions about the meaning of ethnic identity and the relation of ethnicity to nationalism and the nation-state. These questions surfaced in a personal sense when, for the first time in my life, I joined a political organization as a Jew rather than simply as an individual with these or those principles and ideals. The organization, "Arabs and Jews against the Gulf War," so publicly allied two peoples who were usually bitter foes that I was drawn to it, even though my criticism of the Gulf War was not a function in any direct way of what I was, as opposed to what I thought. But once inside the group—which, alas, lived only as briefly as the war did—I was confronted with new puzzles that had nothing to do with the popular magnetism of states but a great deal to do with what it means to belong to a people. On the one hand, in addition to shared objections to U.S. military hubris, there was what I can only describe as a family resemblance among all the individuals in the room uncharacteristic of any other political movement I had known. The gestures, intonations, sense of humor, and manner of expression of thought and feeling were immediately familiar to me in the case of the Jews and vaguely familiar to me in the case of the Arabs. The atmosphere had something about it for which no English word comes to mind but which the Yiddish word *haimish* nearly captures.[1] On the other hand, the group was split along more particularistic lines in its attitude toward the national question. Every Jew in the

room was, as one of them, Paul Breines, put it, "tone-deaf to nationalism." This condition partly could be traced to the leftist politics
that separated the Jews in the group from all Jews outside it who
supported Israel as a Jewish state, thereby proving the banality of the
phrase "the Jewish community." But as I dimly realized even then,
such tone deafness also registered the modern history of a diasporic
minority threatened by movements against the multinational European empires on the part of those vying to become majority peoples
of their own nation-states. In contrast, all the Arabs in the room
were scathing in their criticisms of Middle Eastern regimes for being
reactionary and antipopular — and proudly declared themselves Arab
nationalists.

These similarities and incongruities among Jews and Arabs against
the Gulf War pushed me to bracket my own hostility to nationalism
in order to investigate it as a real question, instead of a question that
already had repudiation for its answer. But the further I plunged into
my research, the more this question seemed to generate new paradoxes and conundrums. Every theoretical explanation of nationalism
ultimately gave way to its own negation. Every assessment of the
value of nationalist movements was inadequate in the absence of
some other assessment with which it was mutually exclusive. Every
practical response to nationalism in politics promised as many disturbing as reassuring results. The only conclusions it was possible to
reach and the only decisions it was possible to make were of the sort
Bonnie Honig has dubbed "dilemmatic."[2] That is, all paths of
thought obscured equally telling contrary thoughts; all paths of action were strewn with causes for regret and remorse. Moreover,
these conundrums were intrinsic to nationalism and so were inescapable elements of all epochs in which nationalism plays a central
part.

One of those epochs has clearly turned out to be our own. In the
pauses between violent contests among states such as the Gulf War,
dilemmas of national belonging, assertion, and exclusion might have
sunk back to the level of the merely theoretical. Instead, our age has
witnessed an escalation of tensions articulated in ethnic terms, a mi-
gration of peoples sometimes as cause and sometimes as consequence of state-orchestrated ethnic persecution, and a surge of separatist nationalist politics worldwide. It may be awkward to recall it
after Bosnia and Kosovo, but the West's initial response at least to
ethnonational movements in the disintegrating Soviet Empire was

one of great glee, as if bids for national self-determination assured the triumph of democracy and freedom over the communist world. I happened to be teaching Rosa Luxemburg during this bright, fleeting moment of the new nationalisms. She supplied all the reasons why the West's affirmation was at worst opportunistic — as she would have put it, it would not be the first time that Western liberals had thrown their cards in with nationalism against communism — and at best exceptionally naive. Luxemburg was condemned in her day and has been dismissed in ours as someone obtuse to the genuinely populist realities of nationalism. Still, this passionate Marxist was far more alert at the beginning of the century to the incendiary potentialities of nationalism wherever diverse peoples are intertwined than liberals were near the end. Anyone who read Luxemburg in the late 1980s could have predicted all that speedily occurred afterward.

This book was written mainly during this decade of high nationalist drama, punctuated at one end by the first glimmerings of the new nationalist movements in the Soviet Union, at the other end by the crushing of the Serbian campaign against Albanian Kosovars, and in between by the genocidal war against the Tutsis in Rwanda, the "hurricane of violence"[3] in multicultural Bosnia, communal strife in India, and a host of other ethnic upheavals from Germany to Turkey to Indonesia to the United States. The politics of the period are reflected in the three threads of intention that with varying degrees of visibility weave their way through my chapters. One thread is the attempt to understand the disparate tendencies of thought that inform a sympathy for ethnonationalism, a sympathy for heterogeneous political community, and sometimes a contradictory sympathy for both. A second thread is the attempt to dive for pearls among the wreckage of old universalist ideas in order to help crystallize a new way of linking an appreciation of cultural particularity and variety to a feeling of solidarity across "difference" lines. A third thread is an attempt to consider how nonparticipants might judge and act in response to ventures in ethnic cleansing.

The discerning reader will notice that the book's introduction and conclusion, written last, are much more chastened with respect to this third thread than the book's earliest main chapters. After NATO's bombing of the Serbs, the Serbs' initial success at driving ethnic Albanians from Kosovo, and the revenge of the Albanian Kosovars against the Serbs and the Gypsies, it is less easy to be sure of the relative virtues of action and inaction on the part of those who wish to stop atrocities inside any state other than their own. For individuals, simply being on the outside is a problem, although one would have to worship the state form in order to see it as an insurmountable problem. The typical outsider's ignorance of the complexities of the inside is a worse problem, even if it is only a highly exaggerated version of the ignorance that any self has of everything outside itself — and of much inside itself too, for that matter. When the outsider is a state rather than a person, another kind of trouble compounds this one. The participation of all states in domestic cruelties of various kinds, the self-interest of states in upholding the inviolability of borders, and the gross inequality of power internationally mean that most states will have neither the will nor the capacity to orchestrate interventions against atrocities elsewhere, while the few that are strong enough in capacity always will be susceptible to the charge of hypocrisy and Machiavellianism, whether they have the will to intervene or not. But it is the effectiveness of intervention, the ability of even the most knowledgeable and well-intentioned international organizations to secure a better rather than worse fate for targets of ethnic violence, that now appears catastrophically unclear. Hannah Arendt makes the compelling argument that not self-determination but creativity, not the absolute control of action but the unpredictability of action and its consequences, is the true condition of human freedom. Still, such unpredictability can bring to life as much tragedy as adventure. It also guarantees that we never can know after the fact if some other action would have led to as great a tragedy as an action that was actually taken.

Moreover, the historical precedents for any current crisis are often unclear and always politically contestable and thus can never be a fully reliable guide for determining how that crisis should be met. For example, many postcolonial and left-wing intellectuals attacked the bombing of Kosovo by assimilating it to instances of imperialist intervention for the sake of magnifying the power of the United States rather than to a new form of internationalist intervention to stop crimes against humanity. They cited as evidence the record of U.S. interventions to prop up right-wing regimes, along with the failure of the United States to intervene against ethnic persecution in countries where it considered the victimized populations unimportant or where the victimizing parties were allies of the West. For other critics, some of them also left-wing, Kosovo was reminiscent not of Central America and Vietnam but of the interwar period in

Europe that climaxed in the Holocaust. If the Allied powers had intervened with force in Germany before the end of the 1930s, these critics had reason to wonder, would that intervention have accelerated the murder of thousands and the expulsion of millions of Jews? And would six million refugees have horrified the world at the time, while that same number could only appear a miraculous gift to Jews looking backward today? Against both positions, certain Balkan specialists argued that the situation in Kosovo was so complicated that it could only be treated as sui generis. They also implied that only those who understood the complexities of the area could possibly determine the right response to them.[4] And indeed, area specialists might be, perhaps, the best authorities on what outsiders should do in a given situation, if situations were always unique instead of echoing or connecting to other events, times, and places and if political judgment were a function of empirical knowledge alone, rather than of a political perspective on, interest in, and cunning about the world, more or less empirically well-informed.

NATIONALISM IN POLITICS

The focus of this volume is on nationalism in politics, especially the drive for political unity by any group that asserts itself as ethnically distinct and self-identical, but also on claims to national distinctiveness and self-identity by established states. The felt grounds for such assertions may be racial, religious, linguistic, historico-political, civilizational, or what Michael Ignatieff describes as minor differences among similar peoples narcissistically reconceived as major differences.[5]

The purpose of this volume is to probe, in the context of nationalism in politics, how one might think, feel, and judge in order to act well. This is the oldest political philosophical question, and the ancients who originally asked it did so under the cover of two overarching presumptions. One was the presumption of an objective order of truth and value penetrable by philosophical reason, against which differing ideas, feelings, and judgments about the world could themselves be judged. The other was the presumption that not only theoretical wisdom about the eternal cosmos but also the practical wisdom required to act well in the flux of political life were prerogatives of those with the essential aptitude, cultivated intelligence, and social leisure for philosophical investigations. Both the assurance of an objective moral order and the limitation of political excellence to a philosophically educated elite long since have been weakened by modernity's relativizing and democratizing tendencies. This does not mean, however, that the political philosophical question is no longer pertinent. To the contrary, the semi-decline of the idea of objective truth and value means that questions of how to think, feel, and judge in order to act will be more perplexing because they are intrinsically open-ended: they are real questions rather than staged or artificial steps to an answer that is fixed in advance. This change in the logic of questioning from the classical period to our own implies that different political perspectives may point the way to different judgments and decisions that are equally compelling within their distinctive worldviews. In turn, the semi-decline of the idea of a philosophically cultivated political elite means that the question of how to think in order to act should be treated as a question not just for any political perspective but for any person with any stake in the world. That is, it should be posed as a question not for the privileged and powerful few but, hypothetically at least, for everyone.

If this book's interest in the questions that nationalism raises for everyone distinguishes it on the one side from classical political philosophy, it distinguishes it on the other from many other contemporary studies of nationalism. The purpose of those studies is to understand the origins, or causes, or historical development, or popular resonance, or economic functions either of nationalism in general or of some nationalist movement in particular. Mark Beissinger complains, with specific reference to Ernest Gellner, that contemporary scholars of nationalism in general have downplayed its political and hence contingent elements in favor of its structural and seemingly inevitable determinants.[6] My related complaint is that scholars too often position themselves as if they were peering in from the outside on the constellation of elements of which nationalism is a part, thereby evading their own political entanglement in that constellation. There are, to be sure, many advantages to taking a temporary position of principled detachment from the world, as if one had come to it from elsewhere. One can see, microscopically, all the details of a given situation and how they appear from all the different engaged perspectives on it as well as, macroscopically, the larger patterns made by different situations that are significantly alike. The danger of detachment is that it can freeze into a permanent posture.

This happens when those who look down on ordinary mortals invested in the play of politics delude themselves into thinking that they have no political investments of their own. It also happens when those who look down become immobilized by seeing so much from so many angles that every conceivable course of action seems hopelessly coarse and one-sided. Professional intellectuals are especially susceptible to such self-deception and political paralysis.

Like social scientific analysis, a political philosophical consideration of how to think and act entails a moment of detachment or abstraction from immediately lived life. Still, political philosophy must find a way to convey and promote a passion for that life rather than an aloofness from it. Michael Ignatieff, who addresses the same kind of normative-practical questions that I do, combines passion and abstraction by interviewing participants in ethnic conflicts and then musing on the ethical dilemmas such conflicts raise for insiders and outsiders alike. My own, admittedly more self-serving method is to look to intellectuals forced by history to confront the national question, who reflected on politics in order to decide how to step into or sidestep the fray, and whose writings illustrate how particular lines of thought and feeling open up into particular lines of action. Inevitably, there will seem to be something in this tack of the ancients' prejudice for those who are philosophically cultivated over everyone else. The individuals on whom I draw — Karl Marx, Rosa Luxemburg, Hannah Arendt, Frantz Fanon, Isaiah Berlin, Tom Nairn, Edward Said, and V. S. Naipaul — elaborated theoretical positions (or, in Naipaul's case, literary narratives) on ethnic identity, belonging, national self-determination, internationalism, cosmopolitanism, and rootlessness. They all published their ideas in pamphlets, articles, and books. Again with the possible exception of Naipaul, whose ties to the Hindu nationalist Bharatiya Janata Party remain somewhat obscure, they played noteworthy roles as theoreticians of political parties, as troublesome gadflies in political movements, or as confidants of political leaders and policymakers behind the scenes. The fact that they were intellectuals who left public marks on the world makes it possible to study their commitments and ideas. It is unavoidable that the same fact distinguishes them as special cases — more famous or infamous than most people, and more indefatigably reflective about the predicaments that nationalism precipitates. But they are also ordinary cases in not being professional experts on those predicaments. They grappled with the national question not to accumulate specialized knowledge about it but to light a way for themselves and others through the semi-darkness of political life.

What accounts for the semi-darkness of nationalism in politics? The obscurity begins with the category itself. On the one hand, "nationalism" and its cognates "the nation," "nationality," and "the nation-state" can be said to cover political identities based on the experience of shared ethnic ancestry or "blood," cultural heritage, and the memory, if not the physical actuality, of a homeland.[7] On the other hand, ethnonationalism can be considered only one variety of nationalism, the most prominent other being based on common citizenship, subjection to the same laws, and habitation in a unified geographical territory. Then again, these two kinds of nationalism with such different starting points — ethnic and civic — seem to reach the same practical conclusion when they are successful. In the first case, the experience of a common ethnic identity leads to a national movement to create a political state; in the second case, the development of a political state leads to the solidification of a national culture and the consolidation of a new people.[8] If ethno- and civic nationalism do inevitably converge, one must wonder if there ever can be a people that does not ultimately imagine itself in ethnic terms or a state that does not legitimate its power by recourse to such imaginings.

Equally murky are the conceptual relationships among "nationalism," "the people," and "the state." This is so because the category of nationalism is elastic enough to accommodate both a state-generated or state-manipulated collective identity and an identity that rises from the bottom up and is as likely to work against the established state as for it. That category also covers movements whose impetus is neither official nor popular but derives instead from an ambitious intelligentsia or an ascending economic class. If political concepts simply served the purposes of analytic rigor, talk about nationalism could be clarified by assigning a different word to each different idea. But political concepts have their foundation in life, and the life of ethnicities, nationalities, peoples, and nation-states is enough of a morass that these entities frequently run into one another in practice. The concepts of ethnicity, nationality, peoples, and nation-states do, and must, follow suit.

The connotative complexity of these concepts permits clashing explanations of what they denote as the same thing. For example, scholars who highlight the ethnic aspect of nation-ness will tend to trace the chronological origins of modern nations to older ethnic identities and the ontological origins of national feeling to some humanly fundamental experience of group belonging. Scholars who foreground the political aspect of the nation will hook national solidarities to modern historical changes in the late eighteenth, nineteenth, and twentieth centuries that redivided the world along politically independent and ideologically populist nation-state lines. In turn, those who point to the ethnic origin of nations are likely to see national identity as long-lived enough to be counted as almost biologically rooted, while those who underscore the nation's modernity will see national identity as culturally fabricated and historically contingent. Attitudes toward the relative coherence of national identity versus its propensity for internal contradiction and fracture do not divide as neatly along essentialist and constructionist lines. Those who are adamant about the modernity of nationhood are capable of seeing national identity as internally stable and unitary,[9] while those who tie modern nation-ness to older ethnic identifications can be more aware of national identity's transmogrifications and fractures precisely because they take the historical long view. Over three thousand instead of three hundred years, any identity is bound to vary, splinter, and mutate.

The complexity of nationalism does not lie only or even mainly at the level of conceptualization. There is also no political phenomenon more ambiguous than this "terrible beauty" from an evaluative point of view. Strong communal feeling, a sense of cultural distinctiveness, the love of a particular landscape, pride in shared historical accomplishments, a collective political agency — seen from another angle, these virtues become the vices of a suspicion of critics inside the community, a contempt for foreigners outside, a drive to dispossess aliens and conquer new territory, a self-mystified relation to the past, a collective political bellicosity. The negative features of nationalism are so weirdly the same features as the positive that anyone who reflects on the national question must have a high tolerance for contradiction and double-sidedness.

These evaluative ambiguities forecast the moral-political quandaries that confront every age in which politics have taken a nationalist turn. What constitutes a people, historically, geographically, and, to use an old-fashioned but fitting term, spiritually? Does national identity merit territorial autonomy? Is national self-determination a condition of political freedom? Of human freedom? Whose will makes up the national will? Does national identity require national homogeneity, and if so, what is the fate in a national community of ethnic and racial minorities, diaspora populations, immigrants, and "guestworkers"?

Everyone pitched into nationalist conflicts will be pressed to take a stand on such questions. The answers to them, however, are not objective truths waiting to be discovered but possibilities that become actualities through collective efforts to inscribe in the world this idea of the nation or that. Nationalism's most exhilarating feature is its capacity for wrenching a group out from under the heel of a more powerful group, if necessary by matching physical force with physical force. At the same time, its most disturbing feature is its capacity for inscribing its own positive idea of the nation through violence. The capacity becomes a propensity with the victory of the view that the quandaries of constituting a people, a national will, and a national identity can be settled once and for all by persecution, dispossession, exclusion, and annihilation. If nationalist violence drives such quandaries into the minds of participants and onlookers alike, it quickly drives them out again, as the brute material realities of warfare, mass rape, coerced refugee marches, and genocidal killings obliterate all speculative thought about collective identity. In any case, while physical force sometimes may be the only way to overcome physical force, it logically cannot resolve moral-political problems. This is why these problems always surface again after nationalist wars have been lost or won.[10]

Nationalism raises its conceptual, evaluative, and moral-practical questions for intellectuals because it raises those questions for everyone. But nationalism also raises important questions about intellectuals as a separate group.

One such question concerns the tension between the intellectual's mental constitution as a critical thinker and social constitution as a member of a group whose status and power has come to depend on its control over the language, literature, and public life of a national society.

As professional critics, intellectuals are likely to be skeptical of nationalist claims, given that those claims always have a mythical dimension to them[11] and given that it is the overriding impulse of the intellectual to puncture myths. Moreover, in comparison with social types either settled in one place or bound to that place by memory and longing, intellectuals tend to be imaginatively and often physi-

cally deracinated. They are frequently unmindful of inherited affiliations, attuned to the pleasures of exile,[12] and cynical about communities of any sort, the more cosmopolitan among them being estranged from all particular settings or, to put the point positively,
living perpetually as universal "citizens of the world."[13] Driven by
the desire for individual honor and prestige, and priding themselves
on their independence of mind and their imperviousness to the emo-
tions of the crowd, intellectuals also can be expected to find mass
movements irritating and upsurges of nationalism among the masses
nerve-racking, although those among them who are power hungry
and politically astute may be willing to manipulate nationalist sentiments for their own self-aggrandizing ends. Finally, intellectuals by
constitution are unhappy with anything in life that is unexamined
and simply given and so would be likely to gravitate away from
identities and solidarities that are a function of ethnic lineage or state
dictation, toward those that are freely constructed and self-con-
sciously chosen.[14] This antipathy toward the unexamined and simply
given is so pronounced that even intellectuals who are antirationalist
in their ideals of identity and solidarity rely on critical-rational argument to make their case.[15]

Yet there are good reasons to contest the claim that intellectuals as
a social group are immune to the partialities and prejudices of nationalism. Intellectuals may be stylistically agile enough to speak and
write in the language of pure aestheticism, moral disinterestedness,
or philosophical universalism, but this does not mean they do not
cloak special interests and commitments underneath, including nationalist interests and commitments. Historically, furthermore, intellectuals have played a central affirmative part in the development of
nationalist movements. As linguists, teachers, journalists, poets, and
political philosophers, they have generated and disseminated ideas
and myths of nationhood.[16] As political orators and leaders inflamed
by passion for a larger cause, they have mobilized people into nations who once were identified with a locality, social stratum, or
tribe. In the modeling of new nationalisms after old ones, intellectuals have been the first social segment to absorb, through formal
education and professional training, ideas of nationhood and values
of national self-determination. They also have had strong class interests in supporting nationalist movements when the political autonomy of their own language group would win them a monopoly of

positions in education, communications, artistic production, the state bureaucracy, and the law.[17]

Another important question about the intellectual's relation to nationalism concerns the tension between the intellectual's critical mentality and political affinities when those affinities are even distantly democratic. The tension between criticism and democracy has generated two vexing predicaments for the intellectual in the nationalist context. The first is the predicament of alienation from the people on the part of intellectuals who align themselves with popular causes while criticizing nationalism for being based on illusion, self-delusion, ressentiment, and/or a dialectic of rebellion that begins in a desire for justice but ends in injustice. These intellectuals may try to fight against, or transform from within, or expose, or ameliorate, or simply outwait nationalist movements, but in all cases their criticism puts them at odds with the people on behalf of whom they think and act. The second is the predicament of alienation from politics on the part of intellectuals who appreciate, defend, and even celebrate the popular resonance of the national narrative, or fiction, or myth, without believing in that myth. Such intellectuals are as unable to be out-and-out nationalists as they are unwilling to be out-and-out anti-nationalists. One might say, at a gross level of generalization, that these two forms of alienation are opposed and that the first kind is more characteristic of intellectuals in the first half of the twentieth century and the second more characteristic of intellectuals today. But at a finer level of magnification, the two kinds of alienation can be seen logically and chronologically to overlap. Many thinkers in this book move back and forth between them.

Besides exhibiting, in different ways, the strain between critical reflexes and popular politics, the intellectuals I have chosen to explore have much to recommend them as a set. Most important, from a theoretical standpoint, they are deft at handling the conceptual antinomies that crowd this field. The antinomy of particularism and universalism stars in every discussion of the national question and in my discussion, too. Other key antinomies include, roughly in the order of their appearance in the text: civil society and political society; class division and national unity; ethno- and civic nationalism; separation and assimilation; liberal individualism and national-cultural pluralism; the country and the city; tradition and modernity; and nationalism and cosmopolitanism. A few antinomies take the form of ideal types: the pariah and the parvenu; the native and the exile. A few, finally, are methodological, providing the means to challenge what Alasdair MacIntyre once called the self-images of the age. Thus, many of my thinkers implicitly or explicitly draw on the distinctions between surface and depth, center and periphery, or darkness and light to capture, respectively, hidden aspects of power, inequalities of identities and regions, and disfigurements of private and public life.

As personalities, my thinkers display a wide variety of temperaments: some earnest, others ironic; some optimistic, others despairing; some kindhearted, others caustic. Their politics stretch from the left to the right and their habits of thought from the systematic to the picaresque. They write in response to different decades of the twentieth century, with the obvious exception of Marx, and they bear the markings of different cultures and regions. At the same time, they are tied together by similar preoccupations and the fact that almost all of them are exiles of some sort. Marx migrates from Prussia to France to England; Luxemburg moves among Russia, Switzerland, Germany, and Poland; Arendt flees from Germany to France to the United States. Fanon moves from Martinique to France to Algeria; Berlin emigrates from Russia to England; Said leaves Palestine for Egypt and then for the United States, afterward crisscrossing all the great world capitals; Naipaul makes his way from the Caribbean to England, and from there makes his innumerable visits to the Americas, Africa, and Asia. Only Nairn, the staunchest defender of nationalism of the lot, does not have the exile's tangled geographical roots and ambiguous geographical location. Even so, he is a traveler in his political imagination, sweeping his sights over Scotland, Great Britain, Europe, and nationalist struggles against imperial power across the globe. As for the others, many move from one place to another as the result of coercion of some sort, but they also are voluntary wanderers, propelled from place to place by political commitments, social connections, and/or intellectual curiosity. Their heightened sensitivity to the national question is not happenstance. As Said reminds us, anyone catapulted out of his or her native place will likely be hyperconscious of place and belonging. That same person also will be poised to look at the old home, the new, and the very idea of "home" with an acute because alienated, although not unblinkered, eye.

I selected my thinkers for their representative intellectual and personal qualities, but my tastes — aesthetic, theoretical, political — have much to do with their array. These tastes help explain my point of departure with Marx, which puts me politically at odds with Ignatieff and Gellner, even though such liberals owe their own debt to universalist philosophy and exhibit their own universalist insights and blindnesses. Ignatieff, for example, often writes as if a civilized and humanistic West faced a violent and particularistic rest, as if liberalism were the only source of a universalistic ethic, and as if Marxism were merely a synonym for Soviet-style oppression or even a form of particularistic identity politics, rather than a competing Enlightenment tradition with a concomitant set of virtues and vices.[18] Gellner makes similarly sweeping distinctions between the West's appreciation of the true conditions of freedom and the impulse to tyranny of everyone else, especially those in "backward" nations and Islamic societies. Although he views "free economic enterprise" as civil society's necessary condition, Gellner describes liberal civil society in lofty philosophical terms far removed from capitalism's gritty realities. He attributes Marxist criticisms of those realities to a communist totalitarian mentality, and Marxism's lack of popular appeal as a state ideology to the merciless demands it makes on individuals through its sacralization of the secular world. On the latter grounds, however, nationalism should have failed, too. One must demur that for Marxism's unattractiveness to "the people," its stringent and unforgiving rationalism, not its religiosity, is really to blame.[19]

My point of departure also separates me from many contemporary critics on the left. For both advocates of identity politics and Habermasians, Marxism's treatment of national identity and national political unity as a function of capital accumulation, as secondary to class division, and as shot through with mystifications makes it substantively wrongheaded and epistemologically antidemocratic. For postmodernists, so do Marx's rationalism and universalism, which they, unlike Ignatieff and Gellner, darkly underline. Today, left-leaning thinkers in general champion the particular, the local, the self-generated creative fiction, the collective solidarity that is spontaneously felt as a function of identity or desire rather than chosen on the basis of instrumental or critical reason. I hope to show, against all these positions, the fruitfulness of Marxism as a way into conundrums of nationalism that are, as of yet, unresolved.

Marxism, however, is not the point of arrival of this book or the only path taken to get there. I examine modernist and postmodernist tendencies of thought, liberal pluralist positions, and anti- and post-colonial perspectives that issue from (to use terms that may sound outmoded) revolutionary, conservative, and radical camps. But it is the singular Hannah Arendt, a partisan of no camp at all, who haunts this volume more than anyone else. This is partly because the interwar period Arendt studied—with its collapsing multinational empires, its aggressive majority peoples, its persecuted minorities and stateless refugees—so eerily resembles our own. It is also because Arendt understood the essential lineaments of her own time in her own time, without being trapped inside the myopic limits of her time. This is why she can speak with what seems like exquisite timelessness to us.

THE JEWISH QUESTION

The Gulf War piqued my interest in the national question, and the unfolding catastrophe in the former Yugoslavia sustained it. But books have a way of taking off in surprising although not accidental directions, and in this one it was the emergence of the Jewish question that surprised me. In hindsight that emergence seems entirely predictable. I had avoided the national question for most of my life, in part because other questions seemed more pressing to me and to my generation but also because of my almost instinctive antipathy toward nationalist sentiments. One deep source of that antipathy were the bits and pieces I had picked up as a child about the terrible effects European nationalism had on the Jewish diaspora and a growing anxiety, as *I* grew, that a Jewish state was fated to follow some variant of nationalism's logic of discrimination, persecution, and expulsion. Once I confronted the national question instead of evading it, the Jewish implications of that question surfaced like the return of the repressed. Perhaps that is why, of the thinkers I chose to explore initially for other reasons, Marx, Luxemburg, Arendt, and Berlin all happened to be Jews (although, to be sure, Marx was baptized, and Marx and Luxemburg detested religion). Their own interest in Jewish identity prompted Berlin and Arendt to inspect the lives of other controversial Jews, who also make guest appearances here. Finally, for Berlin the question of Israel/Palestine was pressing; for Arendt it was urgent; for Said it is burning. These details lend a certain particularistic quality to this volume—but then, particularism is always what the national question purports to be about. Nevertheless, I strongly agree with the early, skeptical Nairn when he writes, with his signature sarcasm:

> Most approaches to the . . . [huge and complicated problem of nationalism] are vitiated from the start by a country-by-country attitude. Of course, it is the ideology of world nationalism itself which induces us along this road, by suggesting that human society consists essentially of several hundred different and discrete "nations", each of which has (or ought to have) its own postage-stamps and national soul. The secret of the forest is the trees, so to speak. Fortunately, this is just the usual mangled half-truth of commonsense.[20]

Regardless of its self-delusions, nationalism is never wholly or even primarily about self-contained particulars. The case of Jewish nationalism embraces the special situation of the Jewish minority in European society. However, it also has to do with the special threat that nationalist movements pose to all those whom the Jewish Algerian writer, Albert Memmi, once self-referentially called half-breeds; the conditions common to all diasporas; and the same larger dilemmas about belonging, citizenship, exclusion, and obligation to outsiders that every other special case of nationalism entails.[21]

These larger dilemmas are this book's real subject of inquiry. Hence its destination is not a resolution of the question of Israel or Yugoslavia or any other specific nationalist conflict. Neither is its destination a single formula for the ideal political community, which would only be a new assault on the variety of cultures that, against all odds, still manage to cling to the world. Instead, the book concludes with what I see as two necessary conditions of political community today that are unfulfilled and unfulfillable by the nation-state form. The first, "nationalist" condition is an effective, material respect for the human attachment to place that the British conservative Michael Oakeshott calls "the love of the familiar." This condition requires that political communities provide and safeguard, from both the political pressures of ethnic homogenization and the economic pressures of the infinite accumulation of wealth, a home in the world for all human beings. The second, "cosmopolitan" condition is a popular, visceral delight in human variety inside political unity, which is not at all the same thing as an intellectual affirmation of variety between one political society and another. This condition requires an amelioration of group resentments and humiliations that drive collective searches for recognition and movements for national self-determination. It requires the extension to all those who live within the borders of a state, for the time they live there, whatever political rights and obligations the citizens of that state enjoy. Most elusive of all, it requires a release of the springs that snap open hearts and minds to the reciprocal engagement with strangers that Said rightly praises as "true worldliness."

Chapter One

Karl Marx Uncovers the Truth of National Identity

SURFACES AND DEPTHS

Many thinkers in our period have been entranced by the notion of life as a horizontal play of appearances across the shimmering surface of reality. "Appearances" are taken to be performances, or narratives, or self-interpretations, and "reality" to be those performances, narratives, and self-interpretations in their shifting and multiple forms. The idea that reality is made solely of appearances has the virtue of cultivating the human eye extensively, by preparing it to see the sheer plenitude of the world. But the different notion of life as vertically layered into surface and depth, though now much out of favor, has its own virtue of cultivating the eye intensively, by training it to look for aspects of the world hidden from immediate view. These aspects include thoughts, words, and deeds shuttered out of privacy and tact by a self not entirely disclosed in or identical with its performances. They include sediments of social thought and practice that have been deposited over too long a time to appear before the viewer on a single plane. They include not merely the memory of the past and discursive constructions of the present but also the past denied by memory and the present betrayed by discursive constructions of it. They include the pressure on empirical practice of an inner logic or structured system of practice. Finally, they include stakes in life that are at once significant and unsettling enough to require distortions, dissemblances, and outright lies.[1]

Life understood as performance, or narrative, or self-interpretation does not appeal only to the disembodied intellect. It offers its audience the sensuous enjoyment of theatricality, or the literary delights of the imaginatively told tale, or the heartwarming satisfactions of empathetic understanding. Similarly, the idea of a deeper reality under the surface of things is one kind of conception but also one kind of pleasure. That idea offers the intellectual thrill of searching for the solution to a mystery and the psychological charge in the chain of activities that runs from suspecting to detecting to exposing. The intensity of this thrill and charge, which is a function not just of finding truth at the bottom but of finding doors that must be unlocked all the way down, is the reason why the idea of life as surface and depth can be defended not merely on the substantive grounds that life has a depth to it but also on the aesthetic grounds that life is enchanting when it is looked at that way. Transparency in social life may be the declared goal of depth analysis, but the endless generation of secrets to be uncovered must be *its* secret hope.[2]

An intuitive sense of the enchantments of detection as opposed to, say, the charms of theatricality can be obtained by thinking in the intimate sphere of the difference between the casual attraction and the fierce attachment, or the one-night stand and the episode in which the intimates' words and movements last night refer not only to themselves that night but backward to other nights, other words, other movements, as well as forward to anticipations of nights not yet lived. This difference is not moral or even utilitarian in significance, with "closer" and "deeper" standing for "more virtuous" or "happier." Duplicity, jealousy, cruelty, and betrayal only really come into their own in the second cases. It is then, to take the example of duplicity, that there will be reasons not merely for the fabrications of gesture, manner, and costume by which any self presents itself to any other but also for the fabrications by which one self obscures from a particular other some desire, incident, or mood—obscures it both because it is explosive through breaking with an established pattern to which that self still is committed and because it is more real and true than the fabrication that masks it.[3] Depth in intimacy does not exactly hinge on vaguenesses and concealments that mask something else underneath. It is rather that the constant lengthening and tightening of the tie between intimates provides ever more material off which suppression and convolution can work, an ever greater stake in deceiving or distorting, and thus an ever growing object for mental and emotional interest. That interest can be sustained, as well, when at least one participant in an encounter is deep even though the encounter is not, through that self's inclination to self-inspection, or special sensitivity to the registrations of experience, or morbid entanglement in half-buried memories, or constitutional propensity for hypocrisy and deceit. Depth of character in any of these ways guarantees that there is something in a relation to be discovered and revealed, even if the superficiality of a relation means that there is no one to exact the revelation, barring the arrival on the scene of a confessor, confidant, or voyeur.[4]

The same magnetism of life understood as surface and depth that we have seen in the intimate sphere holds good in the public sphere, using that term in its broadest sense to cover all other social relations. Although the very definition of the public sphere rules out as an element of its magnetism thoughts, words, and deeds that are shuttered from general view because they are private, the other elements reemerge here with increased force. The sedimentation of thought and practice over time; the tension between the past and the memory of the past, the present and constructions of the present; the pressure of an inner structure on empirical practice; the veiling of significant stakes — all are magnified in the public sphere because of its panoramic sweep, which takes in not two or three people but two hundred, or two thousand, or two million. The social significance of what is revealed and what is concealed in the public sphere provides one reason why nineteenth-century depth theorists were driven to devise a whole battery of categories that, to suit a more impersonal and expansive setting, are less miniature and individualistic than intimate categories, more formal and abstract. Thus those theorists spoke of "illusion," "deformation," "inversion," and "mystification" versus "true" or "critical" or "rational" understanding to capture what in the intimate sphere would be called the difference between "deception" and "realization," as well as of "subterranean levels" and "genealogies" to signify the hidden dimensions or buried origins of social practices.

One of the preeminent principles governing the modern organization of public life and stylization of private life has been the national principle, actualized in the movements for and institutionalization of nation-states, and in the psychological and cultural expressions of national identity. Here, too, theorists have recently been drawn away from a vertical conception of the appearance and reality of nationalism in politics to a horizontal conception of a plurality of national cultures, each with its distinctive history, traditions, customs, and myths. This conception has paved the way for an appreciative understanding of aspects of national experience discounted by more suspicious thinkers in the past. Foremost among those aspects are the emotional pull of locality, the enduring resonance of ethnic ties, the fulfillment of the individual in national community, and the variations in mannerisms, tastes, habits, and sensibilities from one national group to the next. Alas, the horizontal view of nations and nationalism has cured older blindnesses at the price of obliterating the insights to which those blindnesses were attached. Like all congealing orthodoxies, it exemplifies the general rule that every turn of social or political theory produces new problems for itself in the process of solving the problems of its immediate predecessor. This is why, however fruitful theory may be, it is not positively cumulative in the long run.

Of the surface-and-depth insights into nationalism that have been denied seats in the contemporary chamber of uttered and utterable ideas, three are particularly unwelcome there. The first is the idea of mystification in national community, the second is the idea of contradiction in the civic nation, and the third is the idea of a universalizing process by which particular ethnic and national identities are forced into mutual contact and irrevocably transformed in ways they neither control nor entirely comprehend. To say that these ideas are no longer accepted *by* us is not to say that they have left no lasting mark *on* us, for each of them played a part in generating problems of thought that did not disappear when their inspiring ideas disappeared. Then, again, the real world of nations and nationalism also played its part in generating these thought problems. Hence their continued vitality testifies not only to the imprint that an old mentality left behind on a new one but also to the objectivity of certain problems of nationalism vis-à-vis all mentalities.

A reconsideration of these depth insights into nations and nationalism, along with their accompanying thought problems, takes us to the grave of Karl Marx, abandoned long ago to the weeds by conservatives, liberals, and leftists alike. Their very unison in doing this or, indeed, anything at all, signals a blurring of lines between political camps that only reinforces Marx's contemporary irrelevance, since those lines originally had been drawn with reference to him. Consequently, if we wish to revisit Marx, we will have to drag his shade back from the netherworld of all those who are universally despised and discarded. We also will have to clear away a heap of stereotypes that reflect what Aijaz Ahmad aptly describes as "polemical dismissals of Marxism, without any detailed engagement with Marx's thought."[5] These dismissals have been especially abrupt in the case of theorists of nationalism, who either entirely ignore Marx or skewer him and then ignore him for what they take to be four unforgivable sins.[6]

The first sin, Marx's supercilious attitude toward inherited forms of collective identity, jars with most sensibilities today. His penchant for the ethnic slur aggravates, above all, those who call for a celebration of difference even if, in their anxiety to respect difference, such multiculturalists resort to such bland phrases of depiction that groups touted for their difference come to sound identical and identically dull. In contrast, Marx is caustic in his characterization of the peculiarities of every conceivable ethnic, racial, and national group, including, most notoriously, his own. Compared with euphemisms that turn all peoples the same shade of gray, Marx's comments about Jews, Germans, Chinese, Indians, and so on are obnoxious, yes, but also refreshingly colorful and irreverent.

Marx's three other sins, according to his detractors, are his view of nationalism as false consciousness, his reduction of the nation-state to an instrument of the ruling class, and his evasion of the material realities of ethnonational differentiation. These oversimplifications of Marx require correction before we can mine each of his relevant ideas. By shifting our sights from cartoons of Marx's arguments to the arguments themselves, we will be able to grasp both his positive contributions to our subject and his entanglement in perplexities that continue to entangle us. For the conundrums he exposes no less than for the critical thought he stimulates, we would be wrong to call Marx's answer to the national question passé.

THE NATION AS ILLUSORY SUBJECT

Of all the misconceptions of Marx that cloud the atmosphere around him, those concerning his notions of falsity and truth make the weirdest mix. One misconception is that Marx sees all ideas as reflections of the experiences of the social classes that have those ideas, and the truest ideas as reflections of the experiences of the subordinated class. Another, opposing misconception is that Marx equates ideology with class mentalities inside the social world and truth with a scientific knowledge of society gained from a god's-eye point of view. Contrary to the first notion, Marx conceives of conventional ideas or ideology as reflecting the interests and position of the dominant social class, regardless of the class that happens to be thinking conventionally. Because it is susceptible to ideology, the experience of subordination does not provide automatic access to the underlying dynamic of class relations. Contrary to the second notion, Marx conceives of critical reason as both a precipitate and pre-cipitant of transformations within the world the thinker is thinking about. At the same time, that reason must encompass the whole so-cial order, of which the different experiential perspectives, including the thinker's own, are no more than single aspects. This combination of ideas suggests that the truth about class society is a systemic one, that it is partly obscured, and that it can be searched for by anyone with criticism and passion. To be more precise, it can be searched for by anyone with a method that can plumb society's depths and a desire to do so born out of practical but not necessarily firsthand experiential investments.

In light of Marx's refusal either to see felt experience as the ground of true knowledge or to see critical reason as a neutral anal-ysis of the world, one might think him perfectly poised both to ex-plain nationalism as a form of popular false consciousness and to condemn it as such. Indeed, this third, more specific misconception of Marx's ideas of falsity and truth has flourished along with the other two, providing theorists of nationalism with a reason to turn their backs on him. However, Marx makes no use of the term "false consciousness" in his work and, when he refers solely to working-class consciousness, infrequent use of the concept "ideology." In-stead, he most typically ascribes ideological thinking to members of the ruling class, whose illusions and deceptions help justify their so-cial dominance to themselves; almost as typically to their profes-sional intellectual apologists, who produce and disseminate those il-lusions and deceptions; and often enough to socialist theoreticians who take a different line from his.[7] He directs the rest of his ideology critique almost entirely at situations, ubiquitous rather than class specific, in which members of society think and act in the dark. Fan-tastical fears about nature and the appearance of contingent social practices as necessary ones contribute greatly to that darkness, as do the ruling ideas of an age through which a ruling class presents its particular interest as "the common interest of all the members of society"[8] and makes its will "into a law for all."[9] In short, the main targets of Marx's ideology critique are groups materially benefiting from ruling ideas on the one hand and undifferentiated members of society on the other.

As for the proletariat, both Marx and Engels almost invariably write as if it either already has uncovered the truth of class society, which to their minds is not a national truth, or is fast arriving at that truth and hence at undertaking its mission as revolutionary agent. Near the end of the nineteenth century, Engels does seem to hit a pessimistic note when he reflects on the critical potentialities of the proletariat in light of the general rule of class society that revolutions always have been made in the service of "small minorities in relation to the ruled mass of the people." The revolutionary participation of that mass or even its "passive, unresisting attitude," he declares, only gives the new ruling minority "the appearance of being the representative of the whole people." This remark could have precipitated a critique of nationalism as popular false consciousness at least as severe as that of nationalism's severest Marxist critic, Rosa Luxemburg. Instead, it is the prelude to Engels's recollection and reiteration of his and Marx's line of thought during the upheavals of 1848: "If in all the longer revolutionary periods, it was so easy to win the great masses of the people by the merely plausible false representations of the forward-thrusting minorities, why should they be less susceptible to ideas which were the truest reflection of their economic condition, which were nothing but the clear, rational expression of their needs, of needs not yet understood but merely vaguely felt by them?" Engels does go on to muse that "[h]istory has proved us, and all who thought like us, wrong," but what he claims it proved them wrong about was not the subjective proclivities of the workers but the objective capacity of capital: "The state of economic development on the Continent at that time was not, by a long way, ripe for the elimination of capitalist production."[10]

That if an oppressed class could be won by lies then surely it would be won by truth is a curious deduction, and only an extraordinary rationalist could make it. However, it shows the same respect for the intelligence of the popular masses of modern society that Marx's and Engels's words always do show, as long as they do not refer specifically to the peasantry. This would count as a significant qualification in light of the number of peasants in the world and the role that peasant culture plays as a source of metaphors for nationalist ideology, were it not for the fact that the peasants were already a doomed class in Marx's and Engels's imaginations. Thus, the fatal flaw in the thinking of these two is not an intellectual arrogance toward the people through ascribing false consciousness to them but too modernist a view of who the people are and too intellectualist a view of what moves them in one political direction or another.

If Marx never uses the term "false consciousness" and hardly ever, with singular respect to the working class, the term "ideology," neither does he even implicitly assimilate nationalism to the false consciousness of the proletariat at the same time that he assimilates the modern state to the superstructure of capitalism. In fact, the formulas of false/true consciousness and base/superstructure, while similarly mechanical, are otherwise too incongruous to be relied upon together. The claim that productive forces and relations constitute the material foundation of social life and that "legal, political, religious, aesthetic, or philosophic" forms constitute its ideological superstructure suggests that the subjective moment of social life follows from and meshes with the objective.[11] Conventional ideas may be mystified ideas, but they serve the socioeconomic order of things and in that sense the consciousness that thinks in terms of them cannot be considered "false."[12] Marx emphasizes the suitableness, not the falsity, of ideas in capitalist society in both his early works, where he writes as if capital is right on schedule in nursing its proletarian executioner, and his later works, where he writes as if capital keeps overcoming every objective limit it meets, so that the ripe moment for revolutionary thought and action recedes further and further into the distance. For reasons too intricate to lay out here, it is in the history of Marxism after Marx that we see the falling fortunes of "base and superstructure" and the rising fortunes of "false consciousness and true understanding," as Marxists revise their categories to accommodate the failure of objective crises of capital to incite working-class criticism and rebellion. Ultimately both dualisms become outdated.[13] The consequences of their demise for the understanding of nations and nationalism are ambiguous. On the plus side, two temptations to reduce nations and nationalism to mere functions of capital disappear. These are the "base/superstructure" temptation to portray the nation-state as the product and instrument of capital's need for a unified market at an early stage in capitalist development, and the "false consciousness/true understanding" temptation to portray nationalism as an ideological glue binding the working class to the bourgeoisie when the real interests of the two classes are opposed. On the minus side, what also disappears is the imperative to acknowledge the services that the modern state provides capital, the ways in which free private enterprise gives rise to a new political and culture regime of dictations and constraints, and the tensions between national community and class inequality. Finally, it becomes difficult to foresee the course of an economic logic that previously had strengthened but ultimately weakens national political sovereignty and distinction by pressing for political and cultural integration to dovetail with economic integration at the supranational level. Such pressure surprises many late twentieth-century thinkers, who only in the middle of the maelstrom recognize the "forces of globalization" that Marx anticipated a century before.

That Marx does not describe nationalism or anything else as false consciousness is obviously not to say that he is not critical of prevailing ideas. Indeed, we can extrapolate a promising strategy for thinking critically about nationalism from his famous contrast between the Hegelian idea of an Abstract Subject and the material existence of actual human beings. Hegelian idealism proposes that history is the expression of the self-development through time of the Absolute Idea, so that particular objects in history are actually semblances or cloaks hiding "*philosophical* existence" under "sensuous disguises."[14] Against that proposal, Marx declares that natural, concrete life is the only fundamental reality and that the starting point for analyzing human history is "real living individuals," with consciousness considered "solely as *their* consciousness."[15]

For positing an Absolute Subject that actualizes itself as the object world, Marx calls Hegelian idealism a sequel to the "religious illusion."[16] A sequel, but not a repetition. Marx criticizes Hegelian idealism for offering intellectuals worldly self-satisfaction through its fantastical portrayal of history as the movement of abstract ideas, thus presenting, as the key to history, the intellectuals' own creations.[17] He criticizes religion, in contrast, for offering the popular masses fantastical solace for their real suffering, leaving the worldly sources of that suffering intact. Religion is "an *expression* of real suffering and a *protest* against real suffering" that helps prevent real happiness from being fought for and won.[18]

In declaring the Nation a collective subject — a declaration initially *by* intellectuals but *for* the masses — is nationalism a sequel to the religious illusion too? Given nationalism's representation of history as the struggle of peoples to possess their own states, Marx more likely would call it a "political illusion" — a variety he praises for being, in contrast to religion, "at least moderately close to reality."[19] But Marx's discussion of idealism provides us with the spark we need to see this particular political illusion as a secular extension of the religious illusion, whenever the nation is understood as a hypostatized subject with a reality grander than that of the human beings who compose it.[20]

The idea of the Nation as a secular sequel to the religious illusion provides an antidote to Benedict Anderson's analysis of the nation as an imagined political community, which has been perhaps the most influential and seductive analysis of our times. Although Anderson depicts the modern nation as a secular sequel to religion, he depicts religion as neither truth nor illusion but as a benign cultural or "meaning-generating" phenomenon. Assimilating the "made-up-ness" of both religion and nationalism to "'imagining' and 'creation,'" not "'fabrication' and 'falsity,'" he sees the "fiction" of nationalism as following the "fiction" of religion in two ways.[21] It bestows a larger meaning on what would otherwise be the merely fortuitous births and deaths of human beings, and it creates communal ties among otherwise separate individuals, as well as among otherwise disconnected past, present, and future generations.[22] Thus, at the tail end of the tradition that begins with Hegel and Marx, Anderson drops the idea of illusion without committing himself to the idea of a reality that critics claimed illusions obscured. Too anti-elitist to condemn popular beliefs as mystifications, too world-weary to embrace any beliefs as truths, Anderson prefers to strike a half democratic, half ironic pose toward "constructions of reality."[23]

What different sights might we see if we retain the new idea of nationalism as a secular sequel to religion without forsaking the old idea that religious meanings may have mystifying as well as truth-telling or creative functions? With Anderson, we would be able to compliment nationalism for being earthbound, dedicated to the mundane vitality of a people in a way that religion is not. Whether or not nationalism is, like Marx's view of religion, thoroughly explicable as "an expression of real suffering and a protest against real suffering,"[24] it has the advantage over religion of allowing "real happiness" to be fought for. Does it allow real happiness to be won? Against Anderson, Marx would give us three straightforward reasons for saying "no." First, by conducting human sociality, nationalism obscures the divisions, inequalities, and exploitations inside society that Marx sees as the root cause of human misery.[25] Second, while championing a people's vitality, nationalism inflames the egotism of that people and estranges every people from the rest. Third, in sweeping individuals into a larger unity that is declared to have a subjectivity of its own and in representing those individuals as molecules of that subjectivity, nationalism promises the dream but precludes the reality of human happiness, which to Marx's mind never can come from an illusion.

While countering the romanticism of the idea of the nation as imagined community, the idea of the Nation as illusory subject is problematic in a number of ways. One problem is that like the religious idea of God (although unlike the Hegelian idea of the Idea), the idea of the Nation, if an illusion, is an illusion "for the people." Representing itself as the locus of popular unity and popular sovereignty as well as the site on which "the people" historically obtains formal political agency along with the upper classes, the modern nation-state is well placed to generate popular support on its own behalf. The populism of the modern nation—the mass appeal of its claim to strengthen all of its individual members equally—means that even those who criticize nationalism for the sake of the people are bound to appear as enemies of the people.[26] This misfortune has dogged Marxism in its relation to nationalism from the start.

Another problem with the idea of the Nation as illusory subject is that there seems to be no reason why the same charge should not be leveled at any and all collective nouns.[27] The problem of how to refute the idea of the Nation without having to refute almost every other category of social thought is unnerving for those who see the self as socially determined, social entities as more than the sum of their individual parts, and community as a good in itself. It is especially unnerving for those who see class as the fundamental category of modern political economy. The most tempting solution is to distinguish between "bad" collective nouns that are mythological in conception (for example, "the German Volk") and "good" collective nouns that are abstractions from empirical positions and relations (for example, "the Proletariat"). This path, however, dead-ends in new difficulties that were not obvious to Marx but are all too obvious to us. Even those who are convinced that language mirrors reality instead of constructing it would be hard-pressed not to admit that all concepts are mythological to a certain extent, in that they make more out of reality than is there empirically, through the inevitable mediation of physical sensation by hopes, fantasies, and fears. Then, too, concepts such as "the Proletariat" and "Communism" are entangled with elements mythological not to just a certain but an extraordinary extent. Far from being accidental, these entanglements are intrinsic to the theory in which the "Proletariat" and "Communism" most centrally appear. Moreover, the political consequences of these entanglements are not unambiguously regrettable from the Marxist point of view. It can be argued that the socialist movement could not have grown as vigorously as it did had it not hypostatized "the Proletariat" or mythologized "Communist Society" and, conversely, that socialism collapsed when its myths collapsed.

A third problem with the idea of the Nation as illusory subject is that myth may make the difference between a collection of people to which individuals belong in only a mechanical way and a community to which individuals are emotionally attached. Can a collection of persons be *felt* as a community if those persons simply see it as the sum of their individual, concrete practices and relations — that is, if they do not idealize it? And if the felt community does require a myth for its coherence and animation, isn't critical reason, with its impulse to puncture myths, the enemy of communities of every sort, including communist communities?

The most disturbing problem is that it is by no means self-evident that the Nation as a hypostatized subject looming over human beings and demanding their self-surrender thereby induces unhappiness in them. One might propose instead that the looming and demanding Nation has been a condition of human happiness in the modern age, through providing a homeopathic remedy for the belittlement of human beings by forces even more impersonal, uncontrollable, and incomprehensible. To the extent that this proposition is true, modern happiness might be said to hinge, against Marx, not on critical reason but on mystification. Modern happiness might be said to consist, against Anderson, in individuals' imagining themselves not as free and equal members of a popular community but as infinitesimal grains of a larger-than-life force able to impose its will on the world.[28] An important point of connection between nationalism and fascism surely will be found right here.

All of these difficulties in conceiving of the Nation as illusory subject have to do with the stubbornness of the human investment in illusion rather than with the wrongheadedness of the idea that illusion and nationalism are intertwined. They confirm Marx's understanding of society as opaque to its own members but challenge his conviction that human beings would choose, or could choose, or even always *should* choose to give up their myths, self-delusions, and fantastical wishes if "material conditions" enabled them to do so. In sum, intractable perversities of human will and desire dash both Anderson's optimistic account of the benign imagination that brings forth imagined communities and Marx's hopes for a worldwide victory of critical reason.

THE HEAVENLY COMMUNITY

Marx offers a second set of insights, with a second set of difficulties attached to them, on civic nationalism — that sense of national community in modern liberal states that is based on the consent of individuals to be governed by the same political institutions and to obey the same laws. This is the variety of nationalism that many thinkers applaud today as moderate, inclusive, and "Western," in contradistinction to a violent, exclusive, and "Eastern" variety based on common ethnic ancestry or "blood." To examine Marx's jaundiced view of the civic nation and hence, by implication, of civic nationalism, let us turn from his concept of ideology, or ideas that distort social reality, to his concept of the concrete contradiction, or of practices and relations that conflict with, obscure, and depend on other practices and relations.

The most famous of Marx's concrete contradictions center on the split between economic relations that appear in the market, where capital and wage labor confront one another as free independent agents exchanging equal for equal, and economic relations hidden behind factory doors, where wage labor is coerced to produce surplus value for capital without equivalent return. But Marx also refers to three concrete contradictions at the heart of the modern liberal nation-state. The first contradiction is that between the principles governing political life and the actualities of economic life. According to Marx, the unity of citizens in political society contradicts and obscures the fragmentation of individuals in civil society, so that political community becomes a celestial gloss over the "egotistic life" of the mundane world. Here, every man "regards other men as a means" and "degrades himself into a means."[29] In turn, the institutional separation of modern state and civil society contradicts and obscures the fact that their separation is a function of civil society itself. Civil society requires the emancipation of private property from political constraints, the supremacy of private property over social relations, and the enforcement of the rules of private property by the state acting as if it were a neutral arbiter upholding universal principles of justice.

The second concrete contradiction is that between the state as an institution based "on the real ties existing in every family and tribal conglomeration (such as flesh and blood, language, division of labour . . .)" and the state as an institution based on social division ("especially . . . on the classes, already determined by the division of labour"). In that latter capacity, Marx declares, the state is "divorced from the real interests of individual and community." The state's ground in actual social unity ("on the real ties") contradicts and obscures its ground in actual social division ("especially . . . the classes"), which allows it to exist formally as the organ of the whole and substantively on the side of any particular social group that dominates over the rest.[30]

The third concrete contradiction is that between the state as the collective power of all members of society acting as a self-governing community and the state as the collective power of society estranged from all its members and concentrated in institutions ruling over them as an alien, bureaucratic force.[31]

These concrete contradictions between political and civil society, between the state as the reflection of social unity and of social division, and between unalienated and alienated social power, weigh against Engels's claim, so often assumed to be a snapshot of Marx's political theory, that "in reality . . . the State is nothing but a machine for the oppression of one class by another."[32] They consequently weigh against any equation of Marx's theory with this reductive idea. At his most suggestive, Marx reveals the civic nation to be a double reality of unity and division with complex implications for modern politics that he never traces out. To the extent that political society and the state are a function of civil society and private property, the supports for national unity and patriotism will be very weak. The real ties of dependence constitutive of all societies will be obscured by the atomistic ethos and organization of this one; a collective commitment to competitive individualism and private enterprise will undercut the propensity for collective commitment per se; and state demands for devotion and self-sacrifice for the good of the nation will clash with individual autonomy and self-interest. Then again, to the extent that the state and political society make up a celestial sphere, that sphere will generate in citizens an ambivalent mix of identification and alienation. For being the locus of collective unity and common interest, the state and political society will invite patriotic pride, loyalty, and political consent. For the "heavenly" quality of its unity, its abstraction from everyday life, its built-in capacity to deceive by representing particular interests as the general interest, and its tendency as alienated social power to develop interests in domination of its own, it will invite suspicion, cynicism, and political dissent. Moreover, to the extent that social division is not merely a function of class or other forms of domination and subordination but issues from the sheer heterogeneity of human beings, deception, oppression, and dissent will be permanent features of public life. Out of particularity in society will be sure to come efforts to represent specific interests as the general interest. Out of the unity of citizens will be sure to come attempts to impose a singular identity on the whole of society. Out of the state's interests in domination will be sure to come efforts to suppress, not express, the citizens' wills. Out of the heterogeneity of humanity will come revolts against all of these moves.

The refusal to acknowledge the inevitability of particularity and heterogeneity in society, and hence the inevitability of tensions between social division and political unity, must be counted as one of Marx's greatest failings. But the same refusal, with a different rationale behind it, is one of nationalism's gravest failings, too. Marx's delusion at least is humanly expansive: Marx believes that all individuals, whoever and wherever they are, can and should identify with one another universally after the demise of class society. Nationalism's delusion, on the contrary, is humanly contractive: nationalism proposes that only individuals who are identical in some particular way can and should belong to the same political community.

Preoccupied at any rate with class division, not national unity, Marx is cavalierly imprecise about a whole range of conceptual discriminations that any theorist of civic nationalism must sort out. What is the relationship between "political society" and "the state"? What is the appropriate delimitation of "a people" and its conceptual relation to "the people" in the sense of "the popular classes"? What is the conceptual relation of "a people" to "political community" and "the public sphere" (with which "a people" has certain suggestive affinities); to "civil society" and "the state" (in which "a people" seems to be the third triangular point); and to "heterogeneity" and "social division" (which the singularity of "a people" contradicts)? Even when they are not looked at historically, from which angle Marx's idea of a formal separation between bourgeois state and individualistic civil society has turned out to be merely one variation on the theme of state-society relations under capitalism, such questions are highly complex.[33]

One of the most ambitious attempts to sort out these complexities in the light of contemporary reality has come from Habermasians who acknowledge enough of a distant tie to Marx to call themselves "post-Marxists," even while they join a larger chorus of conservatives and liberals in many of their claims. Post-Marxists such as Jean Cohen and Andrew Arato reject Marx's "political society/civil society" formulation for conflating on the one side "state" and "political society" and on the other "economy" and "civil society." They argue that those conflations obscure a realm between state and economy in which private persons enter into voluntary association with one another to discuss public affairs.[34] In this realm, individuals are said to enjoy a level of freedom, equality, democracy, and community uncharacteristic of either the economy, which is driven by the imperatives of money, or the state, which is driven by the imperatives of power. Like most of their contemporaries, post-Marxists reject the ideas that private property is the basis of social domination and that dissolving the divide between public and private is the route to human emancipation. As negative evidence for their case, they point to the magnification of state power and obliteration of individual agency that followed the attack on private economic power under Soviet-style communism, as well as the less dramatic but still notable decline of individual responsibility accompanying the expansion of the capitalist welfare state. As positive evidence, they point in Western liberal democracies to civil rights, feminist, gay and lesbian, and ecological movements; and in Eastern communist regimes to "authentic" citizen initiatives and dissident groups. These movements are held to emerge out of civil society rather than the economic or public political realm. Their forms are held to be associative, not bureaucratic; their concerns public-spirited, not privatistic; their sensibilities pluralistic, not authoritarian. Unlike the old socialist movement, the new social movements, for Habermasians, are reassuringly democratic in that they seek to refashion identities, meanings, and values at the molecular level rather than overthrow society and install a new central political regime.

In sum, according to post-Marxists, actually existing liberal democratic nations consist of the economy or "market," the state, and a civil society composed of individual initiatives, spontaneous social relations, and the public activities of private persons. The market and the state may exert pressure on civil society, but neither supplies civil society's underlying principle, so that that pressure is not what theorists these days call "constitutive." Market and state may threaten to exceed their proper boundaries and thus compress the field in which democratic social relations and activities take place. Still, all three realms have something to commend them as long as the commodifying ethos of the market and the directive ethos of the state are decently constrained. In that case, the market is good for producing and distributing goods and services efficiently, for bolstering individual agency, and for protecting society against the tyrannical capacities of the state. The state is good for steering society, for being answerable to democratic pressures, and for counteracting the most egregious market inequalities. Civil society is not just good but excellent for generating individual independence, the sense of social obligation, cultural meanings, and citizen participation in the national public arena.

The theory of civil society as the locus of democratic citizenship avoids the dichotomous thinking that prevented Marx from seeing the importance to human agency of a private sphere outside economic relations, just as such thinking prevented liberals from seeing the importance to human agency of a public sphere outside the state. Nonetheless, there is something in the theory of civil society that is hostile to flights of the critical imagination beyond the boundaries of the existing order of things. There is also something hostile in it to national-cultural variety worldwide, for although Habermasians may chastise Western liberal democracy for not fully protecting and nourishing civic life, they identify the good society with what they take to be the basic outlines of *this* society. At the same time, there is a dreamlike quality to those outlines — or at least an academic's dream. Post-Marxism's portrait of civil society is crowded with neighborhood associations, church groups, grassroots organizations, street rallies, and marches for unmet social needs — and with people who spend their days in sociable conversation, critical deliberation, and voluntary endeavors for the public good. Any activities of private persons as public actors less savory from a liberal to left point of view are simply trimmed from the picture.[35] For our purposes, what is most noticeably missing are ethnonationalist movements with the aim of capturing state power — the strongest "social movements" to emerge out of Eastern Europe's incipient "civil societies" thus far.[36]

Post-Marxism also romanticizes both the significance of civil society in relation to the other two spheres and the nature of that relation by implying that neither the state nor the economy has a greater weight than civil society and that each sphere is separate and distinct from the other two. By deemphasizing the authoritative, centralized power of the state so that it might highlight the discursive, democratic power of individuals, post-Marxism minimizes an institution in theory that continues to maximize itself in practice. And by consigning material production and consumption to a sphere in which it is clearly less interested than it is in café conversations and political debates, it so entirely effaces the workaday world that one suspects it of mistaking the style of life of intellectuals for the routines of the population at large. In line with almost every other theoretical tendency these days, post-Marxism refers to that workaday world as "the market," a homely metaphor obscuring not simply the exploitative productive relations of capital that Marx disclosed under the surface of exchange relations, but also what William E. Connolly and Michael H. Best once aptly called a saturating "civilization of productivity."[37] This civilization adds a wealth of new goods to the world. At the same time, it produces inequality among individuals as both the motivation and effect of the search for private profit, replaces all distinctive cultural ends with the single end of the infinite production and consumption of commodities, reshapes each country's landscape in accordance with its own prerogatives, and dictates both the positive agenda of the state and the negative circumscription of state power to protect private property rights. Its psychoemotional reverberations in the individual — adventurousness, inventiveness, dynamism, and a sense of initiative, yes, but also material insatiability, work freneticism, money arrogance, anxiety, envy, and despair — do not remain compartmentalized in "the market realm" but follow individuals wherever they go. In short, "the market" is a major mystifying category that obscures the mode of production as a whole, as well as its penetration of the self and the entire social order.

Infusing all realms of society instead of merely the market realm, the civilization of productivity severely constrains the possibilities for the real equality and community of individuals as citizens of the civic nation, as well as the possibilities for those citizens to exert collective power over their common way of life. In conceiving of the modern civic nation as the contradictory unity of "celestial" political community and "terrestrial" social inequality and competition, Marx remains the best early spy of those constraints. Moreover, despite the undercategorization of Marx's "state/society" schema, that schema is all we need to recognize post-Marxism's "civil society" as a new version of the old "heavenly sphere."[38] Post-Marxism's "civil society" may be admirably cooperative, pluralistic, deliberative, and democratic, but it is a theoretical abstraction from most people's everyday existence and ethereal in relation to the main economic *and* political realities of the civic nation's "earthly" life.

THE FATE OF ETHNONATIONAL PARTICULARITY

The final sin of which Marx has been accused in relation to nations and nationalism is his reading of history as a movement by which localism, parochialism, and small-scale collectivities are sacrificed to broader and broader geographical affiliations, more and more expansive intellectual outlooks, and larger and larger units of sociopolitical integration, the whole process pointing toward a worldwide universality of human sympathies, understandings, and enjoyments. To be sure, Marx's reading of history is universalist in the dialectical rather than linear sense. The enlargement of horizons occurs through violence and destruction, as the result of forces unleashed by human beings but not governed by them, and effected by actions motivated not by the great subjective virtues but by egotism, cruelty, and greed. Marx is dialectical as well in viewing universalism as the practical result of a relentless historical process rather than as a merely wished-for ideal.

Marx's depiction of an ever-widening stage of modern thought and action would make it plain that he does not see history as a tale about peoples and nation-states, even if one did not already know that he sees it as a tale about the forces and relations of material production. Although he gives them short shrift, Marx clearly is aware of shared habits of conception, inherited orientations of sympathy and antipathy, and ethnoracial ties and identifications that in his nineteenth-century way he calls differences of stock. He refers often and without any embarrassment to national peculiarities of the French, English, Germans, Indians, Egyptians, and Chinese that stem not merely from these groups' different positions in the chronology of capitalist development but also from their distinctive cultures and ancient histories.[39] Nevertheless, for Marx, capitalism explodes and reconstitutes the cultures with which it comes in contact — which, given the infinitely expansive logic of capital accumulation, means every culture. Once swept up into that storm, ethnic nationalities can remain neither autonomous nor "pure" but sooner or later will be forced into uneven relations of material dependence, social intermingling, and cultural contact with one another.

As for the nation-state, it is entirely a product of modern history and as such has temporal origins, not to speak, yet, of a temporal end. In the geographical areas of capitalism's early development, Marx explains "political centralization" as the "necessary consequence" of the "agglomeration" of property, populations, and means of production by the bourgeoisie, whereby "[i]ndependent, or but loosely connected provinces, with separate interests, laws, governments and systems of taxation, became lumped together into one nation, with one government, one code of laws, one national class-interest, one frontier and one customs-tariff."[40] Although in his day the economically agrarian and politically fractured regions of central and eastern Europe had yet to achieve such centralization, Marx is sure that they will. Even with respect to the non-Western regions colonized by the West, Marx believes that imperial interests, after dismantling traditional societies, pave the way for nationalist movements against themselves and the subsequent birth of independent nation-states. In India, for example, the unified state, the native army, the free press, the civil service, and the railroads — all established by British rule for the sake of colonial domination and exploitation — become conditions for India's self-emancipation as a modern nation.[41]

If a Western condescension suffuses Marx's account of what the British were doing, albeit with the worst of intentions, for the Indians, what should we call the condescension in his account of what capital did for traditional societies in the West? For capital does in India what it did in England, with these important differences. It does it later in time, giving rise to the distinction between "backward" and "advanced" civilizations that obscures, all too often from Marx himself, the real distinction between regions into which capital has advanced and regions into which it has not. It does it as an intruding force from the outside, supported by the apparatuses of an alien state. It thereby raises the national question in the region it penetrates at the same time that it raises the class question, not to speak of all the questions about the ambiguous value of modernity that Marx himself never asks but that can be asked once full-fledged examples of "developed" societies are in place. Finally, it does it uninhibited by bourgeois moral principle or sanctimony: "The profound hypocrisy and inherent barbarism of bourgeois civilization lies unveiled before our eyes, turning from its home, where it assumes respectable forms, to the colonies, where it goes naked."[42]

The boundless economic appetite that leads the bourgeois nation-state to tyrannize over distant regions and peoples, and so to corrupt the national political principle both at home and abroad, moves ardent republicans such as Hannah Arendt to condemn colonialism outright. For Arendt, colonialism's only good product is the struggle of colonized peoples for their own political emancipation. For Marx, however, the situation is more complex. If colonialism destroys the integrity of distinct ways of life, if it corrodes the autonomy of both traditional civilizations and modern polities, if it binds all peoples asymmetrically into a single economic system, it also enlarges the theater of human life from the locality to the nation-state to the world.[43] Thus it does its unwitting part to lay the material basis for a universal outlook, sensibility, and sense of affiliation on the part of the whole human race.

Marx's celebrations of universalism, scattered throughout his work, never change in their gist or enthusiasm. His admiration of the broadening results of bourgeois rule in *The Communist Manifesto* is entirely typical of him: "In place of the old local and national seclusion and self-sufficiency, we have intercourse in every direction, universal inter-dependence of nations. . . . The intellectual creations of individual nations become common property. National one-sidedness and narrow-mindedness become more and more impossible."[44] Also typical is the linkage he makes, in *The German Ideology*, between such expansiveness and human emancipation: "[T]he liberation of each single individual will be accomplished in the measure in which history becomes transformed into world history. . . . Only then will the separate individuals be liberated from the various national and local barriers, be brought into practical connection with the material and intellectual production of the whole world and be put in a position to acquire the capacity to enjoy this all-sided production of the whole earth."[45] We have seen that even colonialism helps bring about this emancipated world of "universal intercourse." As Marx writes in "The Future Results of British Rule in India," the bourgeois period of history creates "the material basis for a new world . . . in the same way as geological revolutions have created the surface of the earth. When a great social revolution shall have mastered the results of the bourgeois epoch . . . and subjected them to the common control of the most advanced peoples . . . human progress [will] cease to resemble that hideous pagan idol, who would not drink the nectar but from the skulls of the slain."[46]

Sometimes a mode of thought is revealing because it falls prey to conundrums that continue to disturb history long after the popularity of that mode of thought has died out. Marx's universalism is revealing in this indirect sense.

The first set of conundrums in Marx's universalism is conceptual. Is it logically possible for human emancipation to be understood as the universal enjoyment of national-cultural many-sidedness? Can there be many national and cultural sides if everyone equally enjoys them all? Or does meaningful national-cultural variation depend on the absence of universal experience and instead on some degree of separation, even isolation, among peoples?[47] If variation requires that most peoples do not experience most ways of life, for whose sake is variation to be preserved? Is the cynical, class-specific answer the right one: "For the sake of a cosmopolitan elite that desires interesting experiences in its travels"?

Conversely, what is human emancipation an emancipation *from*? Marx's most immediate answer is "class domination." However, through his repeated couplings of "freedom" and "universality," Marx also implies that humans are constrained not just by social subordination but also by living in any particular place and way. If it is peculiar to link together universal enjoyment and national-cultural particularity, it seems positively bizarre to treat particularity in and of itself as a confinement, as if the individual, to be fully emancipated, must breathe air no closer than that breathed by the whole human race. Still, there is a grain of good sense in this bizarre thought. Particularity can become a kind of confinement when an individual would grasp for herself existing possibilities of desire, thought, and action if her limited horizons did not prevent her from knowing what those possibilities were. This also explains why there is a democratic answer — "For the sake of everyone" — to the question, "For whose sake is national-cultural variation to be preserved?" Inside a universal culture, with no different possibilities of desire, thought, and action existing anywhere else, all individuals would be more tightly trapped than any individual could be inside the narrowest, most particular mode of life.

The next conundrum is dialectical. What is the likely outcome of the contradiction between a bounded polity and an unbounded economy? Are there good reasons to assume the continued existence of the nation-state, even if modern capital makes the nation-state economically obsolete?[48]

Nationalism makes sense from Marx's economic perspective both as a means of political unification to suit early capitalist expansion in the West and as a means by which overseas colonies can achieve political independence from Western capitalist states. But once domestic capital moves beyond national bounds, Marx never explains why the working class "must organize itself at home" with "its own country" as "the immediate arena of its struggle."[49] We are left to suppose that a national language, educational system, and set of habits and customs are what help fuse a working class together. We also can guess that political power at its most effective—that is, at its most coercive—still is organized on a national scale. Certainly Marx implies as much in *The Communist Manifesto* when he states, "Since the proletariat must first of all acquire political supremacy, must rise to be the leading class of the nation, must constitute itself *the* nation, it is, so far, itself national, though not in the bourgeois sense of the word."[50]

Still, the last phrase is a curious one, given that Marx believes the bourgeoisie at some point no longer is national "in the bourgeois sense" either: economic, not political, impulses govern it and eventually lead it to abandon the national for the global scene. "The need of a constantly expanding market for its products chases the bourgeoisie over the whole surface of the globe," which is exactly why one would think the proletariat must organize itself over that whole surface too. Marx's most well-known phrase to that effect is, "The working men have no country." Although this most often has been interpreted to mean that the working class does not identify itself in national terms, it more persuasively means that that class is the creature of a mode of production that becomes geographically nomadic. It also can mean that that class quite literally does not possess any country: no country is ruled by it as an active, self-determining political subject or is stamped by its interests and needs. If one reads the point this way, the implicit next line is "does not possess, but should." Indeed, Marx assumes the continued existence of the nation even after the proletarian revolution when he states, "In proportion as the exploitation of one individual by another is put an end to, the exploitation of one nation by another will also be put an end to," and that it then is "in the hands of a vast association of the whole nation" that production is to be concentrated and public power wielded.[51]

In short, Marx continues to rely on the category of the nation without a clear analytical basis for that reliance.[52] He does not have occasion to be shocked that a national working class has joined forces out of economic interest with a national ruling class against nonnational laborers elsewhere, although it will not be long before other Marxists do. He does not see psycho-cultural elements as having the kind of explanatory power that would allow him to ground national identity in collective attachments to a homeland, a shared history, and a familiar way of life. On such attachments Marx is almost silent, hinting only that there is something tragic about them, in that stable places, enduring ties, and customary things become targets of the destructive-creative movement of capital. In our own period, when national identifications have proven more highly charged than class identifications, Marx's silence seems plainly wrong. Nevertheless, the emotional charge of nationality cannot be understood in isolation from the dynamic of capital as Marx describes it. Nor is our view of the epic vigor of ethnic and national identities surer than Marx's view of their poignant impermanence.

The third conundrum of Marx's universalism is empirical. To what extent does the more developed capitalist country show the less developed the image of its own future?

In the preface to the first German edition of *Capital*, Marx issues his notorious warning that if "the German reader shrugs his shoulders at the condition of the English industrial and agricultural labourers . . . I must plainly tell him, '*De te fabula narratur!*' "[53] For this he has been chastised by some contemporary theorists who wish to underline the cultural differences not merely between the English and the German but more vividly among the English, the Senegalese, and the Taiwanese. He has been chastised by other theorists who wish to underline differences in wealth and power among early capitalist developers, late ones, and noncapitalist regions — differences that signify incommensurate present positions and future possibilities in an uneven and unequal global economic system. Both underlinings are important, given Marx's failure to explain exactly what he means by "The story will be told about you!" When he declares that the bourgeoisie remakes the entire world in its own image, does he mean that capitalism creates a world that everywhere looks alike, or instead a world that everywhere feels its impression? Does he mean that capitalism eventually eradicates local-regional difference (which would spell the doom of Marx's "many-sided universalism") or instead the effects of the unevenness of its progress? Or does he think only international socialism can do *that*?

If one reads Marx as making the relatively but not absolutely weak claim that capital creates a world that everywhere feels its impression, his forecast of where history is going is not at all off track, at least with respect to capital's material and cultural effects. With respect to the global spread of liberal politics, Marx — but liberals too — has been less prophetic.[54] And, of course, with respect to the revolutionary politics of the proletariat, Marx has not been prophetic at all. To defend Marx's vision of historical movement in this qualified way is not to celebrate his predictive successes and failures in the particular mix that history has served up. It is not to suggest that the details of actual life are not more profuse than the details of his theoretical scheme. It also is not to say that life will not look different when one is looking for differences from the way it looks when one is looking for similarities, so that a search for differences will turn up rich national-cultural variation, while a search for similarities will reveal a single global system at work, with homogenizing effects on everyone.[55]

In the end, Marx deals his own theory of history one hard blow when he capitulates to bourgeois ideology by equating capital's backwardness or advancement in different regions with the civilizational backwardness or advancement of those regions. The world deals that theory another, harder blow when global capitalism defeats international socialism and meets its strongest match in two antagonists to socialism instead. One antagonist is fundamentalist religion — in Marx's eyes, a relic that disappears after bourgeois society privatizes religion but at the turn of the twenty-first century the sole force left that confronts capitalism's universalistic principle with a universalism of its own. The other antagonist is the ethnic nationalism emerging out of defunct communist societies — societies that theoretically were to be the wave of an internationalist future but actually have functioned as pickling preserves for ethnonational animosities that exploded once the lid came off.[56]

Because of nationalism's complex relation to both communism and capitalism, because of its complexity in general, and because of the clashing political investments of its students, the question of how it is to be understood remains unresolved. Nationalism can be seen as a political-developmental movement from collapsing multiethnic empire to emerging nation-state to civic polity, or as an ethnically defined and resentment-driven upheaval triggered by the regional inequities of capitalist expansion. It can be seen as a rural, popular reaction and adaptation to the destructive-creative forces of modernity, or as the rebellion of human variety against the straitjacket of industrialization, bureaucratization, and global communication. It can be seen as a localist resurgence against the growing economic irrelevance of the centralized nation-state, or as a panicked response to state dissolution. Especially at the end of the twentieth century, it can be seen as a compound crisis of modern political unity,[57] in which fragments of identities are released into time and space by the simultaneous combustion of all these contrary conditions.

Against the backdrop of contemporary interpretations of nationalism that soft-pedal its internal tensions in favor of an expressive theory of national identity, an advocacy of civic nationalism, or a reification of ethnic difference, Marx has three simple, underestimated strengths. His idea of the illusory subject deflates the romanticism of the view of the nation as imagined community. His emphasis on the contradictions between the modern polity and economy punctures the idealization of civil society and of a civic nationalism that flatters Western liberal polities. Finally, his belief that historical forces bring different ethnonational identities into relation provides a necessary antidote to the disdain for universalist realities and ideals. However, Marx also falls prey to conundrums that can be transcended only if we find ways to reconcile sensibilities such as his with ones to which they are typically opposed. Can we join an awareness of large, inexorable historical forces with an appreciation of the unpredictability and idiosyncrasy of the particular? An understanding of the objective determinations of culture with a pleasure in cultural differences in and for themselves? A recognition of the impetus to homogenization with a defense of heterogeneities that rise up against it? A value on worldly or reflectively chosen solidarities with a sympathy for local or inherited affiliations? Finally, can we join a concept of social transformation with a refusal to translate "before and after" into "backward and advanced"?

To a certain extent, these questions have been posed to us by Marx's mixed record of success and failure in answering the national question. But to a much greater extent, they have been posed by the actual process of capitalist expansion, which has brought all peoples into universal contact, forcing them to grapple with the shattering impact of that contact. The answers to these questions, however, are not determined by an objective economic process. To steal a last phrase from Marx, they are possibilities of thought and action that must be fought for and won.

Chapter Two

Imperialism, Self-Determination, and Violence

Rosa Luxemburg, Hannah Arendt, and Frantz Fanon

STRANGE COMRADES

On the national as well as every other question, Rosa Luxemburg, Hannah Arendt, and Frantz Fanon are enough unlike each other that they would probably protest "against being gathered into a common room."[1] They not only belong to separate generations but also are contemporaries only in pairs, and Luxemburg and Arendt only at one edge of their life spans. Although all three take the long view of history, they are sparked to think, write, and agitate by different and differently timed immediate events. Luxemburg responds to nationalist threats to socialist internationalism in the last decade of the nineteenth century and first two decades of the twentieth; Arendt, to growing ethnic persecution, statelessness, and rightlessness over the next thirty years; and Fanon, to the high tide of decolonization in the decade after that. Their attitudes toward nationalism, and the practical investments behind those attitudes, are also at odds. Luxemburg is a vociferous enemy of nationalism, in part because it way-lays the European working class from its revolutionary mission by identifying each national segment of it with its "own" bourgeoisie. Arendt dissects national identity, overseas imperialism, and the pan-movements with a cooler contempt, compelled not by a forward-looking political agenda but by a backward-looking determination to trace the chain of events leading to the destruction of the European Jews and the collapse of Western civilization. Fanon is an active if also wary partisan of nationalism, viewing the creation of a collective national will as a necessary condition of the struggle against colonialism and for political independence, popular well-being, and equality between first and third worlds.

In certain ways, Luxemburg and Fanon are joined with each other but severed from Arendt. Both are humanist revolutionaries, Luxemburg within Europe but hoping for the release of all people from economic exploitation and political subordination, Fanon against Europe but hoping for a worldwide transvaluation of values.[2] Both stand on the side of the popular masses against the ruling classes. Their habits of thought are orthodoxly Marxist in Luxemburg's case (Arendt's weird "doubt" of Luxemburg's Marxism notwithstanding[3]) and Marxist in the traveling-theory sense in Fanon's. Arendt, in contrast, strikes a strictly intellectual attitude toward revolution no less than toward nationalism, seeking to understand it critically but not in the midst of, or as an immediate prelude to, acting politically either for or against it. Moreover, Arendt is unruffled by class distinction, despises Marxism, and accuses movements that aim to change the fabric of society for the sake of satisfying the material needs of the multitude of ruining the chances for individual distinction, plurality, debate, and the ability "to embark on something new."[4] She is kinder to liberation movements but still is not bowled over by them, viewing the struggle against oppression or what she terms the constraint on free movement as, at best, only an antecedent to the project of building "a new house where freedom can dwell" and "excellence can shine."[5]

In other ways, to do with being rather than thinking or acting, Luxemburg and Arendt are allied with each other and separated from Fanon. Most obvious, Luxemburg and Arendt are women, although this does not prevent them from spurning much more absolutely than Fanon does what once went by the misnomer of "the woman question." More significant for our purposes here, Luxemburg and Arendt are members of a national minority in Europe, historically poised between eliciting Europe's attraction and contempt, and between desiring from Europe differentiation and assimilation. Fanon in contrast belongs to one of the many native majority peoples outside Europe that in the age of imperialism Europe turned into virtual minorities in their own land.

What Luxemburg, Arendt, and Fanon all have in common are a preoccupation with nationalism, at least a foothold in the twentieth century, and a national-cultural hybrid background of exactly the kind that nationalism in its rightward turn tries to stamp out. All three also share theoretical emphases and temperamental qualities that distinguish them from many intellectuals today. Substantively, they identify the pursuit of private profit that leads the European bourgeoisie to scramble for raw materials, labor, and markets as a key starter ingredient in the witches' brew of modern nationalism, imperialism, and violence. The pursuit of profit may issue in the nation-state, or corrode the nation's public life, or foreclose the very possibility of a national existence — but in every case it leads to imperialist ventures with new nationalist aftereffects. In emphasizing the contradiction between the boundedness of the European polity and the unboundedness of capital, Arendt in *The Origins of Totalitarianism* is an explicit successor to Luxemburg in *The Accumulation of Capital*, although Luxemburg sees the bourgeoisie as founding the modern nation-state and then using it as its instrument of economic consolidation and expansion, while Arendt sees the bourgeoisie as capturing the state and undermining the national community, morally and territorially, through forsaking the public business of the nation for private profit all over the globe. In emphasizing the poisonous effects of the chase for infinite power and infinite wealth in the colonial territories — the sole positive outcome being colonialism's provocation of movements for national independence — Arendt's *Origins* anticipates Fanon's *The Wretched of the Earth*, although Arendt is preoccupied with the self-aggrandizement and self-corruption of the colonizer and Fanon with the misery and militance of the colonized.[6] Then, too, for Fanon there are two bourgeoisies to take to task: a foreign class of capitalists that exploits the colonies, and a native middle class so parasitical and bankrupt that it fails even to perform the productive functions of its European counterparts.

Another main focus for all three theorists is the intolerance of nationalism toward the feature of modern social life that today goes by the name of "difference," an intolerance they each spy and decry from their own vantage points. Luxemburg notes how national self-determination degenerates into national tyranny, the impulse toward it giving rise for both logical and historical reasons to attempts to stifle such impulses on the part of other nationalities. Fanon warns that anticolonial nationalism can turn into "ultra-nationalism, to chauvinism, and finally to racism" if national consciousness, which is alert to who people are and how they are distinguished from other sorts of people, is not replaced by social and political consciousness, which is alert to what people do in relation to one another and how greater justice between them can be brought about.[7] It is Arendt alone, however, who is bothered by the monochromatic effects of nationalism as a problem in itself, distinct from the problem of group persecution. In her analysis of the French nation-state and the central and eastern European pan-movements, Arendt shows us how both republican nationalism and ethnonationalism are driven to supplant social plurality with singularity, if for opposite reasons. Republican nationalism raises the identity of all citizens to the highest political principle; consequently it seeks to obliterate all symptoms of group particularity in society. Ethnonationalism raises group particularity to the highest political principle; consequently it seeks to rid society of all particular groups except one.

By following the crisscrossing threads among our three thinkers, we can explore the overlapping complexities of nationalism, imperialism, and plurality as they are grasped by minds that alternately clash and coincide. We also can acquaint ourselves with strong personalities who are not so undone by complexity or so paralyzed by doubt that they cannot speak definitively and act decisively. An adamant self-certainty enables Luxemburg to charge European nationalism with hypocrisy and self-delusion and to fight it at every turn. It enables Arendt to stipulate a geographically limited polity as the condition of political freedom while refusing to anchor those limits to a national essence — or as Arendt might put it, while refusing to lean on the banister of nationalism for support. It enables Fanon to declare violence strategically necessary to overthrow rule by violence and physiologically necessary to release the native from the somatic reflexes of subordination that are the result of that same rule.

Despite their equally vivid answers to the national question, our authors do not enjoy similarly glowing reputations today. Luxemburg was dismissed by political thinkers long ago for her fixation on class politics and a defense of internationalism that bypasses rather than confronts nationalism's popular force.[8] In contrast, the ever-mounting exegeses on Arendt make one strongly suspect that this theorist has been over-mined and that if she is to have anything left to say to the next generation, she should be sealed off from the further comments of this one. A view of Luxemburg and Arendt together might save the one from being too much out of fashion and the other from being too much in it. Unfortunately, the reception of Arendt on the national question is blocked not just by bad timing but by a problematic text. Arendt examines that question most minutely in "Imperialism," the second part of *The Origins of Totalitarianism*, where she pursues a line of thought on Africa and Africans that not only illuminates but also instantiates the phenomenology of European racism. Readers who would spit out "Imperialism" might be better able to savor it if *The Wretched of the Earth* were served afterward. How might Fanon benefit from this arrangement? One could have hoped that readers scandalized by Fanon's defense of violence in politics would be more open to him in Arendt's company, were it not for the fact that Arendt was scandalized by Fanon first and recorded her reasons for posterity. By suggesting that Fanon can teach us nothing about politics because he glorifies violence, she anticipates rather than counters contemporary currents that see violence as an absolute evil. What Fanon can gain from his proximity to Arendt is a path cleared to his insights through her thicket of objections.

We might mention three other complaints about our thinkers that seem less like reasoned charges than like prejudices either against certain types of people or against people who have unforgivably betrayed their "type." One prejudice against Luxemburg and Arendt together is that they have nothing to teach us about nations and nationalism because, as members of a deracinated Jewish intelligentsia, they are unable to appreciate the territorial attachments of national community.[9] A second, almost reverse prejudice against Arendt alone is that her implication of the Jews in the making of modern anti-Semitism reveals her to be a self-hating Jew who can have nothing to teach us about nationality in the nonterritorial sense of ethnic or ethno-religious feeling. A third prejudice, against Fanon, is that his criticism of the West is undermined by either (depending on who is speaking) his outrage at the West or his absorption of Western ideas, from Marxism to psychoanalysis to nationalism itself. As prejudices, these complaints cannot be rebutted directly but must be left to stand or fall on the basis of how useful our thinkers' answers to the national question prove to be.[10]

An a priori rejection of Luxemburg, Arendt, and Fanon in any event could not come at a more inopportune time. History has delivered to us a new combination of "political catastrophes" and "moral disasters" that strongly resembles the backdrop to their fertile reflections.[11] Capitalist expansion, the aftereffects of imperial power, and the collapse of multinational states have once again politicized previously quiescent populations, triggered chain reactions of nationalist identifications, incited searches for independent nation-states, created new minorities and diasporic groups, and catapulted into prom-

inence new coteries of "rootless" intellectuals. In light of the fact
that the present is never entirely divorced from the past, even if it
never simply repeats the past, how might our three thinkers help us
meet these shock waves?

ROSA LUXEMBURG

Let us begin with Rosa Luxemburg, who speaks to us from the earliest point in the twentieth century. Luxemburg confronts the national question directly, in many words over many years, with a passion inflamed by the centrality of nationalism to politics in her
period as well as the centrality of politics to theory in her life. She
also confronts the national question in many places. A Jew from
Russian Poland, she moves to and from Poland, Switzerland, Germany, Russia, and France. An active member of the Polish, Russian,
and German Social Democratic Parties, she participates in discussions on the national question throughout Europe and with respect
to noncapitalist regions in other parts of the world. It is almost as if
she belongs everywhere at once, her practical life the most convinc-
ing piece of evidence for her theoretical internationalism.[12]

Luxemburg also stands at the most antagonistic end of the spectrum of critical responses to nationalism. In those responses, she
is as wedded to the distinction between mystification and truth as
that great maker of such distinctions, Karl Marx. Her reasons are
roughly the same as his, although Luxemburg emphasizes far more
than Marx does the susceptibility of the masses to bourgeois ideology, of which nationalism for her, but not for him, is a particularly
potent instance. Indeed, she is often isolated among the European
Marxists who debate the national question up through the outbreak
of the First World War for being uniquely obtuse to the pull of national identity, the attachment to land or country, and the importance of ethnonational variation.[13] Her vehement criticisms of
nationalism are taken seriously enough to draw fire within Social
Democratic circles during her lifetime. Those criticisms fall into dis-
favor and then oblivion after her death.[14]

The foundation of Luxemburg's critique is the premise that nationality, not as an ethnic or cultural group (for such "national peculiarities had already existed for centuries") but as a national movement aspiring to its own nation-state, is a product of the bourgeois
era. Capitalism is inherently boundless, in that its inner logic of

profit accumulation presses it beyond every geographical border. It is also inherently iconoclastic, creating a culture and intellectual spirit that is open, scientific, and skeptical. Nevertheless, capitalism develops not in a void but "in a definite territory, a definite social environment, a definite language, within the framework of certain traditions, in a word, within definite national forms." An ascendant bourgeoisie sanctifies and reconstitutes these forms to suit its imperatives and designs. It unifies a particular territory, language, and set of practices within which it can secure political freedom, the conditions of modern culture, and "an internal or domestic market for its own commodity production," which it then calls "the fatherland."[15]

Luxemburg's first critical thesis based on this premise is that nationalism's traditional appearance contradicts its modern reality. As we shall see in a later chapter, this will become the core thesis of all modernist theories of nationalism at the opposite end of the twentieth century — although divorced from Luxemburg's other criticisms and so minus its original sting. According to Luxemburg, nationalist movements depict the nation as a "natural, unchangeable phenomenon, outside social development," "resisting all historical vicissitudes," rooted in an age-old folk culture and conservative peasant mass that is "an unshakable fortress of national distinctness." At the same time, the nation-state those movements seek to bring into being becomes the crucible for the development of the universal characteristics of modernity. These characteristics include "the big city," technical progress, industrialization, "speedy and constant communication," far-flung transportation networks, popular education, and "a new social class: the professional intelligentsia."[16] This first contradiction of nationalism is less a charge against it (except insofar as the opacity of action to actors is always a misfortune) than an analysis of it as intrinsically fraught with the tensions between the country and the city, past and future, continuity and disjuncture, the particular and what becomes, because of material historical processes, the universal.

Luxemburg's second critical thesis, on the contradiction between national unity and class division, is her most orthodoxly Marxist claim. As such it is very much *not* in vogue among modernist theorists of nationalism today.[17] The idea of the organic existence of a people "as a homogeneous social and political entity" is, Luxemburg declares, a "misty veil" obscuring "classes with antagonistic interests and 'rights.'"[18] Under this veil, the nation-state serves the bourgeois class[19] by binding workers to their exploiters, providing the administrative and coercive apparatus for capital's consolidation domestically and expansion abroad, and separating into antagonistic political units popular masses that had mingled in the old multinational dynastic states.[20] The class character of the nation-state is at once so fundamental to and so divisive of its identity that, as Luxemburg puts it with respect to the nationalist struggle that exasperated her most, "[We cannot] seek a single solution of the Polish national question for Koscielski and his stable boy." One need not know who Koscielski is to get the point.[21]

In her third critical thesis, Luxemburg contests the democratic truth of national self-determination. She asks, "Who is the self that national self-determination is to make self-determining?" and her answer is, in every setting, "Not the people, but their masters." For evidence, she points to nationalists' garrulousness about a people's need for political autonomy and silence about the particular way in which that people is to be governed; the overweening power of the state that nationalists are out to acquire or increase; and the class domination in all existing nation-states that nationalists seek to continue, not arrest. Thus, in the old multinational European empires, nationalists appear to be fighting for their people's freedom, but their obsession with political independence and lack of interest in democratizing the existing society show that they are really fighting to become their people's new rulers. In Bolshevik Russia, party leaders embrace the right to national self-determination for all peoples as "a jewel of democratic policy" while displaying a "cool contempt" for the "whole apparatus of the basic democratic liberties of the people" on which true self-determination depends.[22] In capitalist countries, a bourgeois agenda — the need for "a 'native' market," a "strong military," "customs policy," "administration in regard to communication, jurisdiction, school systems, and financial policy . . . the whole apparatus of a modern capitalistic state" — sets the parameters for the substance of the national self.[23]

In all these cases, at least, the master is, nationally speaking, the people's "own." In her fourth critical thesis, Luxemburg attacks nationalist movements for exerting mastery over other peoples, too, by asserting the right to self-determination while crushing that same assertion by other national, ethnic, and racial groups. This "antinational" impulse of nationalism has two sources. In part, it is a function of the disjuncture between the geographical limitation of the nation-state and the bourgeoisie's economic appetite, which is "so elastic and extensive that it always has the natural tendency to include the entire globe." The European nation-states can engage in imperial adventures to satisfy that appetite while claiming the right to self-determination for themselves only if "the European peoples are regarded as nations proper, while colonial peoples are looked on as 'supply depots.'" Indeed, European capitalist states champion the right to national self-determination for themselves *in order to* justify their intrusion into other regions of the world, thereby denying the possibility of national self-determination to those regions and so negating national self-determination as a universal right. Their "political conquest and domination over other nationalities," Luxemburg declares, proves the nationalism of those states to be "a theory of the ruling races" originating in "'European' cretinism" no less than in "the ideologies of bourgeois liberalism."[24] More generally, the great capitalist states secure their own self-determination through a position of world dominance that precludes effective self-determination for other states.

Luxemburg admits that "the history of the colonial expansion of capitalism" to some extent prompts "the contradictory tendency" of the struggle for independence of the colonial countries. However, she protests that "the winning of independence" only transfers "national dependence" to "another nationality." She illustrates her point with myriad examples, from the English emigrants who freed themselves in America "on the ruins and corpses of the redskin natives" to the explosive potentialities of the Indian movement "for the rights of the nation" against the British, given the "very existence in India of a huge number of nationalities."[25] Because the assertion of the right to national self-determination always triggers a chain reaction of national oppression, Luxemburg takes a hard line against anticolonial nationalism, too.

Such chain reactions of nationalism and antinational oppression partly signal the reemergence of the imperialist impulse in a new setting. But they also are a function of a second disjuncture not so tightly tied to the imperatives of capitalism between the ethnic singularity of the nationalist principle and the ethnic pluralism of much of geographical reality. As a result of a long history in which, as Luxemburg puts it, peoples "were constantly moving about geographically . . . joining, merging, fragmenting, and trampling one another," nationalities in modern states are an entangled intermixture.[26]

Once the same territory is inhabited by a mélange of peoples, the bid for national self-determination on the part of any one of them must be a bid to consign the rest to a fate on that continuum of unhappy fates ranging from political inconsequence and social discrimination to persecution, expulsion, and genocide. In short, ethnonational self-determination turns into ethnonational oppression in any context characterized by the mingling of peoples — which in our age is synonymous with the human context.

What makes movements for ethnonational self-determination so decentralizing and emancipatory vis-à-vis larger states dominated by a different national group, and so centrist and tyrannical toward ethnic and racial minorities in newly emancipated ethnonational states? Part of the answer lies in the logic of "self-determination," whenever the "self" is particular, not universal, and possesses the means to impose its will on the world.[27] Hegel exposes this logic when he states that the subject seeking self-determination must seek to determine everything outside itself that otherwise would determine it as an alien force. It is because the quest for self-determination on the part of any one subject inevitably degenerates into a quest for domination over all other subjects that Arendt will refuse to equate freedom with self-determination at all. She conceives of freedom instead as the ability of the self to begin something new in the world, precipitating, in response, other unpredictable and uncontrollable actions on the part of other selves so that all selves are, in their very freedom, radically unselfdetermining.[28] Alas, it is the nature of every ethnonational movement to understand freedom in Hegelian, not Arendtian, terms: to view its own identity as made not through a process of creative combustion with other identities but through the assertion of a rigidly separate substance over and against all other substances.

If Hegel assures us that the struggle for domination is not the final moment of the search for subjective freedom, Luxemburg warns us that the reciprocal recognition of equally independent and self-determining subjects is not either, at least not when those subjects are ethnic nationalities. The equal independence and autonomous self-determination of ethnonational subjects is exactly what the geographical intermixture of peoples rules out, by making the independent self-determination of any one of them a prelude to the domination of the rest. Not mutual recognition on the part of peoples each fortified inside its own nation-state but the political unity of a plurality of peoples is for Luxemburg the only democratic path that modern politics can take, the cultural vitality and civil equality of those peoples to be ensured "through their close cooperation, and not [through] their mutual separation by barriers of national autonomy."[29] On the one side, Luxemburg supports political unity against political separation out of an empirical assessment of the modern tendency toward the economic integration of larger and larger geographical areas, an idealistic faith in the potential for a universal expansion of human identification, and a moral conviction that with the achievement of social equality, human identification *should* expand until it reaches the limits of the whole human race. On the other side, Luxemburg supports ethnic difference against ethnic domination out of, if not a love of difference, then at least a repugnance for domination, as well as a respect for traditional cultures that are relatively cooperative in their organization of the labor process.

Luxemburg's case against nationalism is far from airtight. She is not incorrectly accused of sidestepping popular national feeling if and as it actually exists. In part, she dismisses that feeling as out of date on the materialist grounds that "historical development, especially the modern development of capitalism, does not tend to return to each nationality its independent existence, but moves rather in the opposite direction." In part, she depicts the working class as nonnational by leaning heavily on the distinction between the majority of the proletariat (whose "traditional forms of consciousness" are "the usual forms of bourgeois consciousness") and "the most advanced and most revolutionary section" — and then by leaning solely on that section. "There literally is not one social area," as she characteristically puts it, "in which the possessing class and the *class-conscious* proletariat hold the same attitude, and in which they appear as a consolidated 'national' entity."[30] To the idealist temptation of equating the real subjective identifications of the working class with the way Marxist theory says the working class should think and act when it is fully class-conscious, other Marxists debating the national question in the same period do not find it necessary to succumb.[31]

While Luxemburg overappreciates the internationalism of the European working class, she underappreciates the nationalism of oppressed peoples. Her explanation of nationalism as a function of bourgeois economic requirements in what become the great capitalist states makes it difficult for her to acknowledge the distinctive precipitants of nationalism in colonized regions. Her faith in socialist

internationalism makes it impossible for her to acknowledge nationalism as the most effective weapon for oppressed peoples in the real
as opposed to ideal arsenal of modern political strategies.

Finally, although Luxemburg's formula of the good political society as a unity of political identity and ethnic difference may be ap-
pealing, it is easy to suspect it of hinging on the substitution of a
dream of ethnic harmony for the reality of ethnic conflict. It is also
easy to suspect it of hinging on a presumption that ethnic differences
in the long run will not be very great. From Luxemburg's angle, most
small nationalities have already been turned into remnants and relics
by the large capitalist states. Moreover, the spread of bourgeois political liberties and the triumph of social democracy that Luxemburg
portrays as the road to interethnic peace and understanding she also
portrays as part and parcel of modern processes that will temper
ethnic identity over time. From the angle of minority peoples, however, a call for the political unity of diverse ethnic groups over their
political independence is likely to appear as a move for ethnic dominance by a large and arrogant but still particular people dressed up
in universal-culture disguise. Her passionate hatred of all forms of
domination notwithstanding, even Luxemburg cannot escape suspicion on this last count.

Luxemburg's flaws do not cancel out her noteworthy strengths.
She is alert to the pernicious couplet of elite mastery and popular
servitude, in the context of nationalism no less than of capitalism or,
for that matter, Bolshevism.[32] She grasps the intimate relationship
among self-serving leaders, dominant classes, and the nationalist
quest for state power, and she is able to support her theoretical analysis of that relationship with a formidable empirical knowledge of
modern economic history. Luxemburg refuses to be swept away by
the glamour of struggles for national self-determination or to con-
flate those struggles with the struggle for social and political democracy. Her main criticisms of European nationalism, colonialism, and
even anticolonial nationalism are compelling enough to be echoed
later in the century by Fanon. In the case of anticolonial nationalism,
he simply will turn what for Luxemburg are indelible marks of nationalist movements — elite manipulation of the masses, class division, and ethno-racial chauvinism — into susceptibilities of those
movements at specific stages in their development.

Indeed, we find an unexpected compatibility between this consummate antagonist of nationalism in every setting and critical propo-

nents of nationalism in the colonial setting. This compatibility is especially clear if Luxemburg's attack on the "offensive nationalism" of European nation-states is read side by side with her extraordinary last seven chapters of *The Accumulation of Capital*. Here she gives her own inflection to Marx's view that capital becomes world-historical when she claims that the accumulation process requires not simply capital's ceaseless expansion but also its coercive interaction with noncapitalist economies. She emphasizes the crucial importance of noncapitalist cultures for a logic of capital that, in her words, opens them up by brute force, ransacks them, and mutilates them—but also the importance of those cultures in and of themselves.[33] She so darkly underlines the ensuing destruction of whole ways of life with their own integrity and value that one is struck much more by the world wreckage capital produces than by its part in advancing the dialectic of world history.[34] Whether or not Luxemburg is correct in her technical arguments about capital's economic dependence on noncapitalist economies, her compassionate portrayal of the vitality of distinct cultures and peoples prior to capitalist penetration exemplifies her hatred of every kind of oppression and counterbalances her impatience elsewhere with ethnonational particularity. Along with other anti-imperialist Marxists of her day, Luxemburg must be seen as taking the first step toward turning Marxism as a theory of relations of economic inequality and exploitation within specific national societies, the essentials of those relations spreading sooner or later everywhere else, into a theory of relations of economic inequality and exploitation within a global system, in which whole regions and peoples as well as (not, for her, instead of) classes are major protagonists.[35]

Luxemburg deserves our admiration last of all for her bold and fiery style. Wrestling with all questions from a point deep inside political life, she exhibits, at least with respect to nationalism in politics, the urgency of a voluntarist who thinks that argument and action can make a difference to history, the purposefulness of an actor who hopes to set off some new chain of events in the world through thought and deed. If intellectuals on the sidelines of nationalist conflicts today dismiss Luxemburg even more cavalierly than they dismiss Marxism in general, it is surely as much because her passion jars with their tentativeness and irony as it is because her notion of nationalism is flawed. Partly because of her passion, Luxemburg is a salutary figure for our times, even though the big battle for her—

between national self-determination and socialist internationalism —
is no longer the battle for us.

HANNAH ARENDT

Luxemburg's views on nationalism, ethnonational persecution, and
class rule provide a strong stimulus to Arendt's own line of thought.
To be sure, Luxemburg plays the class card so intently that she
brings into relief on the one hand the presumption she shares not
with Arendt but with Fanon that the nation must be made to serve
the common people and on the other hand the presumption Arendt
shares with Fanon and not with her that nationality, ethnicity, and
race rather than class pose the most arresting political problems for
the century. Nevertheless, Luxemburg is allied with Arendt in that
both begin their musings on the national question inside Europe,
both see the trajectory of the European nation-state as shaped by the
activities of the bourgeoisie, and both believe that trajectory concludes more regularly in domination than in liberation.

In "Imperialism," Arendt follows Luxemburg in underlining the
suitability of the European nation-state for the early development of
capital, the bourgeoisie's later overseas expansion, and that class's
use of nationalist ideology to obscure social divisions at home. But
while Luxemburg views the nation-state as a creature of the bourgeoisie from the beginning, and the bourgeoisie as pitted with the
state against the working class, Arendt views the nation-state initially as having an independent integrity to it, and the bourgeoisie as
pitted against that integrity. Both thinkers idealize their favored antinomies to the bourgeoisie. For Luxemburg, as we have seen, empirical members of the working class might be blinded by nationalist
ideology, but the most advanced segment of that class is conscious
that its true connections are with other oppressed workers around
the world. Consequently, when Luxemburg speaks of the proletariat,
she always calls it "internationalist." Arendt, for her part, refers to
the original western European nation-state not as it is in reality but
as it is in conception. As such, it comprises a rule of law protecting
all people equally, an authority derived from popular sovereignty, a
citizen body inclusive of all of those who participate in the nation's
history and destiny, and a bounded territory harboring both a public
sphere and private property in the sense of a secure physical place in
which individuals can tend to the intimate, biologically rooted as-

pects of their lives. The nation-state in conception also combines national identity, political equality, and social plurality, with politics having primacy in national life over economics.

Arendt shows us how each of these good characteristics is undone as the bourgeoisie presses for an expansion of public political power to serve its global search for private gain. Economic motivation takes primacy over politics. The nation-state rules over distant peoples by violence and without their consent. Property conceived as the infinite accumulation of wealth undermines the stability of property as place and contributes to mass rootlessness everywhere. The nation discovers its identity in the distinctiveness and superiority of its race — a discovery legitimating the colonization of other peoples and reassuring the lower classes at home that although they may be socially and economically inferior to fellow nationals, they are biologically and culturally superior to foreigners.

Ironically, racial solidarity unites the nation at the moment that the nation-state becomes, in its imperialism, "antinational." Ironically, too, racial solidarity corrodes the significance of the nation by making preeminent broader distinctions between European and non-European civilizations and between white and colored or black races. The awkward fit between "nation" and "race" comes to haunt nationalist movements against Western domination too. In these cases, however, nationalists are prone to protest that nation-state allegiances corrode racial-civilizational solidarities rather than the other way around. That is, they see the line of degenerative movement as running from the unities of "the African people" or "Arab civilization" to legalized and militarized divisons between "Senegal" and "Kenya," or "Syria" and "Egypt," dreamed up by the West and serving the class interests of native political elites.

Although Arendt does not turn her sights to twentieth-century pan-Africanism and pan-Arabism, she studies in detail the nineteenth- and twentieth-century pan-movements in Europe and their devastating impact on modern history. Born out of the situation of oppressed minorities in Central and Eastern European multinational states, these pan-movements give rise to what Arendt terms "continental imperialism." Unlike overseas imperialism, continental imperialism is the work not of capital but primarily of the "mob" — the déclassé, the unemployed, the criminal elements at the top and bottom of society — and secondarily of the intelligentsia. Its principle of expansion is not economic gain but an "enlarged tribal consciousness" with a commitment to unify all individuals of the same "blood" or "spiritual" origin and to elevate this distinctive "folk" above all other people. It threatens the established European nation-states through its disregard for settled political borders; its elaboration of a compensatory myth in the absence of a real state, a real territory, a real public life; and its location of the criteria for belonging to a people in "being," not "acting." Still, Arendt warns us, the tribal or ethnonational idea of the people is not utterly at odds with the republican idea, which implies through its own hyphenation of "nation" and "state" that before acquiring an artificial state, the people had a natural existence.[36]

The less than airtight separation of republican and ethnonationalism is on display whenever racial images are used to conjure up the "French" or "English" people and whenever the cultural creations of language and literature are used as evidence of a "Slavic" or "Germanic" soul. Moreover, while in theory republican nationalism, unlike ethnonationalism, extends the possibility of citizenship to individuals of any origin who accept the nation's law and public life as their own, in practice the republican nation-state is twice capable of ethnic persecution. In the service of ensuring the national identity and equality of its citizens, that state is driven to suppress public signs of ethnocultural difference, which in effect means the suppression of ethnic minority difference. In the service of limiting its citizen body to a particular subsegment of the whole human race, that state also will resort to exclusionary policies as soon as it is besieged by refugees from elsewhere *en masse*. It follows that precisely the peoples ethnonational states select out to despise and expel will be treated as stateless and rightless by republican nation-states. Arendt holds that from the end of the First World War to the end of the Second, republican nation-states reiterate the racial judgments of ethnonational states, consigning peoples condemned by ethnonationalism as nonnational to the extralegal authority of their own police forces and the extraterritorial limbo of their own concentration camps. In short, "Those whom the persecutor had singled out as scum of the earth . . . were received as scum . . . everywhere."[37]

A gloom pervades "Imperialism" about the outcome of nationalism in politics that Luxemburg earlier and Fanon later never distantly match. Why are their spirits higher than Arendt's? After all, Luxemburg sees her position on nationalism attacked polemically from every side, and she witnesses the practical defeat of that position in social democracy's ignominious embrace of nationalism in 1914. Fanon, in turn, will leave his readers with the distinct impression that nationalism is ultimately a dubious means to any good end except decolonization.

Certainly Luxemburg and Fanon preserve an optimism about the possibilities for the political world in general as a consequence of their own engagement in revolutionary movements. However problematic those movements may be, they spare these two the isolation that Arendt describes in *The Origins of Totalitarianism* and that she regrets on behalf of herself and others like her in her personal letters. Those movements also save Luxemburg and Fanon from the despair of being unable to make a dent in the larger political situation, by multiplying a hundred thousandfold the force of individual words and deeds. Certainly, too, the times on which Luxemburg and Fanon focus are more hopeful than Arendt's interwar period. The two decades leading up to the Russian Revolution are open-ended enough that barbarism *or* socialism can strike Luxemburg as history's possible denouement. In turn, the decade after the defeat of Nazism has something heartening about it, in that each year transports one part of the world further away from the nadir of its own civilization and transports another part closer to independence from that civilization's rule.

Yet Arendt is also bleak about the national question because she sees it as a riddle with no solution. In addition to her alienation from collective political action and the darkness of her times, it is her view of the national question as a conundrum that makes Arendt so well suited a thinker for us. She emphasizes that once modern rootlessness (Luxemburg would add "ancient rootlessness too!") undermines the organic homogeneity of peoples in every region, all answers to the national question are bad. A society of heterogeneous strangers joined by their subjection to the same central state is as distasteful as a state-orchestrated attack on cultural difference to create a unified cultural identity. The formal distinction and protection of ethnic minorities is as problematic as the disappearance of minorities through their cultural assimilation. The exclusion of nonnationals by the nation-state is no more ideal than its indiscriminate inclusion of them until the nation swells up to universal size. The domination of a minority people by a national majority is as unfortunate as the minority's acquisition of its own separate nation-state, with the domination of some new minority as the result.

In a world that is socially an intermixture of peoples and politically all sewn up by established nation-states, the "worst factor" in the tangle of bad factors to do with nationalism, Arendt tells us, is the fine-sounding conviction that "true freedom, true emancipation, and true popular sovereignty [can] be attained only with full national emancipation."[38] That conviction, in that setting, is a recipe for claustrophobia: not the colony claustrophobia that Fanon will describe as afflicting native populations prohibited from moving beyond narrow limits, but a world claustrophobia in which peoples turned by the politics of national self-determination into natives of nowhere can find no place on earth to move to in order to be free without generating new waves of discriminations, coercions, and exclusions.

What keeps Arendt from opting for Luxemburg's counterproposal to national self-determination as a way out of these various dead ends? Clearly Arendt finds "the unity of political identity and ethnocultural distinction" a sympathetic phrase.[39] If she refuses blithely to follow Luxemburg's lead here, it is because Arendt is alert to the difference between what it is possible to do in words to transcend the dilemmas of nationalism and what it is possible to *do*. Given the slip between current ideals of heterogeneity-in-unity and real collective antagonisms of every sort, should we not be alert to that difference too?

FRANTZ FANON

Despite her critique of overseas imperialism and her sympathy (so much in contrast with Luxemburg's lack of sympathy) for nationalist struggles against colonial rule, Arendt is no friend of Fanon. She makes what can be read as an implicit argument against him in her impressive *On Revolution*. There, while noting the legendary connection between the origins of political community and violence, Arendt stresses violence's incapacity for speech, its marginality to politics, and its unsuitability as subject matter for political theory, which "remains bound to what appears in the domain of human affairs; and these appearances, in contradistinction to physical matters, need speech and articulation."[40] She confronts Fanon directly, however, only in *On Violence*, admittedly a much weaker work. Here she argues that violence is antipolitical even though it belongs to "the political realm of human affairs." This combination of ideas is less peculiar than it seems, for Arendt can condemn violence for being anti-political—that is, at odds with argument and persuasion and destructive of "the world of appearances and . . . the company of our fellow men"—only if she also can establish that violence belongs to the realm of human contingency and artifice, not the realm of biological necessity and natural forces, where condemnations are beside the point.[41] Arendt denies that violence has an instinctual or organic origin in part by fiat, stipulating that human violence occurs in the sociopolitical realm and that biological factors never can explain anything there. But she also denies that violence is instinctual or "vital" by tracing violence to rage, and rage not to unreason but to an offended sense of justice or a reaction against the hypocrisy of lying speech.[42] In addition, Arendt rejects the equation of violence with automatic impulses or bodily reflexes by defining it as strategic or "instrumental by nature," so that it is assimilated to rational calculation and is rational "to the extent that it is effective in reaching the end that must justify it."[43] Finally, she states that violence does not repeat some natural cycle but brings into being something new, even though what this type of action brings into being is most probably only "a more violent world."[44]

One of Arendt's aims in *On Violence* is to discredit all thinkers who embrace bloodshed as either an inescapable element of politics or a positive good. She focuses special attention on Fanon because of what she sees as his lamentable influence on the spirit of her age. If she admits in a footnote that Fanon is "much more doubtful about violence than his admirers," she does not significantly lower the temperature of her attack on him anywhere else.[45]

What must be said at once against Arendt on Fanon's behalf is that his attitude toward violence only erroneously can be taken as a great enthusiasm dampened by a small doubt. Indeed, his entire treatment of nationalism is more aptly seen as a canvas painted in certain colors and then brushed over with others. This self-revising method of argument does not reflect either ambivalence toward violence or confusion about nationalism on Fanon's part. It reflects instead the dynamic quality of the struggle for national liberation, the explosive effects of decolonization on the social environment, the instability of every aspect of life during "a program of complete disorder." The sudden thawing out of a world that had been previously frozen requires a corresponding fluidity in the conceptualization and assessment of that world's constitutive elements. Thus, in response to changes that nationalism itself helps produce in its milieu, and without ever being self-contradictory, Fanon moves from celebrating to criticizing to repudiating national consciousness, culture, and politics. Thus, too, he raises the curtain on colonialism as a two-person drama between the native and the settler and then gradually brings onto the stage peasants, town dwellers, a parasitical native bourgeoisie, Senegalese and Sudanese, black Africans and Arabs, and even sympathetic Europeans. This multiplication of characters does not at all signal a mistake in his original casting but mimics the actual process by which decolonization replenishes a world colonialism had "cut in two."[46]

In the same way, Fanon calibrates his judgment of violence to suit torrential changes in the political landscape. In his first essay he condemns the colonial order for speaking "the language of pure force" but declares that against such an order, the " 'thing' which has been colonized" must exert a counterforce in order to become "man."[47] In his second essay, he insists that spontaneous mass uprisings must give way to thought and action tempered by political education if a popular movement against tyranny is not to become either tyrannical itself or prey to a new kind of tyranny through harboring too naive a notion of the world. Fanon's startling final essay exhibits the psychiatric case studies of torturers, soldiers, resistance fighters, and civilian victims of brutality, all suffering the aftershocks of anticolonial war. In their psychological disintegration, these figures reach an eerie equality with one another, being most clearly distinguishable not as Algerian or French, and not as the active agents or passive targets of violence, but as individuals plagued by this or that nightmarish neurosis or psychosis.

In "Concerning Violence," Fanon praises violence for making subjects out of human objects. In "Colonial War and Mental Disorders," he shows that violence shatters human subjectivity. The two essays together confirm the following truth: the slave who "at the moment he realizes his humanity . . . begins to sharpen the weapons with which he will secure its victory" can win freedom from the master/slave relation with those weapons but not freedom from the reverberations of his own acts.[48] If Fanon treats the question of violence with greater complexity than Arendt admits, he also treats it with greater complexity than Arendt musters, proving, incidentally, that theoretical intricacy does not always guarantee depth of political understanding.

First, Fanon represents violence in the colonial context as anti-

political in its original thesis but pre-political in the antithesis to
that. The imposition of colonial rule by "bayonets and cannons" and
its maintenance by "the policeman and the soldier" are antipolitical
because, as Arendt would put it, they prohibit the emergence of a
sphere for public speech and action accessible to natives and colo-
nists alike. The rebellion of the colonized against colonial rule is pre-
political because, as Fanon does put it, it catapults those who are
oppressed from the position of "spectators crushed with their ines-
sentiality into privileged actors." This is not to say that he is san-
guine about whether these newly privileged actors can make their
way from violence to politics. That depends, for a start, on whether
they manage to escape being psychologically crushed with the horror
of what they have violently done and what has been violently done
to them.[49]

Second, Fanon conceives of violence as expressive of somatic feelings no less than ideas about injustice or intentions to achieve specific ends. Fanon highlights the bodily aspects of violence not because he sees violence as belonging to a biological rather than
sociopolitical zone but because he does not ever divide off the body
from sociopolitical life and because he believes the bodily aspects of
violence loom large in the colonial setting. The world into which the
colonizer herds the popular masses — unlike the world of magic the
people traditionally inhabit, unlike the world of Western high culture
into which the native intellectual is lured, and unlike the world of
bourgeois consumption that seduces the European working class — is
not so much ideologically mystified as it is physically claustrophobic.
It is a "narrow world, strewn with prohibitions," a "motionless,
Manicheistic world," a world in which "[t]he first thing which the
native learns is to stay in his place, and not to go beyond certain
limits." Because colonial power operates on the masses by brute
force and physical containment instead of cultural and political sua-
sion; because the native's sense "that his life, his breath, his beating
heart are the same as those of the settler" fuels in him a resentment
that is as visceral as it is cerebral; and because the muscles of the
native are "always tensed," violence against the colonizer offers
the colonized a physiological as well as psychological release from
the effects of servitude. This is why Fanon can understand violence
"at the level of individuals" as a "cleansing force" that "frees the
native from his inferiority complex and from his despair and inaction."[50]

Is Arendt right or wrong to find Fanon politically irresponsible for advocating violence as a part of national liberation? The answer depends in part on whether Fanon is right or wrong that the colonized cannot escape either the external rule of the colonizer or his own internal situation of being permanently "tensed" without a physical explosion. But the answer just as centrally depends on whether Arendt is right or wrong that violence is antipolitical and yet part of the political, not the biological, realm. It is important to realize that Arendt's claims are animated by a primary antagonism to the presence of the body in politics rather than by a primary antagonism to the political infliction of bodily pain.[51] The first antagonism, not the second, lies behind her insistence that the language of politics is exclusively verbal, never physical, so that violence must be counted as speechless and incapable of speech. It also lies behind her presumption that no somatic experience ever pressures a subject to act with physical force, so that it always is possible and (for the sake of protecting not the body but speech) almost always desirable to forswear the "use" of violence through the use of reason.

Conversely, although Fanon may disturb contemporary sensibilities because he does not bristle at the thought of spilling blood (how swiftly the spirit of our age veered away from the spirit of Arendt's and Fanon's), he offers much that should attract us to him. Fanon is unprejudiced against the body and consequently is not compelled to pry the realm of the body from the realm of speech and action. He can see violence as a feature simultaneously of visceral and political experience, and as a means of detonating the master/slave relation, one crucial precondition of a democratic public sphere. He also appreciates the paradoxical consequences of a system of rule that in speaking the language of pure force invites its subordinates to use the same language in return. Fanon would find it perverse to use the term "antipolitical" when referring to a conversation in which "[t]he violence of the colonial regime and the counter-violence of the native . . . respond to each other in an extraordinary reciprocal homogeneity."[52] Through that conversation, the native achieves the status of an active subject in history that a monologue of violence had precluded before. Nonetheless, Fanon shows us that the violence that emancipates the self socially can destroy the self "humanly." In that unfortunate case, the free self will be too tormented to enjoy politics or any other human pleasure.

Other things threaten the popular enjoyment of political speech and action in the new nation besides the psychological breakdown of individuals through their participation in anticolonial wars. There is the dictatorial political leader, the corrupt official machine, and the rule of the country on behalf of a single family or tribe. There are the collective hatreds that nationalist ideology can stir up the day after independence from the settler is won, which Fanon believes have their basis in the different economic functions different ethnic groups perform, even though such groups experience their animosities as originating in their very beings. Finally, there is the great disparity in wealth between the native elite and the vast majority of the people. If Fanon's critique of dictatorship and ethnonational hatred brings him into harmony with Arendt, his allegiance to what Gramsci would have called the "simple people" of the nation and his call for a political struggle against poverty, illiteracy, and a parasitical bourgeoisie put him at odds with her again. Arendt has no great love of the bourgeoisie, but she loathes the conquest of the political realm by the poor. "[T]he cry for bread will always be uttered with one voice," she complains; the "misery of the people" imposes the dictates of necessity on a realm that is meant for freedom.[53]

Historical circumstances always conspire to push certain questions to the forefront of the consciousness of an age with such a force that other questions are pushed into the background. Sometimes the questions that drop from sight have been adequately resolved, but sometimes they are merely repressed. This is why, just as every future generation will be surprised that problems that should have been glaring in the past were not, every past generation would be surprised that the future ignored problems whose urgency the past understood. There is an unsettling sense in which we look at the world less in the way that a sailor peers through binoculars at an ever more detailed and visible coastline, than in the way an esthete gazes into a kaleidoscope. As if the world suddenly were given a quick turn, old patterns disappear; new patterns glitter before the wonder-struck and forgetful eye.

The national question that consumes Luxemburg, Arendt, and Fanon during the first sixty years of the century slides into obscurity even before Fanon's early death. One factor contributing to its obscurity is that the most explosive political fault line in the world from the end of the Second World War to the late 1980s is the single "difference" between capitalism and communism, not the multiple differences among ethnonationalities or nation-states.[54] Even anticolonial movements for national liberation have their greatest significance during the cold war as struggles against imperialism in a larger context of the opposition between two antagonistic economic systems rather than as struggles for the self-determination of peoples in a larger milieu of roughly equal, heterogeneous nation-states. If there is intellectual indifference to the national question except when it dovetails with efforts of decolonization, even then the interest in it is as a subsidiary of the question "capitalism or communism?" The indifference to nationalism in the West initially is magnified rather than reduced by the emergence of new social movements and the identity politics of gender, sexuality, and race.

Yet less than two decades after Arendt's death, nationalism resurfaces as the most heroic of all the dramas of collective identity.[55] At first glance, the new nationalisms of the 1980s and 1990s tell against rather than for our authors' analyses. They seem to confirm the vitality of particularistic national narratives against Luxemburg's idea of a logic of history sweeping up the world into a single scheme, against Arendt's idea of a single set of conditions for the practice of politics, and against Fanon's idea of a single, salvageable entity called "mankind." They seem to prove the pull of inherited identifications and attachments above the desire for freedom; myth and sentiment above reflective reason and intellectual critique; the worth of anchors and banisters over the vertigo of creative action. Finally, they seem to lend their weight to the essential truth of ethnic identity; to a world variety ensured by distinct, homogeneous cultures; and to the democratic value of movements for national self-determination against large, centralized, bureaucratic states.

However, the error and obsolescence of our authors' tendencies of thought and feeling become less clear the moment an ethnic minority breaks away from one state to consolidate a state of its own; the moment a people wins liberation from power to "rule itself" (which always turns out to mean that one segment of that people rules the rest); the moment a will to national self-determination exerts its own aggressive will to power on the world; and, finally, the moment the effects of transnational economic unities overshadow the effects of national political separations. At times like these, no one can afford to be too nervous about criticizing popular solidarities to criticize tyrannical national solidarities, too fastidious about respecting difference in the abstract to stand up against the homogenizing ventures of differences in the concrete, or too swayed by superficial signs of variety to note the destruction of meaningful variety in the world. We could do much worse than to fortify ourselves for these tasks by drawing on the perceptions and sensibilities of Luxemburg, Arendt, and Fanon.

One of our authors' main perceptions is that the great threat to equality, variety, and a secure place in the world comes not from heterogeneous intermixtures of peoples but from the ever-expanding search for private profit, although the old-style colonialism they highlight is no longer a central feature of that search. Another perception is that a multicultural "respect for difference," which many contemporary thinkers tout as the resolution of the tension between identity and difference, is problematic both for petrifying boundary lines between identities and for barring critical judgments across those lines. A refusal to bring to bear general principles on other peoples allows multiculturalists to chatter away about respecting difference in one place, while in another place, as if separated from the chatterers by a universe instead of an ocean, one "identity" is left to withstand an attempt by another "identity" to wipe it off the face of the earth.

Part of the anxiety about forcefulness in judging and acting derives from a fear of exerting imperialist power in a new guise. All of our authors would appreciate that fear. Nevertheless, they would have found incomprehensible such a break between intellectual discourse and political practice, such squeamishness before the need for fighting words and deeds. Their temperaments — Luxemburg's spunk, Arendt's arrogance, Fanon's anger — help explain why, but so do their theoretical dispositions. Luxemburg and Fanon can judge and act with self-certainty because they see situations as having a truth to them rather than being made of competing stories, because they have a concept of humanity that overarches all particular identities and provides a standard to which all identities can be held, and because they make clear-cut distinctions between the forces of oppression and emancipation. Arendt presents us with a more complicated case. On the one hand, she is contemptuous of the idea of a single good that it is the task of history or politics to realize, and she champions the idea of a plurality of ends in human life. On the other hand, she affirms a truth not of ends but of beginnings by insisting that plurality can flourish only under quite particular conditions. Consequently Arendt can and does make imperious pronouncements about the worth of different social orders on the basis of whether they secure those conditions or not.

The same anxiety about forcefulness helps explain the antipathy

of those who "respect difference" toward any kind of physical violence. While Arendt, not to speak of nationalist brutalities themselves, warns us to proceed with the utmost delicacy and caution,
Fanon presses us to reconsider that antipathy in two ways.

First, against power that works through physical coercion rather
than through the manufacture of consent or the normalization of
selves, Fanon shows us that violent rebellion is an eminently suitable
response. This is not to say that it is the only suitable response or
that it has no malignant consequences, but it *is* to refuse to condemn
violence flatly.[56] Second, Fanon shows us that the same importance
we attribute to the body in its feelings of sexual desire must also be
attributed to the body in its feelings of resentment, indignation, and
rage, and hence to the visceral pressures to violence against a social
order that is felt to be unjust. To admit the physicality of certain
forms of domination and the visceral aspect of the fury at injustice is
also to admit that under certain circumstances, the absence of the
impulse to violence must be counted as a puzzle, not a virtue.

What are the implications of Fanon's argument in the context of
nationalism today? Most obvious, Fanon suggests that groups at the
receiving end of nationalist violence have both a good reason and
strong motivation to fight back, especially if the rest of the world has
abandoned them. Most disturbing, he suggests that those who fail to
feel anger at injustices done to them will lack a fundamental psychological weapon for their self-defense whenever social or political discrimination turns into physical persecution. The largest group lack-
ing this weapon is made of women, whose difficulty in lashing out
against domination is itself a domination effect of gender identity.
But the defenseless groups most significant to the modern history of
nationalism are ethnic minorities that try to identify with their discriminating majorities until the very end.

Chapter Three

On the Jewish Question

Isaiah Berlin and Hannah Arendt

ISAIAH BERLIN

"Probably no one in our time has come nearer to being regarded as the academic equivalent of a saint than Isaiah Berlin," remarks Stefan Collini in the *Times Literary Supplement*. Writing several months before Berlin died, after which the accolades multiply everywhere, Collini notes Berlin's many honorary degrees, his Oxford chair, his knighthood,[1] his "apparently effortless *entrée* into the overlapping social worlds of Britain's upper class and governing elite."[2]

Collini might just as easily have cited the felicitous phrases with which others praise Berlin's scholarly work. For example, Noel Annan describes Berlin as having written "the truest and the most moving of all the interpretations of life that my own generation made."[3] Ramin Jahanbegloo extols him for demonstrating that "history is all too full . . . of the agony of men who have tried to evade the tragic responsibility of choice by placing their faith in final and absolute truths."[4] Although he goes on to puncture Berlin's attempt to join pluralism and liberalism, John Gray lauds his thought for being "animated by a single idea of enormous subversive force" and "profound originality": that "ultimate human values are objective but irreducibly diverse, that they are conflicting and often uncombinable, and . . . sometimes . . . incommensurable."[5] Roger Hausheer assures those who are less favored that to meet Berlin "is to know at once why he is so celebrated," given his "brilliance as a lecturer and talker."[6] Michael Ignatieff concludes his splendid biography of Berlin by declaring that he showed "a dark century . . . what a life of the mind should be: skeptical, ironical, dispassionate and free."[7] But perhaps nothing can quite match the rapture of Leon Wieseltier's eulogy to Berlin, "When a Sage Dies, All Are His Kin." Here Berlin is portrayed as "the most original, the most lucid, the most erudite, and the most relentless enemy of the idea of totality in his age, which was an age of totality" or "[m]ore precisely . . . of failed totality" — a failure that can be traced, Wieseltier claims, "not least to the notions of this professor and his crowded, benevolent mind."[8] As for which souls are Berlin's kin (and a plague on all the rest!), Wieseltier congratulates the pluralists, the rationalists, the democrats, the nationalists, and the Jews, whose special connection Wielseltier suggests by couching the whole essay in Talmudic terms.

In combination with his illustriousness as a public intellectual and the intimate regard felt for him by so many luminaries of his day, this rushing torrent of praise makes any criticism of Berlin seem almost sacrilegious.[9] Still, one might venture to protest that Berlin prefers the sweeping summary to rigorous theoretical argument and that he forces the history of modern thought into a bludgeon to hammer home the superiority of pluralism over monism as his own monistic theme. Collini is not the first to describe Berlin as a hedgehog — Berlin's figure for those animals who "interpret everything in the light of some single all-embracing system"[10] — parading as a fox — Berlin's figure for those more admirable creatures who know many smaller things.[11] In both the generality and repetitiveness of much of his work, Berlin is unlike, say, Hannah Arendt or Karl Marx, each of whose books and essays, while expressive of a unified sensibility and outlook, say and do such specific things that one text cannot stand in for any another. For both these thinkers, Berlin shows much irritated disdain. In Marx's case, he arrives there after a confrontation, if not with the intricacies of Marx's ideas than at least with their historical formation and what he sees as their political significance.[12] Arendt he dismisses outright. He complains that he tried to read her but found that "[s]he moves from one sentence to another, without logical connection"; that what she had to say was "nonsense," "not new," or "wrong"; that, in any event, according to Gershom Scholem, she appealed only to those "unused to ideas," for "anybody who was truly cultivated and a serious thinker could not abide her." In short, he has no great respect for "the lady's" mind.[13]

Though Berlin may have his flaws as a political theorist, historian of ideas, and judge of minds such as Arendt's, he is a stunning painter of intellectual portraits. His flair for evoking a personality in limpid, astringent prose is evident as soon as he is moved to conjure up the unique spirit of an individual instead of pressing that individual into the service of his one fixed idea. To be bowled over by his seemingly effortless powers as a miniaturist one need only look at Berlin's reflections on J. L. Austin, L. B. Namier, Chaim Weizmann, and Felix Frankfurter in *Personal Impressions*, which many rightly call his most marvelous work. The same discriminating eloquence infuses "Benjamin Disraeli, Karl Marx and the Search for Identity," which shines because its argument is an outgrowth of rather than a straitjacket over Berlin's depiction of his characters: two sets of fathers and sons who differently respond to the plight of being social outsiders.

But Berlin's standing is only partly explained by his specific qualities of intelligence and literary grace. A magnetism of personality that is always at root mysterious contributed to it, as did the equally mysterious good fortune that followed Berlin throughout his life in much the same way that, as Arendt once put it, "the little hunchback" of bad luck had followed Walter Benjamin.[14] As Ignatieff shows, Berlin's good fortune began with his being the adored only child of a well-to-do Jewish merchant family in Russia; continued with the family's comfortable resettlement in London before the Stalinist era ensued; and rose with his education at the best English schools, his first academic post at New College, and his appointment — the first for a Jew — at All Souls College, "the most select club in English life."[15] There Berlin attained an aura through belonging to an Oxford intellectual elite that automatically presumed the supreme value of each of its members. This presumption was, in fact, once so confident and strong that as Berlin writes in his homage to J. L. Austin, "We felt no need to publish our ideas, for the only audience which was worth satisfying was the handful of our contemporaries who lived near us, and whom we met with agreeable regularity."[16] Among the more tangible privileges All Souls provided Berlin was the opening of every door to status, fame, and material wealth. He gained acquaintance with many prominent intellectual, artistic, and political figures, as well as introductions into high society. The connections he made at All Souls helped catapult him into circles near the center of Western power and authority. Those circles, in turn, were gratified by Berlin's heartfelt allegiance to the capitalist West and his fortification of the liberal idea of freedom against its enemies, of which Berlin considered Marxism the most odious instance. Other liberals found Marxism odious, too, but Berlin's flight as a young boy from Bolshevik Russia lent him impeccable credentials in this respect.

We must consider, however, that Berlin's attractiveness in and for his own setting also might stem from his Jewish identity. To shed light on this possibility, we could do much worse than consult the despised Arendt. In *The Origins of Totalitarianism*, Arendt provides a Proustian account of nineteenth-century French salon society, which found exceptional Jews magnetic and the mass of Jews obnoxious. Berlin repeatedly represents England as a liberal and tolerant society in which Jews could feel themselves equal to all other citizens.[17] Nevertheless, the realities of English anti-Semitism should make us wonder if Berlin himself might have been sought after not merely because he was an individual of exceptional merit but also because he was a special kind of Jew — one whose background was exotic, whose talents were remarkable, and whose understanding of the rules of upper-class English society was expertly acute. In that expertise, if not in his exceptional status, Berlin resembles the assimilating Western European Jews he describes in "Jewish Slavery and Emancipation," who, for survival's sake, had "to make themselves familiar with the habits and modes of behavior" of Gentile society, to "get this right" and "not miscalculate." Through "[s]o much labour and devotion to the life and outlook of other people," they came to identify with the subject to which they had devoted all their "time, gifts, energy, emotional resources," although they stood out precisely because their understanding was "too sharp" and their devotion "too great," and because they were "altogether too anxious to please."[18] The figure of the exceptional Jew as Arendt analyzes it would help explain Berlin's remark, so incongruous with his long and happy existence at the pinnacle of English society, that Marilyn Berger reports in her *New York Times* obituary for him. "Of course assimilation might be a quite good thing, but it doesn't work. Never has worked, never will. There isn't a Jew in the world known to me who somewhere inside him does not have a tiny drop of uneasiness vis-à-vis *them*, the majority among whom they live . . . one has to behave particularly well . . . [or] *they* won't like us." When, according to Berger, "it was suggested to him that he was surely the exception . . . that he had been saluted, cherished and accepted with pride in England . . . he had an immediate response: 'Nevertheless, I'm not an Englishman, and if I behave badly. . . .' "[19] Arendt might have put the point differently. "I'm not an Englishman but an exceptional Jew, and that is precisely one reason why they salute me. But if I act like an ordinary Jew. . . ."

Whether or not Arendt is more persuasive than Berlin about the mentality of the English society that "saluted" him, Berlin's situation as a member of a Jewish minority in England during the Nazi period was not incidental to the formation of his point of view. That situation, by refusing him the luxury of either a strictly individualist or strictly rationalist understanding of human nature and social life, contributed to what must count as his most important project: his attempt to force liberalism into contact with the Counter-Enlightenment sensibilities that had helped produce the grave social disturbances of his times. Thus, on the one hand, Berlin champions individual liberty in the classical sense. He places a high value on freedom as the ability of persons to think and act autonomously, that is, according to their individual lights, as authors of their own purposes and plans, and as actors only minimally constrained by collective pressures and limits. On the other hand, he also endorses elements of thought and feeling best categorized as Herderian. These elements include a respect for the power of irrationalism; an affirmation of the basic human need to belong to a group; an insistence on the importance of inherited collective identities; a defense of national-cultural particularity and variety as goods in themselves; a hostility to the idea of cosmopolitanism despite his own ease in traversing many national languages and borders; and a much diminished universalism that upholds only the minimal moral law needed to censor crimes that should be hideous from any cultural perspective. To be sure, there are several ways to interpret the fact that Berlin is, as Michael Ignatieff puts it, "liberalism's greatest elucidator of the antiliberal."[20] That fact may simply register Berlin's determination to confront and contest convictions opposite to his own. Then again, that fact may register Berlin's belief that these opposite convictions can and should be harmonized, as contemporary liberals claim who have tried to harmonize liberalism and nationalism with a deep bow to Berlin as their muse. But I want to offer a third interpretation: a commitment to liberalism and a fascination with illiberalism are internal, irreconcilable aspects of Berlin's personality — fissures in the self that show up as fissures in the self's work. In the rest of this chapter, I will look at the way one such fissure between individual freedom and ethnonational identity disturbs Berlin's portrayal of four historically eminent Jews — and disturbs Berlin's own portrait, too.

BENJAMIN DISRAELI, KARL MARX, AND CHAIM WEIZMANN

That the question of individual freedom becomes, for Berlin, especially problematic in the context of the Jewish question is not surprising, given his many remarks to the effect that all modern Jews have been seared by their minority social status and by the effects of European nationalism, especially German nationalism in its mid-twentieth century, exterminist phase.

Nevertheless, we would expect this foe of determinism and friend of individual choice to insist that no collective experience or set of historical conditions and situations either dictates or warrants any single response on the part of any particular person. And indeed, Berlin writes "Benjamin Disraeli, Karl Marx and the Search for Identity" partly to describe, in the context of nineteenth-century Jewish life in England and Germany, the formation of multiple mentalities in response to conditions that also produced the nationalist mentality. How, then, does Berlin come to conclude that most of the responses of modern Western European Jewry were evasions of their real identity, tragic attempts to belong to an alien social group, and that only Jewish nationalism was true as well as right?

Berlin begins his essay by framing the thought and action of all Western European Jews in terms of the identity crisis that occurred once they were forced to mix in the Gentile world. "What is a Jew?" and "What is the Jew's relation to society?" became questions for Jews only after the French Revolution, "when the gates of the ghettos were opened, and Jews began . . . to mingle with their fellow-citizens of other faiths." Berlin marks out three responses to the possibilities that enlightenment, political emancipation, and social integration presented for this diaspora group. Some Jews recoiled "before the prospect of a strange, wider world," preferring "the narrow but familiar place of ancient confinement" where they had been materially oppressed but spiritually free. Some ventured out eagerly and assimilated easily. But others, more prickly and less ingratiating, were "liable to waves of self-pity, aggressive arrogance, exaggerated pride . . . with alternating bouts of self-contempt and self-hatred, feeling themselves to be objects of scorn or antipathy to those very members of the new society by whom they most wished to be recognized and respected." Berlin calls such self-torment a "condition of men forced into an alien culture" but also a "well-known neurosis in an age of nationalism, in which self-identification with a dominant group becomes supremely important, but, for some individuals, abnormally difficult." It was the Jews' not accidental misfortune that just when they were beckoned to take their place as free and equal individuals in society, new struggles broke out all over Europe for national self-determination, power, and status. Thus, to the new difficulties of individualism must be added, as a precipitant of the tormented personality, the new pressures of exclusive nationalism and their dangers for the Jews as the minority already "most discriminated-against."[21]

At least under such conditions, Berlin sees two ways for minorities "to shed the emblems of servitude and inferiority" and "don the garments . . . of free men." The first is to demand of the larger society equality and recognition, or to achieve over that society superiority and domination; the second is to identify with some other group unstained by one's despised origins. Berlin argues that the elder Disraeli and Marx chose to blend into bourgeois culture, which is why each baptized his son, although Berlin never explains whether he sees assimilation as an instance of the search for equality and recognition or as an instance of reidentification. But he is quite clear that the younger Disraeli and Marx — both driven "by an inner dynamism remote" from their fathers' accommodating constitutions, with "fiery temperaments, unbending wills, and considerable contempt for most of the human beings by whom they were surrounded" — set out to acquire a dramatic "new persona."[22] Each did this by championing a group beleaguered in bourgeois society different from his own beleaguered group.

Berlin focuses mainly on Disraeli as someone who was fascinated by the free and arrogant aristocracy "as a class and a principle" and who "wanted power . . . and recognition by those on the inside, as one of them." Disraeli surmounted the obstacle of his Jewishness "by inflating it into a tremendous claim to noble birth." He purported that all Jews belonged to an aristocratic Eastern race so that he might pose as the equal of the ancient elites "of his family's adopted country, which he so profoundly venerated." A "flamboyant" adventurer and "rococo" exhibitionist, Disraeli genuinely was "[p]ossessed by the idea of race"; he glorified empire, irrational forces, men of genius as "masters of the destinies of nations," "temperament, blood," "history, the land . . . ancient institutions." Just as genuinely, he abhorred equality, liberal cosmopolitanism, and racial admixtures. His desires and convictions, in combination with his talent for political romance, allowed him to triumph as a dandyish "Pied Piper leading a bemused collection of dukes, earls, solid country gentlemen, and burley farmers" against the "ill-bred upstarts" and "heartless industrial exploiters" of the new economic age. Berlin concludes that Disraeli invented and came to believe in his "splendid fairy-tale" because he was "[u]nable to function in his proper person, as a man of dubious pedigree in a highly class-conscious society." He was "out of his proper element," subduing the element in which he found himself "by sheer power of will and imagination." "[O]ne of the most troubled and most gifted of 'alienated' men," Disraeli searched for and found a regiment "in whose name he could speak and act, because he could not face the awful prospect of speaking in his own."[23]

Berlin strongly suggests that it would have been better had Disraeli faced that "awful prospect" and resolved his identity problems on the basis of realities instead of fantasies. But he is also taken with Disraeli, much more than he is taken with Marx.[24] There is an empathetic affection and amused admiration on the part of this Anglophile for the "oriental-looking spellbinder," who by dint of ambition and a flair for the theatrical became the leader of imperial England, beloved by the queen. After all, Berlin himself was adored by the English, if not adored to that extent, perhaps because he arrived at his position by a route more like that of the assimilating father than that of the self-dramatizing son. Berlin most notably favors Disraeli because he sought entrance into non-Jewish society by boasting "of his Jewish origins instead of hiding them," unlike "some of the assimilated Jews of his time." Disraeli acknowledged his Jewishness and hence "did no violence to what he felt to be true of himself."[25]

In contrast, Berlin describes Marx as a Jew who was self-hating and self-denying. Living in a time of "pathologically anti-Semitic" German chauvinism and subjected even to "anti-Semitic jibes from fellow socialists and radicals," Marx kept silent about his Jewish origins. Worst still, in his early work he wrote about Jews with a "ferocity" of language resembling "that of many later anti-Semitic tracts, both right- and left-wing." At some point, Berlin surmises, Marx "decided once and for all to destroy within himself the source of the doubts, uneasiness and self-questioning which tended to torment [other] men." He repressed both his Jewishness and the anti-Semitism directed at him, which required him to repress the social significance of the Jewish question and the national question under which it was subsumed. As a consequence of his attempt to escape the disadvantages of his origins by denying both the disadvantages and the origins, this supreme critic "all his life systematically underestimated nationalism as an independent force." That "illusion,"

Berlin not incorrectly remarks, "led his fellows in the twentieth century to a faulty analysis of Fascism and National Socialism, for
which many of them paid with their lives." Marx, meanwhile, trans-
ferred his burning sense of injustice to the plight of the working
class, which he represented as a social victim free from national prejudices, internationalist in its solidarities, and animated by the interests of humanity at large. Berlin reminds us that Marx was no less an
outsider to the real class in contrast to which Marx's idea of the
proletariat was a fable than Disraeli was to the real British aristocracy. But it was his outsidership to society in general, a function of
his intolerable position as a Jew, that makes this "bitter, lonely and
fanatical exile" speak like a revolutionary avenger for the proletariat
but sound like "a proud and defiant pariah" in defense of "a long
humiliated race."[26]

In short, to the questions that nineteenth-century Jews were forced
to ask themselves about who they were and how they should relate
to the often hostile wider world, Disraeli and Marx gave different
wrong answers, although the second was worse than the first. In
light of the fact that Jews who assimilated into bourgeois society
later perished in the Holocaust along with everyone else, Berlin can
conclude that Disraeli's and Marx's fathers gave the wrong answer,
too.

Was there a right answer to the Jewish question? For Berlin's response, let us turn to his essay in memory of Chaim Weizmann.

Berlin celebrates Weizmann as a truly "great man." Weizmann
strikes Berlin as great because he was one of those extraordinary
individuals who "seems able, almost alone and single-handed, to
transform one form of life into another."[27] He exemplifies the impact
of free individual choice on history, against the determinist view that
ideas, idealism, and sheer willpower cannot change the inexorable
course of events.[28] At the same time, Weizmann also strikes Berlin as
great because Weizmann could see that every individual Jew is fundamentally marked by his or her Jewish identity, both as it essentially is and as it has been distorted by the Jews' predicament in
modern Europe. Weizmann understood that "the ills of the Jews" —
and Disraeli's and Marx's ills as Berlin depicts them surely must be
counted here — stemmed from their situation as members of a "semi-
helot population, relegated to an inferior and dependent status." Under these conditions, Jews developed "the virtues and vices of
slaves" and became "morally and socially crippled," plagued by ab-

normal psychologies. For their "neuroses, both individual and collective," Weizmann prescribed the medicine of Jewish nationalism, believing that "if Jews were to be emancipated, they must live in freedom in their own land, that there alone they would no longer be compelled to extort elementary human rights by that repellant mixture of constant cunning, obsequiousness and occasional arrogance which is forced on all dependants and clients and slaves." Berlin praises Weizmann for being unconcerned with the form of government the future state would or should take, as if that lack of concern with the relationship between leaders and led were a self-evident plus rather than a minus. He also claims that Weizmann never called on the Jews "to make terrible sacrifices . . . or commit crimes . . . for the sake of some felicity to be realised at some unspecified date, as the Marxists did." With respect to nationalism and communism, which he somewhat peculiarly identifies as the two great approaches to life dividing the modern world, Berlin stands absolutely with Weizmann on one side. While Weizmann's love of England helps win Berlin's love of him, Berlin admires Weizmann most of all for his sympathy with the masses of poor Eastern European Jews, his rootedness in Jewish culture, and his commitment to establishing a Jewish territorial nation in Palestine. Weizmann, Berlin concludes, was "the first totally free Jew of the modern world" and the man in whose image "the state of Israel was constructed. . . . No man has ever had a comparable monument built to him in his own lifetime."[29]

How should we judge Berlin's representation of these three disparate characters? On the one hand, there is something glitteringly bright about his juxtaposition of the politically discordant but psycho-culturally similar Disraeli and Marx. There is also something compelling about Weizmann's diagnosis of the problems of the Jews — especially in comparison with Disraeli's and Marx's non-diagnoses — as a function of their collective humiliation, inferiority, and dependence, and so something right about Berlin's gravitation to the man. On the other hand, especially when viewed as a triptych, Berlin's portraits obscure as much as they reveal. For a start, Marx's fury at class exploitation is rendered as a symptom of a repressed Jewish identity, as if that fury could not possibly have been elicited, at least in a Jew, by capitalism's real inequalities and iniquities.[30] Berlin does not go that far even in psychoanalyzing Disraeli's racial fantasies, for Disraeli exaggerates his Jewish identity, which Berlin sees as such a finer thing than ignoring it that he does not worry much about where such racial fantasies might have come from, not to speak of where they might and eventually did lead.[31] Berlin likewise treats Marx's internationalism, against its backdrop of spiraling German chauvinism, as a sign of an unconscious evasion of the national question. Berlin never imagines that Marx's fervent belief in the universal solidarity of the working class might express his wished-for antidote to the ethnic, racial, and national prejudices of the entire world.

Ultimately, however, Berlin's account of Marx is important less because of its disagreeable implications for Marx than because of its disagreeable implications for Jews in general. Berlin's "Marx" suggests that no one can be a good Jew who does not take the Jewish question as the primary question, and that any other social passion Jews might feel can only be a deformed and redirected feeling for their own ethno-religious group. Berlin's account of Weizmann has different but analogously constricting implications. As Berlin describes him, Weizmann finds little that is positive and fruitful in the social marginal and exile, above all in the marginalized and exiled intellectual, as if the complex sensibilities of, say, a Kafka obsessed with the meaning of guilt and punishment, or a Benjamin treating critical ideas as ends in themselves, both manifested and were wrecked by the "abnormality" of the psyches behind them. Against Weizmann's rebuff of introspective and agitated personalities, not only of well-known "avant-garde" intellectuals but also of who knows how many anonymous women and men, Berlin whispers barely a complaint.[32] He likewise does not demur at Weizmann's affirmation of the stolidity and self-satisfaction of a majority people with its own ethnonational state. Certainly he never protests that Weizmann's notion of the abnormal Jewish personality almost exactly mimics modern anti-Semitic ideas of Jews as nervous, rootless, and degenerate, or that his ideal of the Jewish nationalist bears a close if not perfect resemblance to the ideal of the German nationalist articulated by the fascist and radical right.[33] Indeed, Berlin certifies those notions in his essay titled "The Origins of Israel," where hewrites with approval that in that new state there are "few sophisticated, chess-playing, café intellectuals — late-night figures, dispensers of a peculiar compound of Freud, Marx, Sartre, or whatever else is at once shocking and fashionable; seekers after strong sensations . . . with a tendency to flourish within declining or insecure cultures . . . [such as] the Weimar Republic of Germany." Berlin takes pleasure in Israel's enjoyment of a "relative placidity, relative coarseness; a kind of stubborn normality and a complacent soundness, wholesomeness, dullness — which the Jews have surely richly deserved." He concludes that in Israel, "What you find are natives of a country . . . not the artificial products of a liberal European intelligentsia in decay." Even if they had a less distasteful genealogy, these ideas and ideals would deserve reproach for mowing down whole swaths of Jewish thought and action, including some of the highest and most verdant swaths. The one kind of variety among Jews that Berlin seems to commend is ironically a function of their initial geographical dispersion. But even as he marvels at the vast array of Jews who immigrated to Israel from other cultures and places ("There is no place in the world where a greater degree of variety of humanity is observable . . . so extraordinary a collision and 'cross-fertilization' of types . . . so many ways of living, so many attitudes, so many methods of going about everyday things"), Berlin surmises, without any apparent regret, that this multiplicity will give way to singularity as Israelis assimilate to a "common denominator."[34]

The conviction that Jewish nationalism is the one true and right form of politics for all Jews compromises the philosophical principle of individual freedom and plurality, most obviously with respect to Jews themselves. Berlin comes very close to admitting the point in his essay titled "Jewish Slavery and Emancipation," when he attacks "the intolerable form of bullying" of those who insist that all true Jews must leave the diaspora for the new state of Israel. Against such a "wholly indefensible" position, Berlin recognizes "the right of all human beings to a certain elasticity" and the right of "(e)ach and every individual Jew . . . to choose his own mode of life for himself with all its attendant qualities."[35] Nonetheless, he goes on to make the curious case that nationalism enhances individualism, on the grounds that the same Jewish assimilation into European society that was an impossibility before the creation of a Jewish state becomes a real alternative afterward. This is not because European nation-states now embrace Jews as natives but because the opportunity for all Jews to become citizens of Israel makes assimilation into other societies a genuine individual choice, as though the absence of an alternative choice for the assimilating individual had been the sole stumbling block. "[T]he fate of individuals, and even of individual communities, whether to stay or move, is now, morally at least, in their own hands, and each will settle its freedom as it wishes, as best it can. . . . In this sense the creation of the State of Israel has liberated all Jews."[36] There are all sorts of logical conundrums in Berlin's claim that a Herderian answer to the Jewish question in Palestine creates a Millian freedom for Jews everywhere else. Those conundrums acquire a moral-political cast as soon as one looks at the repercussions of that answer for Palestinian Arabs with, to be sure, boomerang effects on Israeli and non-Israeli Jews. Berlin evidently came to have second thoughts about the chauvinistic derailings of a nationalism he praised for being benignly Herderian in its initial stages. Still, he never confronts the possibility that the "Herderian" origins of Jewish nationalism might have sealed its chauvinistic fate.[37]

HANNAH ARENDT

To see how it is possible to make an entirely different sense of Weizmann, Disraeli, Marx, and Jewish nationalism, we could do no better than to turn again to Hannah Arendt. Not unlike Berlin, Arendt commends pre-1948 Zionism over assimilationism for treating the Jewish question as a political question and for demanding a "'readjustment'" of Jewish-Gentile relations "in political terms."[38] But as opposed to "the road that Herzl marked out, and Weizmann followed through to the bitter end," she wishes that the Jews had allied themselves with all oppressed peoples struggling for revolutionary change in Europe. Alas, she laments, it requires greater "political strength of will" to "achieve freedom" than to be "transported to freedom." Arendt writes not in the 1950s and late 1960s, as Berlin in his essays does, but in the 1940s — a period so bleak for European Jews that anyone's myopic care for their plight above other peoples' might be forgiven. Nevertheless, even then she berates the Zionists for having conspired with European imperialist powers to reach their aims, beginning with Herzl's advances to the Turkish Empire in the midst of its slaughter of the Armenians and continuing through "Weizmann's unswerving loyalty to the cause of the British Empire in the Near East." Still, Arendt is able to register both sides of a coin Berlin represents as having only one. Thus she declares with her characteristic moral and syntactical complexity:

> Those who are dismayed at the spectacle of a national movement that, starting out with such an idealistic élan, sold out at the very first moment to the powers-that-be — that felt no solidarity with other oppressed peoples whose cause, though historically otherwise condi-

tioned, was essentially the same — that endeavored even in the morning-dream of freedom and justice to compromise with the most evil forces of our time by taking advantage of imperialistic interests — those who are dismayed should in fairness consider how exceptionally difficult the conditions were for the Jews who, in contrast to other peoples, did not even possess the territory from which to start their fight for freedom."[39]

Arendt also accuses the Zionists, including Weizmann, of anti-Arab policies and practices, the "most outstanding" being, by 1948, "the creation of a new category of homeless people, the Arab refugees."[40] She presses until the cause is lost for a Jewish national homeland as opposed to a sovereign Jewish state, built and governed "on a solid basis of Jewish-Arab cooperation" in a binational Palestine.[41] She blames the lack of popularity of that ideal on the "misfortune" of "a Central European ideology of nationalism and tribal thinking among the Jews," as well as, on the Arab side, of "an Oxford-inspired colonial romanticism . . . of poverty," which denied the material benefits for the Palestinians of relations with the Jews.[42] Arendt's criticism of Jewish nationalism for its population transfers and expulsion of Arabs and for its refusal to readmit Arab refugees; her wariness toward the humanly fragmenting consequences of the principle of national sovereignty for small nations; and her hostility to national chauvinism in every guise all are crystallized in her ominous remark at the creation of Israel that "[t]he birth of a nation in the midst of our century may be a great event; it certainly is a dangerous event."[43]

Arendt is far more open-eyed and prescient than Berlin when she forecasts that a Jewish nation-state in Palestine as the answer to the problem of Jewish unfreedom in Europe would inevitably give rise to a new humiliation and persecution, a new crisis of dispossession and exile, a new people forced to live as dependants and "semi-helots," and finally, a new reactive drive for national self-determination. Arendt is also more prophetic than Berlin is when, near the end of his life, he repeats his long-standing conviction that Zionism would win the Jews "normalization" by carving out for them a place where they "were not forced to be self-conscious . . . where they simply could live normal, unobserved lives."[44] Half a century earlier, Arendt sees that Jews instead would be forced back into unwelcomed self-consciousness as a result of their crime (to borrow the term Berlin uses with respect to Marxism) against the Palestinian Arabs. She predicts that Israel will become isolated in the Middle East, consumed with fortifying itself militarily against its hostile neighbors, and censured by much of the rest of the world, with anti-Semitism transfigured into anti-Zionism.[45] At the same time, she makes it clear that this bad dialectic of Jewish nationalism cannot be explained either by any essential will to power of the Jews or any inherent hatred of the Jews by the Arabs. Although the situation of the Jews is a function of the particularities of Jewish history, it bespeaks the general truth that in any geography shared by a multiplicity of groups, ethnonationalism is doomed to create new disasters in the act of transcending old ones.

If Arendt differs with Berlin over what to make of Weizmann and Zionism, she also differs with Berlin over what to make of those two imperious Jews who refused to assimilate quietly into middle-class society. Although Berlin never alludes to it, Arendt offers her own masterful portrait of Disraeli in *The Origins of Totalitarianism* twenty years before Berlin offers his.[46] There she calls Disraeli the only historically great exception Jew. By this unflattering phrase she means that Disraeli became politically powerful through conjuring up a mysterious Jewishness that would make him attractive to and distinguished in a race-conscious society. Anticipating Berlin in most of her descriptive details but not in the normative sense she makes of them, Arendt accuses Disraeli of caring "for admission to high and highest society more passionately and shamelessly than any other Jewish intellectual did" and of looking at Jewishness "much in the same way as a Gentile would have looked at it," as "a fact of origin which he was at liberty to embellish, unhindered by actual knowledge." Most significant, it was Disraeli who wrote that " '[w]hat is a crime among the multitude is only a vice among the few.' " He knew that by turning their Jewishness "into an attractive 'vice,' " exception Jews "would have no better chances anywhere than in circles which pretended to be exclusive and to discriminate against them." Arendt remarks that "Disraeli's display of exoticism, strangeness, mysteriousness, magic, and power drawn from secret sources, was aimed correctly at this disposition in society." Anyone familiar with the rest of the first volume of *The Origins of Totalitarianism* knows that Arendt believes the complicity of exception Jews with society's attraction to Jewishness as a vice was the most dangerous game there turned out to be. If English society never resolved that attraction by exterminating the purveyors of that vice, this did not lessen Disraeli's part in paving the ideological way for such extermination in the larger European setting.[47]

As for Marx, although one wonders why she thinks it must be an either/or proposition, Arendt connects his early outbursts against Jewish money not to Jewish self-hatred but to class animosities between "rich Jews" who received privileges from the reactionary governments they financed and "Jewish intellectuals" who starved despite their idealistic pursuits. Arendt declares that "if they were worth their salt," those intellectuals rebelled against those governments and even more violently against Jewish bankers as "the official representatives of their own people." She places such rebels at the opposite end of the moral spectrum from exception Jews like Disraeli or more ordinary parvenus. She especially praises "conscious pariahs" choosing to live on the fringes of society and stand up for all who are oppressed by it. Arendt laments not the failure of these rebels to fight for Jews as such but their succession by a generation of intellectuals who were social conformists instead of social critics.[48]

Arendt's admiration for the conscious pariah's love of justice and sense of humanity ensures that she will not take Marx to task for attending to the class question as a way of avoiding what should have been the real question for him. Her case against Marx is rather that he became so obsessed with the class struggle between capitalists and workers to which Jews were not a party and so blind to "political questions" that he underestimated the importance of state structure.[49] Thereby he underestimated the role of Jews, who associated and were associated with state against society before the age of nationalism and industrial capitalism, when they lost their security in society by losing their financial significance for the state. Arendt treats Marx's ideas not as psychological defenses against an inner repression of a truth about himself but as insights into a world in which capital was in fact becoming the preeminent force—insights, however, with serious blindnesses attached to them. As Ron Feldman notes in his introduction to *The Jew as Pariah*, Marx saw Jewish merchants and financiers as emblematic of the early stages of capitalist development but as secondary to capital in its industrial phase, and erroneously equated economic marginality with historical inconsequence.[50] It was Arendt who, from her later vantage point, spied the centrality to modern history of homeless, rootless populations. For her, "their very superfluousness, their separation from both state and society" explains why the catastrophes of twentieth-century

Europe begin with the catastrophe of the Jews.[51] In claiming that the worst effect of capitalist expansion is the alienation of populations from their place in the world, Arendt does not make a Herderian point of essential connections broken between national peoples and their territories. She makes her own, different point of humans deprived of both a public place in which they can speak and act as equal but distinctive members of political society and a private place to which they can retreat from the public eye.

To Arendt's mind, Marx failed to understand the significance of the Jews as a superfluous people and of social superfluity per se.[52] But Marx understood injustice, which is why Arendt depicts him, in relation to Disraeli, as the better if still problematic Jew. "In the country which made Disraeli its Prime Minister, the Jew Karl Marx wrote *Das Kapital*, a book which in its fanatical zeal for justice, carried on the Jewish tradition much more efficaciously than all the success of the 'chosen man of the chosen race.' "[53] With these words, Arendt provides her own answer to the questions "What is a Jew?" and "What is the Jew's relation to society?" Today we even might say that she rehabilitates the radical strand of Jewish life that embraces marginality to fight for justice in general, as an esteemed alternative to the orthodox religious and secular nationalist strands that have fought for Jewish rights in particular.[54]

Even though she attacks Marx in other contexts, Arendt stands on his side against Disraeli and Weizmann, in large part because she stands against ethnic determinism, which Disraeli and Weizmann in their different ways affirmed and which Berlin affirms too, despite his commitment to individual liberty as empirical reality and normative ideal. But to congratulate Arendt for this is not to say that Berlin is entirely unastute about Marx's psychology as well as the psychology of other Jews like him. Berlin knows where a refusal to confront anti-Semitism can lead: if not necessarily, as he claims, to Jewish self-loathing, then at least to an obtuseness and vulnerability in the face of the realities of prejudice and violent potentialities of ethnic and national identifications.[55] Berlin is less astute about the dangers in Disraeli's flirtation with racial ideologies, class hierarchy, and British imperial power. And while he does well to confirm Weizmann's diagnosis of the suffering of the Jews as a function of their political dependence and inferiority, he refuses to see how Weizmann's description of that suffering in terms of an abnormal nervousness and over-intellectuality supports the restorative of strangling in Jews all intricate or unconventional psychologies. Finally, Berlin refuses to acknowledge that the Palestinians' own catastrophe can be traced to men who, like this "first totally free Jew of the modern world," sought good health the nationalist way, curing their own people of "world-alienation" by inflicting on another group that same shattering fate.

L. B. NAMIER

Arendt's and Berlin's answers to the Jewish question partly reflect their different situations: the one a Western European Jew who barely escaped Nazi Germany and became a stateless refugee; the other an Eastern European Jew too young to have been troubled by his emigration from Russia, who was happily ensconced in English society by the time the Second World War broke out.[56] Such chance facts of biography and geography do something although not everything to explain why Arendt saw Herderian nationalism as contributing to the plight of the Jews, while Berlin saw it as the solution to that plight. They also help explain why Berlin was more preoccupied with Stalinism than with Nazism and was keen to distinguish a good negative from a bad positive liberty. In doing so, he won the hearts of those in the cold war establishment at least as much as Arendt did when she analyzed Nazism and Bolshevism under the common rubric of totalitarianism. However, Berlin never challenged bourgeois society as Arendt did when she spurned the privatism of negative liberty no less than the tyrannical potentiality of positive liberty, conceiving of freedom instead as the capacity of humans to start new, unpredictable chains of actions in the public sphere. Arendt's and Berlin's contrasting political philosophies signal other deep-seated differences between the two. Arendt was a thinker too strenuous, abstract, and exacting to give most people enjoyment; a maverick who angered many of her readers by taking positions at odds with all factions and camps; and an outcast in the "Jewish community" by dint of her published opinions on Zionism and the Eichmann trial. In contrast, Berlin delighted everyone who mattered with his talk; gave pleasure to his readers by discussing ideas through stories about individuals; thought in ways that may have clashed with perspectives at the political margins but enhanced received wisdom at the center; and was courted by the founders of the state of Israel, by supporters of Israel in the United States, and by British and

American policymakers for his ties to those with power over Jewish affairs. Then, too, Arendt hated bourgeois culture, scorned those who wished to attach themselves to wealth and fame, and was never loath to take controversial public stands on political issues. Berlin, according to his biographer and very often according to himself, was eager to please, admired "aristocratic hauteur," adored celebrity, sought "validation by genius," and "shied away" from making political statements in public.[57]

In short, it is tempting to see Arendt as the exemplary self-conscious pariah and Berlin as the consummate parvenu. That temptation would be somewhat less strong were one to treat the twin figures of pariah and parvenu as suggestive of an internal divide in the personality as well as an external divide between personality types. One need only recall the anti-Semitic sentiments voiced by that arch-pariah Karl Marx in both his published works and private letters to suspect that Arendt and Berlin may have similarly complicated mentalities.[58] Arendt's attraction to the German high philosophical tradition and Berlin's attraction to irrationalist figures and ideas beyond the liberal pale attest to such complications in opposite ways. Very differently, the temptation would also be less strong if Berlin had either a kinder view of assimilation, an art he seems to suspect theoretically even as he mastered it practically, or a less kind view of Jewish nationalism. For, on the one side, assimilation can be seen as confirming not only the obeisance of minorities before the power of a majority culture but also the chameleonlike fluidity and virtuosity of the assimilating self. On the other side, nationalism can be seen as a kind of collective parvenu strategy, in which upstart peoples seek to gain recognition from powerful European societies by mimicking their ideas of what a polity should be and possess. Haven't those ideas proven too invidious to copy, too disastrous in their political effects?

That said, it would be grossly unfair to conclude without underscoring the European animus against the Jews that was a part of the tenor of the times in the first half of the twentieth century. Along with the atmospheric pervasiveness of nationalist ideas, this animus helps explain why Zionism appeared to so many Jews as the only route to freedom. Here L. B. Namier — the tormented subject of Berlin's most unsparing and poignant character sketch — is especially apposite. Berlin describes Namier as the son of Jews who had converted to Roman Catholicism to assimilate into the privileged

reaches of Polish society. Namier rebelled against his parents by re-
turning to the Jewish community "at any rate in his own mind." He
left his native country for England, where in the interwar years he
became a publicly renowned if personally detested modern British
historian, as well as an Anglophile, a conservative, an "out-and-out
nationalist," and a committed Zionist. Namier was "intellectually
formidable," "proud," "contemptuous," and "intolerant," with
enough scorn for the rules of civility governing what should and
should not be said in public that "[i]f he came across latent anti-
Semitism he stirred it into a flame." This difficult man was "driven
into" Zionism, Berlin explains, because he "found the position of the
Jews to be humiliating; he disliked those who put up with this or
pretended that it did not exist."[59] Berlin notes that Namier eventually
found happiness after his conversion to Anglicanism upon a second
marriage, but he never lets on whether we are meant to see that
conversion as a symptom of the diseased state of European Jewry or
a testimony to an exemplary eccentric's freedom of choice.

Although the difference in epoch is all-important, Berlin points out
the same kind of psychological similarities between Marx and
Namier as he does between Marx and Disraeli. Namier would be
appalled by the comparison. Berlin tells a very funny story about
Namier's first long monologue in Berlin's presence, during which,
among other outrageous pronouncements, Namier railed against
Marx as "'a typical Jewish half-charlatan, who got hold of quite a
good idea and then ran it to death just to spite the Gentiles.'"[60] My
purpose in alluding to Namier here, however, has to do as much
with what he writes about the Jews as with what Berlin writes about
him. In a collection of essays titled *Conflicts: Studies in Contemporary History*, Namier angrily describes the genesis of the nightmares
of his times, as well as the failure of European political parties and
governments to counteract them. He charts the growth of pan-
Germanism and the plight of the Jews that worsens between the two
world wars and explodes when Jews are forced into full-scale statelessness and homelessness. Namier sums up their situation in a disturbing epigram: "According to Aristotle, the 'Stateless' must be a
god or a beast; nowadays he is usually a Jew." Thenceforth the Jews
were denied the possibility of living a free and dignified existence as
a people rather than merely as separate individuals, for their resettlement en masse in any country either incited new waves of anti-
Semitism or was prohibited outright by state laws. The general repu-

diation of the Jews by European society, Namier charges, helped account for Hitler's success, for when the Nazis "started with an onslaught against the Jews," there was a "widespread — often only half-avowed, half-conscious — sympathy . . . for that onslaught among all nations."[61]

Namier's words should serve as a warning to critics of nationalism that they — we — must clear a better path to freedom for any minority that is wanted nowhere, by no one, if we wish to criticize the path Zionism cleared for the Jews. That is, we must plot a new political conclusion to the modern drama of world alienation, of which, as Arendt tells us, the "worldlessness" of the Jews was the first act. Nationalism has been key to that drama, along with other modern keys, to be sure, as both a cause and an effect of the superfluousness of peoples across the globe. Nationalism will continue to play its ambiguous role as a source of the identity crises it arises to cure — and as a force for collective freedom but a threat to both human solidarity and individual freedom — until questions like the Jewish question find more generous answers already materialized in political society. In the meantime, many others will be driven to the bitter sentiments Namier expresses in the lines below:

In 1921, on my first visit to Vienna after the war, I happened to engage in a discussion about Jewish Nationalism and Zionism with one of those high-minded, broad-minded, open-minded, shallow-minded Jews who prefer to call themselves anything rather than Jews. "First and foremost," he declared in a pompous manner, "I am a human being." I replied (and this was twenty years ago): "I, too, once thought so; but I have since discovered that all are agreed that I am a Jew, and not all that I am a human being. I have therefore come to consider myself first a Jew, and only in the second place a human being."[62]

Chapter Four

Are Liberalism and Nationalism Compatible?

A Second Look at Isaiah Berlin

THE CASE FOR LIBERAL NATIONALISM

A case has recently been made, with a nod of gratitude to Isaiah Berlin, for joining liberalism and nationalism together.[1] Although its proponents may concede, with another nod to Berlin, the general incommensurability and incompatibility of values, they are out to harmonize *these* specific two. More exactly, they hope to harmonize what they see as the core truths of liberalism and nationalism: individual equality and autonomy on the one side, cultural particularity and belonging on the other. In the words of Yael Tamir, a prominent advocate of liberal nationalism:

> [T]he liberal tradition, with its respect for personal autonomy, reflection, and choice, and the national tradition, with its emphasis on belonging, loyalty, and solidarity . . . can indeed accommodate one another. Liberals can acknowledge the importance of belonging, membership, and cultural affiliations. . . . Nationalists can appreciate the value of personal autonomy and individual rights and freedoms, and sustain a commitment for social justice both between and within nations.[2]

One main argument for such an accommodation is that while liberalism may speak as if it arises from nowhere and as if the individuals and choices it speaks about are entirely abstract, liberalism depends on the existence of nationalism and national culture in multiple ways. Historically, nationalism paves the way for liberal democracy by crowning all members of a people with equal dignity and status.[3] Politically, national identity provides the social cohesion, public commitment, and sense of civic responsibility — the "moral resources for modern citizenship" — that a liberal order requires but cannot supply out of its own stock of individualistic principles.[4]

Epistemologically, national culture is the source of the language and range of possible meanings and values in which all theories, including liberal theories, are elaborated and embraced. Anthropologically, national culture provides the context in which individuals become specific selves who choose among specific purposes, projects, and practices. As Will Kymlicka puts this fundamental point: "[F]reedom of choice is dependent on social practices, cultural meanings, and a shared language. Our capacity to form and revise a conception of the good is intimately tied to our membership in a societal culture, since the context of individual choice is the range of options passed down to us by our culture."[5] In short, "Cultural membership is a precondition of autonomous moral choices."[6] Tamir deduces from the cultural foundation and needs of individuality the right of every individual "to culture" in the sense of being able to live "in a meaningful environment." Conceiving of culture as national and of the individual as the beginning and end of national community, she also deduces the individual's right to a "shared public sphere where the national culture, language, and traditions attain expression."[7] Does every national culture deserve its own independent nation-state? The liberal nationalist answer would seem to be "ideally, perhaps; but given the multiethnic composition of most territories, one of several more realistic institutional arrangements must suffice." A national culture might have its own state, with group-differentiated rights for minority cultures. Or, it might be guaranteed minority rights inside a state reflecting the culture of a different majority group. Finally, a national culture might occupy one minority public sphere among many in a genuinely multicultural society united by obedience to the same political laws.

A second major argument for liberal nationalism is that just as individual human beings deserve recognition of their inherent dignity as free subjects with their own purposes and plans, so do whole peoples deserve recognition as moral equals with equal rights to decide their own fates. That is, liberalism's assertion of the natural equality of individual persons and of their equal right to think and act without outside interference as long as they respect the same right of others is thought to carry over logically to national groups. Thus, in "The Politics of Recognition," Charles Taylor slips back and forth between personal and cultural (especially national-cultural) identities — automatically making the same claims about dignity, autonomy, and dialogism for both.[8] Those who assume a parallelism between person and national culture tend to translate the equal right of persons to self-definition and self-development into the equal right of nations to self-determination, interpreted maximally as the right to political independence and minimally as the right to cultural integrity. This second line of reasoning usually arrives at the same destination as the first: a theoretical embrace of the principle of one nation, one state, and a practical embrace of the right to cultural autonomy at least for deserving nationalities.[9] As we just have seen, however, it gets to that destination by way of an analogy between persons and nations rather than by asserting the requirement of nations for persons. This time, the principle of individualism is set against the backdrop of international society: the self that is to enjoy cultural self-expression is the nation as a person writ large.

A third argument for liberalism's harmony with nationalism is that liberalism's highest value on individual freedom of choice behooves it to value a plurality of alternatives for the individual to choose among, hence a plurality of styles of life, hence a variety of national cultures instantiating that plurality worldwide. With its interest in assuring choices for individuals, its own agnosticism with respect to the good, and its support for civic over ethnic sources of political unity, liberalism is said to safeguard and even nourish cultural variety domestically as well as internationally, with the most liberal societies being those that "encourage cultural pluralism."[10]

These three pleas for liberal nationalism obviously do not coalesce, even though they all may coincide in the same liberal nationalist text. The first takes the person as the end of national community, the second takes the nation as an end in itself, and the third is parasitical on, without being rooted in, cultural inheritance, national belonging, and a collective notion of the good.

Each plea on its own is also flawed in ways that have been so artfully exposed elsewhere that we need only peruse them briefly here.[11] With respect to liberalism's dependence on national culture, there is the unselfevident and freedom-defeating presumption that identity, national or otherwise, is what gives rise to the individual's choices as well as the alternatives the individual chooses among. There is the conflation of culture with national culture, as if meanings, mannerisms, values, and styles of life were never elaborated at the local or regional or civilizational or global level, or in groups whose membership is less given and inherited, more contingent and voluntary, or even in groups seen as given and inherited in, say, familial or caste rather than national terms. There is the assumption that every national culture is discrete, with its own sealed genealogy, rather than being an interpenetrated part of an interconnected history.[12] There is also the unwillingness to admit that if freedom is a function of choice and if national culture makes choice concretely possible by providing individuals with specific purposes and alternatives of action, a hybridity or intermixture of cultures must provide individuals with an even richer set of purposes, a greater variety of alternatives, and hence more freedom.[13] Moreover, if cultural membership is a precondition of choice, it surely also is a precondition of dictation, both in the sense that every culture sets its own tight limits on the individual's imagination and in the sense that many cultures train individuals to submit to authority.[14]

Then there are the problems with moving seamlessly from valorizing choice at the level of the individual person to valorizing choice at the level of the nation as a collective "self," and from valorizing a plurality of alternatives for the person to choose among to valorizing cultural variety worldwide. The nation, or more exactly the nation's leaders, may freely choose courses of action that crush the free choices of some or even most of the nation's population. Then, too, a multiplicity of distinct national cultures can thrive in the world without any of them allowing persons the freedom to choose among a multiplicity of styles of life. Heterogeneity at the global level can coexist with homogeneity at the national level and cultural tyranny at the level of the individual. National-cultural variety in fact almost inevitably ensures that the liberal principle of negative freedom will be breached more often than it is met, for while liberalism declares notions of the good life to be the person's private concern, national cultures uphold notions of the good life that are meant to be collective. Paradoxically, even liberal cultures cannot escape wielding collective power, for they actively cultivate in their members a belief that the good life is the life of private individual freedom in the same breath that they declare the good life to be a matter of individual, not collective, choice. Finally, against liberalism's universalist commitment to individuals, nationalism selects the members of the nation over all other human beings. It also insists on the nation's right to perpetuate traditional social inequalities, including the right to extend or deny, according to custom, negative freedom to different subnational groups. These constitutive features of nationalism will not magically disappear just because liberal nationalists contend that nations *ought* to acknowledge the equal rights of all individuals and contribute toward the material equality of all national communities.[15]

Liberalism might extricate itself from some of the problems that illiberal cultures pose for it, if it were to reinterpret itself as merely the ethos of a particular kind of culture. This would be a culture that values individual freedom of choice as the supreme good but knows it is no more right and true than a culture valuing a different and even incompatible good—and *vive la différence!* The costs to liberalism of acknowledging its own particularization, alas, would be high. That move would spell the end of its ability to make moral judgments about the world as if they were anything other than a set of parochial prejudices and thus the end of its right to remake the world in its own image as if it were remaking the world in the image of an objective universal ideal. Meanwhile, the benefits to the world would be low, as the particularization of liberalism would hardly spell the end of the historical assault on cultural variety to which liberalism has been a sometimes keen and sometimes reluctant party. For liberalism came into the world wedded to capitalism, even though capitalism has not been especially faithful to it, and the logic of capital has had a far more destructive effect on national-cultural difference than has the philosophical idea of individual freedom. To reconceive of individual freedom as a culturally specific value without challenging the universalization of capital, or what today is called globalization, would be the least promising route to a détente between liberalism and national-cultural variety.

ISAIAH BERLIN'S TWO CONCEPTS OF NATIONALISM

Are contemporary thinkers right to invoke Isaiah Berlin in support of their claim that individualism and pluralism are cut from the same fine cloth and that a well-tailored suit of liberal nationalism can be fashioned from it? *Was* Berlin the original designer of this political style, with perhaps a greater flair than his protégés for finessing difficult seams?

Certainly Berlin is an indefatigable champion of individual choice, negative freedom, the autonomous power of ideas, and the superiority of Western Europe as the birthplace of those principles. Certainly, too, he makes one of the most determined efforts of any liberal to grasp the centrality of ethnic feeling in human life, of cultural particularity in the world, and of nationalism in modern politics. Berlin never breaks from admiring the ability of persons to think and act on the basis of plans and purposes they have selected for themselves as unique, self-directing human beings. At the same time, he underlines an almost instinctive desire on the part of people not to stand out as individuals among other individuals but instead to live among those they resemble most in mannerisms, speech, customs, and inherited beliefs. He reveals that the philosophical elements of nationalism derive their practical force not from their intellectual persuasiveness to rational individuals but from the psychological experience of group discrimination, humiliation, and subordination. He insists that the sore point for nationalism is not domination by a master but domination by a master who is foreign, and consequently that the goal of nationalism is not to secure a realm of individual freedom from authority but to enable collective obedience to an authority that is indigenous. Finally, he suggests that a variety of styles and ends of life is ensured by national-cultural differentiation. That human beings are happiest at home with their kind, that collectivist factors fuel dramatic drives for self-determination, and that a plurality of ends of life requires national-cultural particularity might be considered merely empirical claims unthreatening to liberalism as a normative ideal, were it not for the fact that Berlin proposes these claims as fundamental truths about social life that set limits on the values it makes sense to defend. In any event, Berlin does not merely describe but also prizes the sense of belonging to a people, and he strongly empathizes with the experience of ethnic oppression and the impetus to ethnonational recognition and self-rule. Furthermore, his treatment of national-cultural variety as what George Kateb convincingly has shown to be an aesthetic good implies that he should find more pleasing a world made of liberal and illiberal cultures than a world made of liberal cultures alone.[16]

At this point we might recall, from the last chapter, the threads of individualism and ethnonationalism weaving their way through Berlin's depictions of Benjamin Disraeli, Karl Marx, Chaim Weizmann, and L. B. Namier. The discrepancies between these threads suggest that no human being—Berlin included—can be captured coherently by individualist and ethnic categories together, even if no human being can be captured adequately by either individualist or ethnic categories alone. Berlin illustrates but does not squarely confront this conundrum at the level of individual portraiture. Does he do so at

the level of abstract political ideas? That is, does Berlin present liberalism and nationalism as equally compelling incompatibles? Or does
he evade, deny, or seek to transcend their incompatibility as do liberal nationalists who trace their pedigree to him?

It is surprising that Berlin has little to say about the relation between liberalism and nationalism. Moreover, what he says is indirect,
inconsistent, and inconclusive. At times, he suggests a mimesis between national-cultural difference and the kind of freedom he describes as being in the interest of all persons, "not as members of this
or that nationality."[17] He intimates that whole peoples no less than
individual persons should enjoy freedom of choice, the right to live
"their life according to their lights"; develop "whatever faculties
they possess without hurting their neighbours"; and realize "themselves in as many directions as freely, variously, and richly as they
can."[18] He asserts that liberalism protects collective as well as individual rights by "giving each human group significant room to real-
ise its own idiosyncratic, unique, particular ends without too much
interference with the ends of others"[19] — a crisper version of one of
Tamir's extended arguments for liberalism as the foundation of multicultural nationalism. At other times, however, Berlin describes a
tension between liberal individualism and national community, as in
his essay on Rabindranath Tagore, where he contrasts "individual
talent and success" and "economic power and ability" with "that
solidarity which only homogeneous, close-knit societies give to their
members."[20] He has been known to deny any necessary congruence
between liberalism and pluralism ("I believe in both liberalism and
pluralism, but they are not logically connected") and to spy an active
antagonism to pluralism in certain liberal theories, presumably those
that trumpet individual freedom above any other possible good.[21] In
"Two Concepts of Liberty," Berlin sees national emancipation as another creature altogether from the desire for individual liberty, so
that there can be a variety of emancipated nations in the world without any applauding the "maximum degree of non-interference compatible with the minimum demands of social life." Berlin seems to
underscore the cultural particularity *and* superiority of liberalism
when he states that that "extreme demand for liberty" has never
interested the "bulk of humanity" and has been pressed only by "a
small minority of highly civilized and self-conscious human beings."[22]
At certain points he goes so far as to pit a "good" individualism
against a "bad" nationalism, as when he shows how the healthy

Kantian notion that "man is an end in himself" with the right to exercise his power of choice is "perverted" into a pathological idea of the nation as "some quasi-metaphysical super-personality" that becomes "the ultimate authority for all thought and action . . . a new absolutism." Thereby, "however illegitimately," the "notion of the individual's moral autonomy" is transformed into "the notion of the moral autonomy of the nation" and the individual will "into the national will to which individuals must submit."[23] Far more often, however, Berlin distinguishes between a "good" and "bad" nationalism. Is liberal nationalism perhaps what he means by the "good" variety?

To answer this question, we must turn to Berlin's highly appreciative gloss on Johann Gottfried Herder. Berlin sees Herder as the first person to emphasize the basic human need to belong to a community in which everyone shares the same language, soil, history, and customs, and the first to claim that "each civilization has its own, unique, individual spirit . . . from which everything flows." Though Berlin often writes in the voice of the thinkers he explores, the frequency and fondness with which he returns to Herder attests to his special empathy with him. He congratulates Herder for believing that it is on the basis of the cultural, not the racial, principle that "[e]very nation has a full right to its own individual development" and every "man" the right to his own national existence.[24] Berlin does murmur on one occasion that he is not as sure of the sharpness of the boundaries between cultures as Herder is. On many more occasions he approvingly repeats the Herderian idea that a "man's powers of creation can only be exercised fully on his own native heath, living among men who are akin to him, physically and spiritually." Herder's claim that only through national separation "can true cultures be generated, each unique, each making its own particular contribution to human civilisation,"[25] in combination with his charge that empires forced "disparate, dissimilar nations into artificial combination,"[26] suggests that every people should have its own state. If Berlin presents Herder as an enemy of political nationalism, it seems to be because Herder rejects not the goal of national political independence but, instead, national self-aggrandizement at the expense of other nations.

Berlin takes, then, what he sees as a Herderian tack when he distinguishes sharply between the principle of national cultural uniqueness, variety, and equality, which demands that all cultures be valued in their own terms instead of according to some single, external, putatively objective standard; and the principle of political nationalism, which, in asserting that "nobody is as good as we are, that we have a right to do certain things solely because we are Germans or Frenchmen," paves the way for national aggression, conquest, and imperialism.[27] Toward the end of his life Berlin exchanges the terms "cultural" and "political" nationalism for the terms "non-aggressive" and "aggressive" nationalism to cover the same ideas.[28] Now he illustrates "aggressive nationalism" with anticolonial violence and with ethnic hostilities erupting on the demise of the "tyrannical conglomerations" of diverse peoples imposed by the great imperial states. "Non-aggressive nationalism," which he calls "another story entirely," is the old Herderian story of the benign human need to be "at home somewhere, with your own kind"; the variety-ensuring fact that each group has its unique national spirit and "collective historical experience shared only by members of the group"; and the value on the self-determination, equality, and peaceful coexistence of distinct peoples.[29]

While Herderian nationalism, as Berlin represents it, may be one way of touting a plurality of cultures in the world, it has less happy implications for the liberal principle of the common humanity of persons, not to speak of the individuality of persons. Herder may gratify Berlin by interpreting national belonging in terms of common culture rather than common blood and by believing that all national cultures should be allowed to flourish. Still, the nation that is culturally defined in the Herderian sense is no less exclusive and exclusionist than the nation that is racially defined. The equation of "being at home" with "being with our own kind on our own soil" implies that those who are not of "our kind" can and should be forced to find a home elsewhere. The grounding of variety in distinctive national spirits implies that nations should protect themselves from dilution by foreign and heterogeneous elements. Culture- and race-based nationalism are at any rate hardly distinct species, given the frequency with which cultural heritage is tracked backward to blood lineage and racial identity tracked forward to its cultural manifestations. The indistinctness of these two kinds of nationalism is manifested in the fact that both culture- and race-based nation-states do culture tests (what is your mother tongue?) as well as familial descent tests (what is your mother?) to determine the national identity of individuals, while even race-based nation-states have not yet done blood tests. To the extent that culture- and race-based nationalism do differ, it is not because one is good and the other bad but because their worst cases are bad in different ways. Culture-based nationalism gives rise to the nation's repudiation of the world through the dispossession and expulsion of nonnational minorities. Race-based nationalism gives rise to the nation's domination of the world through the conquest and/or extermination of alien minorities *and* majorities.

Berlin never admits to these family resemblances between "good" and "bad" nationalisms. Thus, toward the end of his life, he calls it "unfortunate," in the sense of an unforeseeable accident, that Zionism has become aggressively nationalistic, given that in its origins it was "very civilized and Herderian." The Jews who created Israel wanted "simply a way of life which was Jewish . . . a framework in which they could freely develop as a community, without fear of persecution or discrimination." Even Herder's recommendation in the eighteenth century that the Jews leave Germany to restore themselves as a nation in their own territory with their own kind does not make Berlin worry that there might be an intrinsic connection between nationalism in its difference-loving and difference-persecuting forms.[30]

AMBIGUITIES, CONTRADICTIONS, AND METAMORPHOSES

Berlin's emphasis on an almost instinctive human need to belong helps support the idea of the goodness of national-cultural groups because they satisfy that need and the innocence of national-cultural groups because they seem, in the inherited ties that connect their members, almost instinctive, too: biologically determined, archaic, pre-reflective.[31] It would be a mistake, however, to suppose that Berlin's musings on nationalism always follow this primordialist and essentialist tack. Indeed, his real contributions to the field lie in the opposite direction. However frequently he tells us that nationalism expresses an organic, benign, spontaneous mode of human belonging, he shows us that it emerges in modern history always as a reaction *against*. Moreover, he describes nationalism as highly volatile, undergoing a series of transmogrifications as a result of its own animating ideas and troubled psychology, as well as the result of the objective pressures of imperial power, inequalities between societies, and modern industrialization. Finally, he suggests that nationalism is never simply or finally one thing or another, insisting instead on its moral ambiguity, its responsibility for "magnificent achievements and appalling crimes."[32]

One of Berlin's hallmarks is that against an assortment of determinists, he insists on the independent force of ideas in human affairs. He portrays nationalism, in this vein, as detonated by a conflict between two clashing conceptions of the world, posed by two different schools of thought in two adjacent countries and centuries — conceptions that are, however, not at all accidentally or incidentally related. The eighteenth-century French Enlightenment gave birth to the ideas of objective rationality, impersonal and universal scientific and moral laws, the uniformity and harmony of values, and a cosmopolitan community of mankind. In reaction against those ideas, the nineteenth-century German Counter-Enlightenment asserted the uniqueness of particular individuals and groups, the subjectivity of all belief as the expression of a specific self or way of life, the heroic creation of values, and variety as a good in itself. Berlin describes "th[is] romantic revolt," of which nationalism is its most prominent "offshoot,"[33] as intrinsically ambiguous: "inspiring, audacious, splendid, and sinister too." Romanticism registers important truths: that "man" is independent and free, that his essence is choice, that there is no higher source of values than himself, and that "the worst of all sins is to degrade or humiliate human beings for the sake of some Procrustean pattern into which they are to be forced against their wills." Yet romantic movements for self-creation and self-determination also come to equate liberty with power and to identify "their own liberty with the destruction of all that [oppose] them." That equation eventuates in twentieth-century mass slaughter for anti-universalistic and antihumanistic causes.[34]

Berlin repeatedly alludes to a sorcery by which ideas either incite or turn into their opposites, as the Enlightenment incited the Counter-Enlightenment, and the romantic cultivation of creative subjectivity turned into the cult of heroic individuals as "leaders of men bending others to their indomitable will."[35] Indeed, every time he marks out a clear-cut conceptual dichotomy (whether between two concepts of nationalism, or two concepts of liberty, or a good individualism and a bad nationalism), he then subverts that dichotomy by revealing a hidden magnetism between the poles. He does this in his account of the perversion of Kantian philosophy we came across earlier. From one angle, Berlin's analysis of the transformation of Kantian individualism into nationalist absolutism implies an original dividing line between the two. From another angle, that analysis exposes the process by which the egoistic kernel inside the idea of the autonomous individual metastasizes into the egotistic kernel inside the idea of the self-determining nation-state. In short, national autonomy jeopardizes individual autonomy at the same time that it grows out of it. Far from signaling the harmony of individualism and nationalism, the internal link between them ensures their similarity *and* incongruity.[36]

For Berlin, not only intellectual tendencies are prone to ambiguity, metamorphosis, and contradiction. Romanticism gained its practical power from what Berlin calls the "psychological wound" inflicted on the Germans by the cultural, military, and political successes of the French. This wound had its own series of jolting and jagged aftereffects: first the humiliating inferiority to France after the French Revolution and Napoleonic invasions; then an attempt to imitate French culture; next a revolt against the imitation, followed by a romantic idealization of German culture; and, finally, the nationalist reaction. By such an "inflamed condition of national consciousness," Berlin laments, in one of those lines that inflates and then punctures the proposition of a purely good thing, the "cultural or spiritual autonomy for which Herder had originally pleaded, turned into embittered and aggressive nationalist self-assertion." Berlin sees the "fever pitch" of the Germans as "the original exemplar of the reaction of many a backward, exploited, or at any rate patronised society, which, resentful of the apparent inferiority of its status, reacted by turning to real or imaginary triumphs and glories in its past, or enviable attributes of its own national or cultural character."[37] The political nationalism that raged in the Germans soon raged in the rest of the world, partly as a result of the influence of Germanic ideas on other peoples and partly because the circumstances of those peoples were enough like those of the Germans to elicit the same response.[38]

In a number of essays, Berlin displays the dynamic if tortured — dynamic *because* tortured — psychology at the heart of nationalist upheavals. He charts not only the feeling of cultural inadequacy, the attempt at cultural emulation, and the counterattempt at cultural isolation to protect indigenous ideals but also the fatality of that willed provincialism, given the fact that the inferior nation has already been so radically changed by its relation to the superior that it would have to burn out its own memory to achieve national-cultural purity. Berlin is careful to highlight the productive no less than the destructive side of the nationalist psychology: its instigation of a search for recognition on the part of peoples long denied it by more powerful groups. He speaks solicitously, even poetically, of "the inflamed desire of the insufficiently regarded to count for something among the cultures of the world." He conjures up the painful experience of colonized regions seeking liberation from foreign rule; ethnic or racial minorities that cannot "indefinitely tolerate the prospect of remaining a minority for ever, governed by a majority with a different outlook or habits"; and marginalized, dispossessed, or dispersed groups mobilized into movements, such as "Zionism or its mirror-image, the movement of the Palestinian Arabs," by a "sense of collective injustice" done to them.[39] But while he sympathizes with the search for recognition, Berlin is less inclined to sanitize it than many theorists of collective identity today. He declares outright that groups with effective claims to superiority have no need for nationalism, for "acute nationalism is just a reaction to humiliation, and top nations don't experience that."[40] Subordinated groups, in a classic case of ressentiment, are propelled by a reactive "hostility towards the proud, the happy, the successful." Moreover, the search for recognition can and often does lead to new efforts at "centralisation," the "crushing of various minorities," and "the suppression by the new elite of its own fellow citizens."[41]

What is the relation, if there is one, between the nationalist search for recognition and liberal freedom? Whether at the level of the individual or group, the search for recognition, according to Berlin, expresses the desire to be seen as a unique subject and "as an independent source of human activity, as an entity with a will of its own, intending to act in accordance with it," rather than being "ruled, educated, guided" by another. Nevertheless, the collective search for recognition has much less in common with the desire for freedom than with the desire for "solidarity, fraternity, mutual understanding, need for association on equal terms." The closer link between recognition and solidarity accounts for the fact that nationalists would rather be "bullied and misgoverned" by one of their own people than be allowed latitude for free action "by someone from some higher and remoter group."[42] Berlin's remark is reminiscent of Arendt's warning that freedom is synonymous with neither the uninhibited association of individuals of the same ethnic or national group nor the emancipation of that group from foreign oppression. However, at a deeper level Berlin and Arendt are making different points. Berlin sees freedom as the ability to act as one chooses without interference from others. Recognition and freedom in his sense are incommensurable values, so that a foreign ruler who refuses to recognize the collective political agency of the people he rules still may allow its individual members freedom of action in a circumscribed private domain.[43] Arendt sees freedom as the individual's ability to act publicly in new ways, to initiate new chains of events in the company of its equal but distinctive peers. Recognition and freedom in her sense are paradoxically related. The withholding of recognition from individuals on the grounds of their ethnicity or nationality is tantamount to a refusal of equal political status to them, and equal status is one of Arendt's conditions for the individual's enjoyment of freedom in the public sphere. At the same time, the awarding of recognition to individuals on the grounds of their ethnicity or nationality is tantamount to a denial of their individual distinctiveness, which is the other of Arendt's conditions of free political action.[44] The paradox cannot be resolved, to her mind, by the creation of a separate nation-state for the unrecognized ethnic or national group, for this solution achieves the equal political status of individuals only by enforcing ethnic homogeneity and hence denying individual distinctiveness in a new setting.

If the nationalism that emerges in reaction against imperial oppression cannot be easily assimilated to liberalism, neither can the nationalism that emerges in reaction to modern "alienation, spiritual homelessness and growing anomie." By destroying the traditional social order, Berlin tells us, in what is a minor but still noteworthy argumentative chord, industrial progress "deprived great numbers of men of social and emotional security" and thus produced the need for "psychological equivalents for the lost cultural, political, religious bonds."[45] Nationalism emerges to create those equivalents. The very qualities of security and unity for which it provides surrogates, however, should make it suspect from a liberal point of view. And if nationalism is both a reaction against and a solution to the crisis of modernity, it is a reaction and solution that the ever-expanding process of centralization, bureaucratization, and rationalization requires to be perpetually replayed. Berlin sees in modern society the growing power of engineers, economists, calculators, and specialized experts; the constantly extending reach of industrial enterprises; the broader and broader organization of humanity to serve the productive apparatus; and the globalization of "the gigantic operations in which gov-

ernments, corporations and interlocking elites of various kinds are
engaged." Nationalism can be expected to recur, then, as a "[m]utiny
against the life of the barracks," a rebellion against the "triumph of
scientific rationalism everywhere," an attempt at "escape from huge
impersonal authority that ignores ethnic, regional and religious differences, a craving for 'natural' units of 'human' size."[46] But as
writers as dissimilar as Georg Simmel and Michel Foucault remind
us, although Berlin does not, the very freedom of the individual from
traditional bonds, in combination with the idea of the equality of
each individual with every other, helps set the stage for subjective
isolation, anonymity, and impotence in the face of the objective culture's overwhelming complexity, impersonality, technical prowess,
and sheer physical size. Thus we can expect a nationalist mutiny
against bureaucracy and "giantism" to be a mutiny against individualism too.

The human need to belong to a group, the ideological impact of
German romanticism, the resentment and search for recognition on
the part of cultures that have been made to feel inferior in some way,
the alienating experience of modernity — all of the aspects of nationalism on which Berlin dwells are intellectual, psychological, and
emotional. We can cull from his subjectivist approach two important
lessons for political practice. The first is that the animus in nationalist conflicts is unlikely to disappear until collective feelings of humiliation are redressed, whether or not, from an outsider's view-
point, those feelings are warranted and the effort to redress them
is fair. The second is that far from overcoming nationalism in politics, the centralizing and individualizing processes of modernity can
be expected to generate nationalist or neo-nationalist sensibilities
indefinitely.

What we are unable to cull from Berlin is an understanding of
nationalism's objective economic and political determinants. About
these he is almost pathologically uninformative, partly because his
interests lie always in ideas and partly because he looks askance at
the very notion of objective causality. Even when he briefly notes the
requirement, for nationalist movements, of a social class "lifted and
armed" by industrialization against the older "cosmopolitan governing elites in Europe,"[47] he emphasizes not the economic and political
conditions that produce nationally conscious middle classes but the
new image of the nation that those classes must produce to restore
the "collective life" of a "wounded society."[48] Still, it would not be

difficult to bring Berlin's ideas into agreement with theories of nationalism that pay more attention to material considerations, even if
Berlin himself might protest. As we shall see in the next chapter, the
neo-Marxist Tom Nairn argues, very much along Berlin's lines, that
nationalism is the political expression of relatively weak regions,
with humiliation at an imposed backwardness and inferiority being
the psychological stuff out of which nationalist passions are made. In
contrast, universalism and cosmopolitanism are ideologies by which
powerful nations legitimate their imperial domination of the world.
Unlike Berlin, however, Nairn connects nationalism to the uneven
process of capitalist development across the globe and to the material inequalities among regions that spring from it. Nairn also complicates Berlin's idea of an antagonism between nationalism and the
alienating features of modernity. He shows that the new states that
have won national independence must fulfill the universal requirements of modernity, if they are to overcome their vulnerability vis-
à-vis the advanced regions. Thus nationalism initially contests but
finally succumbs to the process by which unique and varied traditional cultures are destroyed.[49]

Berlin's sense of the contradictory nature of human values is nowhere on greater display than in his attitude toward universalism,
which he typically shows to be mottled in the extreme. That universalist values promote an admirable belief in critical thinking and the
common humanity of all mankind and a reprehensible belief in a
unitary scheme of values and one right set of answers to the question
of how life should be lived is standard Berlin fare. Also standard is
the idea of a plurality of distinct customs and conventions in the
world that cannot be reduced to a single denominator, as well as the
claim of a minimal moral universalism that leads all cultures to repudiate truly heinous crimes. However, in "European Unity and Its Vicissitudes" — the same essay in which he so nicely resists disentan-
gling romanticism's splendid and sinister strands — Berlin makes a
less ambiguous and more problematic pitch for universalism. Here
he asserts that Nazism, fascism, and Stalinism have proven to the
West that it must salvage "certain universal values which can be
called constitutive of human beings as such," values by which those
who have stepped outside "the frontiers of humanity" can be judged
and condemned. So far, so minimalist, so innocuous. But Berlin then
declares that this is the scale of values by which "the majority of

mankind—and in particular of western Europeans—in fact live,"
that it discriminates between men who are "civilised" and men who
are "barbarian," and that it provides the "common moral—and
therefore also political—foundations of our conduct . . . I mean by
this the habits and outlook of the western world."[50]

Against the baleful backdrop of the 1930s and 1940s, one can
understand Berlin's longing for objective moral laws. In pinpointing
an elective affinity between those moral laws and Western culture,
however, he not only indulges in what he condemns elsewhere as an
imperial ploy by which one culture elevates itself above the rest but
also elevates the very culture against the repetition of whose past
crimes those laws are meant to be a future bulwark. Berlin can get
away with this sleight of hand only by calling concentration camps,
world wars, and nuclear explosions "violent aberrations of the recent European experience" and by sighting "symptoms of recovery:
of a return . . . to normal health—the habits, traditions, above all
the common notions of good and evil, which reunite us to our Greek
and Hebrew and Christian and humanist past: transformed by the
romantic revolt, but essentially in reaction against it."[51] By such a
stroke, he allies himself with Western culture over and above all
other cultures and throws himself on the side of rationalism against
irrationalism, forsaking the pluralism and high ambivalence that enhance so much of the rest of his work. He also renders Europe's star
role in the calamities at issue an inexplicable historical anomaly, will-
fully refusing to treat those calamities as endpoints of complicated
but comprehensible chains of events.[52] His insinuation here that the
Enlightenment follows the true, high moral European tradition,
while romanticism is an abnormality responsible for whatever abom-
inations Europe happens to throw up, clashes with his more typical
view of the call-and-response relationship between the Enlightenment and Counter-Enlightenment as antithetical but equally European tendencies, each with its unique proclivities for freedom and
domination.

Berlin is most revealing about the national question in his simultaneous attractions to and repulsions from Enlightenment and Counter-Enlightenment, rationalism and irrationalism, universalism and
particularism. His best answers to that question are his—dare I say
it?—darkly dialectical account of the ambiguous constitution and
self-corrosive movement of each of those pairs of opposites. Berlin is
least revealing when he tries to solve the riddles at the root of his

ambivalence by splitting one contradictory domain into two coherent, antithetical, positive and negative wholes. But just as Dorothy always had the means to whisk herself back to Kansas, Berlin has the means at hand to save himself from his worst impulses here. His rule that human ends are often incompatible or incommensurable with one another can be used, as he more frequently does use it, to clarify the simultaneous allure of Enlightenment and Counter-Enlightenment values. That proposition also can be extended to clarify the *internal* anatomy of desirable ends, by exposing the fact that what most delights us is sure to have a less delightful other side.

To see the less delightful side of cultural or "non-aggressive" nationalism, Berlin would have to acknowledge that what counts as an ethnic identity and so as ethnic intermixtures is culturally, not naturally, decided. In turn, ethnic intermixtures are not essentially explosive but become explosive under specific historical conditions. One such condition has been the dissemination of the idea of natural national distinctiveness — and its political actualization as the nation-state — that Berlin seems to like so much.[53] Another has been the emergence of the conceit of Western moral superiority with its intimation of a natural hierarchy of races and civilizations, which Berlin echoes rather than protests in "European Unity and Its Vicissitudes." A more complex view of "cultural" nationalism would require him to revise not only his intellectual presumptions but also his political investments. For one thing, he would have to become much less phlegmatic about Herder's idea that the Jews should leave German territory to form their own nation with "their own kind" on "their own soil." For another, he would have to reevaluate the "Herderian" and therefore "civilized" origins of Israel, not because Israel's origins are uniquely uncivilized but, on the contrary, because ethnic exclusion or subordination is intrinsic to the creation of any modern ethnonational state.

On the liberal half of the equation, Berlin would have to recognize the internal link between individualism and bureaucratic centralization that makes individualism no less than "giantism" a likely target of reactions against modernity. He also would have to recognize, as one of nationalism's greatest gifts, an idiom that, in contrast with the idiom of negative liberty, welcomes into conceptual existence political solidarities, public endeavors, and substantive collective goods that may enhance rather than constrain human freedom.

We should conclude by noting that none of these blind spots stems

from an attempt on Berlin's part to wash out the incongruities between nationalism and liberalism, or to downplay the passions and
preoccupations that make each so peculiar a companion for the
other. For his refusal to harmonize *these* unharmonizables, or at the
very least for his failure to try, we must be grateful to him. Moreover, we can extrapolate from both his unpersuasive account of a
good and bad nationalism and his illuminating account of ambiguity,
contradiction, and metamorphosis in human affairs the fantastical
nature of the liberal-nationalist project. Advocates of that oxymoron
equate nationalism with the individual's need for cultural meaning,
roots, and solidarity, while dissociating it from the collective feelings
of humiliation, resentment, and pride that motivate the quest for
state power, fortified national borders, and territorial expansion.
They align liberalism with the political virtues of human dignity, individual freedom, and equal rights, while suppressing what can be
seen as its economic vices from the nationalist point of view: individual self-interest, class division, and the accumulation of private
wealth uninhibited by national loyalties and unbounded by dividing
lines between nation-states.[54]

In addition to eviscerating both aspects of their couplet, liberal
nationalists naturalize national cultures by describing them as if they
were the basic elements out of which political societies are made
rather than the products of political societies.[55] They idealize the
union of liberalism and nationalism as a "good" variety of nationalism by splitting off what they find unpalatable about nationalism
into a "bad" variety. Hence the recent bumper crop of "two concepts of nationalism" to suit different liberal theorists' tastes: civic
(good) and ethnic (bad), or political (good) and organic-cultural
(bad), or cultural (good) and racial (bad), or cultural (good) and
statist (bad), or liberal-constitutional (good) and authoritarian-
popular (bad).[56] Finally, liberal nationalists idealize politics and life
itself[57] by supposing that the right institutional arrangements can fix
and freeze a social order in which all individuals appreciate culture
and community, all groups respect individual choice and equal
rights, and all desires and values are reconcilable, realizable, and
morally commendable.

Chapter Five

In Defense of Ethnicity, Locality, Nationality

The Curious Case of Tom Nairn

NATIONAL PREJUDICES AND TRAVELING IDEAS

Ideas have always been able to fly on the wings of speech far away from their place of origin. Today, new technologies of global communication and transportation insure that even theories of nationalism will not be nation bound. The half intrinsic, half technologically magnified boundlessness of ideas helps account for the world-straddling effects of Ernest Gellner's *Nations and Nationalism* and Benedict Anderson's *Imagined Communities*. Soon after they were published in the early 1980s, these texts precipitated a sea change in scholarship from London to Prague to Delhi to New York, by taking as their starting point the tension between nationalism's archaic self-image and modern reality. While Rosa Luxemburg noted the same tension almost a century ago, it reappeared in thought this time unaccompanied by the other contradictions she believed implicated domination in nation formation. By insisting on the modernity of nationalism but soft-pedaling its entanglements with the will to power of ruling classes, political leaders, and majority peoples, Gellner and Anderson, as well as many of their followers, have been able to greet nationalist movements without the automatic impulse to essentialize *or* chastise them.

To note the reinforcing influence of Gellner and Anderson is not to deny the differences in sensibility and method between the two men. An unabashed sociological objectivist and economic determinist, Gellner asserts that nationalism "suffers from pervasive false consciousness" by misunderstanding its own causes and consequences. Nationalism "defends continuity, but owes everything to a decisive and unutterably profound break in human history." It "claims to protect an old folk society while in fact helping to build up an anonymous mass society." It preaches "cultural diversity, when in fact it imposes homogeneity both inside and, to a lesser degree, between political units." The real backdrop to the formation of large, culturally homogeneous, and politically centralized nation-states, whose populations are literate, and literate in the same language, is the transition from agrarianism to industrialism, and the real cause of nation-states, the "structural requirements of industrial society."[1] Gellner views industrialization and economic growth as politically neutral but humanly positive goods, universally desirable because they are universally desired, with ultimately everyone's individual interest and no suspect cultural or class interest forwarded by them. Ethnonational discriminations and resentments merely reflect the fact that the seeds of industrialization have blown down on different peoples and regions at different times, so that its fruits are not yet universally set. Gazing at nationalist conflicts with the kindly but aloof eye of an adult watching children in the painful throes of growing up, Gellner implies that those conflicts will be resolved not by political engagement from the inside or by political intervention from the outside but by objective developmental processes.[2]

Anderson agrees that the archaic self-portrait of the nation is a widespread delusion, for "the very possibility of imagining the nation only arose historically when, and where . . . fundamental cultural conceptions, all of great antiquity, lost their axiomatic grip on men's minds."[3] Yet he displays the political anthropologist's affection for a myth of natality and mortality, fellowship and belonging, that has the magnetism to join individuals whose relations are far-flung, impersonal, and indirect. For Anderson, national communities are founded on fictions with nothing more real or true underneath them, except for the absence of a foundational reality or truth for which all cultural fictions differently make up. His goal is to trace the pathways by which the nation comes into imaginative reality, the gelling of feelings of "deep, horizontal comradeship" among people who begin to see themselves as *a* people, the clarifying process through which, as he says, with his unparalleled genius for metaphor, about one nation, "*inlander* . . . grew ever more specific in content; until, like a ripe larva, it was suddenly transmogrified into the spectacular butterfly called 'Indonesian.'"[4] Anderson writes with the delicacy of an aesthete, not a populist. He also is capable of spying both economic forces and Machiavellian motives behind the making of national communities, giving one nod to "print capitalism" for turning strangers into fellow members of "monoglot mass reading publics" and another nod to elites who contain popular nationalism with an official nationalism of their own.[5] Still, his slant on the nation is most often romantic. He depicts the "imagined community" of the modern nation as a benign union of subscribers to the same newspapers and singers of the same anthems. He declares that that community is inherently inclusive through being based on a shared language that can be learned by anyone. He asserts that ethno-racist exclusions are fueled by aristocratic, not national, ideologies of stock and blood.[6] He declares that patriots fight wars out of love for their country, not out of hatred of the Other.[7] Charting the sequential waves in which national solidarities are forged in the Americas, Europe, Asia, and Africa, he represents national identity as a kind of global modeling effect, in which all nation-states except the very first one enjoy a basic equality with one another through being equally reiterative. Most important, he makes cultural meaning in the sense of a humanly enhancing orientation of self to society and cosmos the very crux of nation-ness.

I have said that ideas are not nationally bounded, but no student of nations and nationalism should be surprised by differences in the reception of them and their authors from one nation to the next. Some medley of nationally inflected interests and prejudices surely explain the near invisibility in the United States of a third modernist theorist well-known elsewhere in the academic world. Tom Nairn is often associated by that world with Gellner and Anderson, he often associates himself with them, and his own classic book, *The Break-Up of Britain*, published a few years before the other two, was no less jolting to older views of nationalism when it first came out.[8]

Is Nairn's fatal flaw from the American perspective an *engaged* attitude that is, in substance as well as style, unpalatable for liberals and leftists alike? Early on, Nairn takes the argument about nationalism's modernity in a far more radical direction than Gellner and Anderson do. He writes with a ferocious hatred of imperialist regimes, metropolitan centers, and big political "battalions." He insists that uneven capitalist development and regional economic inequality is the larger context in which all national aspirations must be set, with the "notoriously subjective or 'irrational' elements in nationalism" sparked by forces of modernity that arrive at the doorstep of vulnerable regions in the form of "domination and invasion."[9] For him, the traumatic destruction of a way of life, rather than a neutral technological process or constitutive cultural meaning, is the key to nationalism, which conversely is defensible as well as comprehensible as a reaction formation against modernity experienced as a shattering blow from the outside. And Nairn is searing, not patronizing or dewy-eyed, in describing what he calls nationalism's inherent schizophrenia: its material determination and mythological self-interpretation; its glorification of a rural past and pursuit of an industrial future; its alternating impulses of emancipation and coercion.

Although Nairn takes up an engaged attitude toward nationalism, the political implications of seeing that phenomenon as "false" in its self-understanding yet "right" in its aims are not entirely clear. At the heart of *The Break-Up of Britain* is an ambiguity maddening to friends and foes of nationalism alike: is Nairn a nationalist or isn't he? Nairn later revises his views in ways that allow him to say "I am!" That resounding "yes," however, only makes him newly distasteful to all those who dislike intellectual partisanship of any sort, as well as to all those who dislike intellectual partisanship of this particular — *particularist* — sort.

In the following pages I want to examine the analysis in *The Break-Up of Britain* and the metamorphosis of that analysis over the next twenty years. At the level of detail, this metamorphosis is Nairn's alone. In its broad strokes, however, it mirrors a larger shift in the spirit of an age, even in those places that have kept Nairn at arm's length. For its idiosyncrasies as well as its demonstration of the promise and dangers of a more general mentality, the case of Tom Nairn can be read as both a curious and an edifying tale.

As a prelude, we would do well to review specific aspects of Nairn's biography that might explain his lack of popularity in the United States. One probable strike against Nairn is his embrace of Scottish nationalism.[10] From a great-power perspective, Scotland can seem politically inconsequential and Scottish nationalism geographically parochial. From the perspective of radical critics inside a great power, it also can seem politically uninspiring, for reasons to do with Scotland's past that Nairn himself laments. After its absorption into Great Britain, as he tells the story, the Scottish Lowlands enjoyed successful industrialization, cultural advance, and a "hugely profitable junior partnership" in "Anglo-Scots imperial expansion."[11] Although politically incapacitated, Scottish elites did not experience the economic deprivation that might have induced them to mobilize all Scots as a democratic national mass. Hence, during the high period of European nationalism elsewhere, no heroic people here rebelled against its ethnically alien rulers. For those who find it difficult to support nationalist movements unless they are uprisings of the downtrodden against their oppressors, Scottish nationalism is likely to be a disappointment.[12]

A second strike against Nairn is that — despite his infinite contempt for all things British — he thinks and writes within the British cultural arena. European-inspired intellectuals in the United States, their admiration for Benedict Anderson aside, have leaned toward the Germans or the French. These national prejudices are especially unfortunate for those interested in questions of national community. Writers from both the metropolis and the peripheries of the old British Empire offer us what Said has called, in his eulogy to one of them, a deeply geographical conception of place by showing how the "physical, political, historical, social and ideological features" of the earth contribute "each in its own way . . . to culture."[13] Said refers here to Raymond Williams, but he might as easily have said the same thing of Nairn. The latter does not exhibit the former's lyricism about the landscape, but he is relentlessly alert to the political economy of world geography — to the ways power in one place sets the material terms of existence for other places, so that regions that are distant physically must be brought close together mentally to be fully understood.

In analyzing the geographical place of nineteenth-century Scottish intellectuals, Nairn supplies us with clues to his own location at once inside and against Great Britain. According to him, Scotland's eminent thinkers and writers immigrated to London, where they "played a very large part in formulating the new national and imperial culture-community." In leaving an "advanced quasi-nation," these Scots differed from other "hungry and ambitious intellectuals" who flocked from the economic backwaters of the British Empire to the center.[14] Recall, for example, George Lamming's description of the novelists who left the British West Indies in the first half of the twentieth century, not out of a failure to write for a national people but out of a failure to be read by one. According to Lamming, the West Indian middle classes ignored their own nascent intelligentsia because they identified culture with English writers, while the illiterate peasantry was entirely alienated from culture in the "English literature" sense. The imperial relation determined not only this predicament of West Indian writers but also their travels to London in an attempt to resolve it. One of the ironies of postcolonial experience is that they eventually found their first audience there.[15]

In the one case, intellectuals forsake their people; in the other, a people forsakes its intellectuals. Nairn himself fits neither situation very well. He is unlike the nineteenth-century Scottish intellectuals in his outrage at the British Empire, and he is unlike the twentieth-century West Indians in not having been forced to seek his fortune in the imperial capital by a lack of recognition in the hinterland. Still, he joins both groups in treating Great Britain—its hinterlands and metropolis—as the broad locale of his working and his work.[16] Even when he writes solely about Scotland, he does so not to celebrate its national uniqueness but to comprehend it, in its British setting, as the exception that proves his general rule about the internal connection between uneven capitalist development and nationalism. Scotland is the case of a nationalist movement that failed to happen when it should have happened if a shared religion, folklore, hostility to foreign rulers, and the recent memory of an independent state—that is, if almost everything but a relation of economic disadvantage vis-à-vis a center—were sufficient precipitants of nationalist politics. But Nairn concentrates much less on the particularities of Scotland even in this comparative way than on Great Britain on the one hand and nationalism in general on the other.[17] Thus his implied audience is not merely Scottish but British, and not merely British but worldly. More precisely, it is made up of the cosmopolitan intellectuals of the world; despite his defense of the people against the intellectuals, the popular classes do not read Nairn any more than the peasants read Lamming and his compatriots.

Later we shall see how Nairn's address to a cosmopolitan readership clashes with his scorn for cosmopolitan social groups and why he feels that scorn. For now we need only note the globalist sweep of his intelligence, as opposed to his localist political sympathies. This sweep is unsurprising in an age in which the references and readerships of all intellectuals have become increasingly expansive, but it is overdetermined in Nairn's case. It derives not merely from the times but also from his perspective on capitalist development, which in turn derives from his Marxism. Although he dramatically revises Marxist theory in *The Break-Up of Britain* and afterward jettisons it altogether, Nairn's roots in Marxism are undoubtedly the third and biggest strike against him from an American point of view.

THE BREAK-UP OF BRITAIN

In *The Break-Up of Britain*, Nairn presents capitalism as the first mover of modern history. At the same time, he presents the disintegration of traditional political communities, the rise of nationalist movements, and the creation of "relatively mono-cultural, homogeneous, unilinguistic" nation-states as modern history's central plot.[18] For him, economics produces politics not in the sense that a base generates a superstructure but in the sense that an impetus triggers a complex and absorbing chain of effects. The differential geographical location of the impetus and the effects of capital accumulation means that the major fault lines of inequality in the world will be regional and that the most deeply felt antagonisms will be those between different ethnic, racial, and sometimes religious groups.[19] Nationalist movements are responses to these inequalities and expressions of these antagonisms. They arise to unify and agitate peoples on the periphery or semi-periphery of the capitalist world system against peoples at the core, provoking nationalist reactions by the far more materially potent core states. It follows that class division is neither the primary contradiction of capitalism nor the truth that national unity obscures. Class does play a stylistic role in nationalist politics by dictating the popular idiom in which those politics must speak. To rally the people, nationalist leaders must draw on the people's language — hence "the emotionalism, the vulgar populism, the highly-coloured romanticism of most nationalist ideology (all the things intellectuals have always held their noses at)." Unlike Marxism, with its hyper-rationalistic theories of class-consciousness, nationalism succeeds at the popular level because it provides "the masses with something real and important."[20]

Nairn condemns Rosa Luxemburg as the Marxist with the greatest number of wrong answers to the national question, because she is the Marxist who most adamantly denounces the national unity of classes she sees as being irreconcilably opposed. Nonetheless, there is a family resemblance between Nairn's analysis of capitalism as a world system divided into cores and peripheries and Luxemburg's theory that capitalism depends on the exploitation of noncapitalist economies.[21] Nairn also follows Luxemburg in underlining the catastrophic consequences of capitalist expansion for noncapitalist economies. This is why, as Nairn puts it, peripheral regions experience "[p]rogress in the abstract" as "domination in the concrete," and "domination in the concrete" as national domination: "in the first instance Anglicization or Frenchification . . . later on, more globally . . . 'Westernization' or 'Americanization.'"[22]

In contrast with Luxemburg, Nairn holds that nationalism is a necessary response to "domination in the concrete," for only a uni-

fied people with a sense of its own separate identity will garner the
will to kick the foreigners out. The result of political independence,
as he sees it, however, is not that the new nation-state sets out on its
own autonomously chosen path but that it pursues the universal requirements of modernity independently. Capitalism is not transcended but extended in a tango in which it remorselessly advances
against customary social structures, while nationalism at first resists
and then yields to the modernizing process.

The Break-Up of Britain consigns socialism to a Kafkaesque fate
of indefinite postponement, for the contradiction between center and
peripheries is perpetually resolved inside the capitalist world system.[23]
The international solidarity of the working class experiences an even
worse fate. Nairn calls internationalism an overstatement in the
nineteenth century, when nationalism flourished no less vigorously
than did socialism, and an utter delusion after 1914, when socialist
internationalism died while capitalism "continued to endure and develop, and . . . nationalism prospered along with it." Given his view
of nationalism as a response to uneven development, of uneven development as intrinsic to capitalism, and of capitalism as a fixed part
of the modern scenery (in fact, as *the* modern scenery), internationalism hardly can be anything but a great-power pretext for driving
little peoples into line. Nairn brands Marxist internationalism itself
as "a legitimizing creed" of the Soviet state, one of those "universalizing, missionary ideologies" harnessed by a dominant nationality
(in this case, the Russians) to serve its national interests.[24] As for
universalism, Nairn rejects it as both historical telos and normative
ethos. On the one hand, capitalism is inherently globalizing: "In
purely economic terms, it has always tended towards larger scale,
and a utilitarian *rationale* indifferent to pettifogging customs and
ethnic colorations."[25] On the other hand, capitalism always has had
to compromise with heterogeneous local cultures, and it is incapable
of realizing the potential of its "innate universalism" in a different
way than Marxism understood. Its inherently lopsided integration of
larger and larger areas into, eventually, a world market and a world
productive system means that generality continually begets specificity: defensive activations of the particular are *this* universal's inevitable (and fortunate) results.

That The Break-Up of Britain posits nations as the main protagonists of modern history is not to say that it presents a nationalist
view of that history. Indeed, it argues that the "imaginings" of na-

tional communities obscure as much as they express the underlying realities of nation formation.[26]

First, nationalism purports that its root cause lies in the uniqueness of nations: "that human society consists essentially of several hundred different and discrete 'nations,' each of which has (or ought to have) its own postage-stamps and national soul." This idea is necessary, Nairn argues, in that Welsh nationalism, for example, must make use of Welsh history, folklore, language, and literature to mobilize the Welsh people. But this idea is also false because that mobilization is not a function of some essential Welsh spirit. "It is not a Welsh fact, but a fact of general developmental history" and even "the most grossly material fact about modern history" that "at a specific time the Welsh land and people are forced into the historical process in this fashion."[27]

Second, although nationalism is prompted by modern forces, it represents the nation as antique, archaic, even primordial. Such myths of national antiquity respond to real "latent fracture lines of human society under strain" by compensating for a lack of modern political, social, and economic institutions that established nation-states already have.[28] To understand the compensatory function of the myth is not necessarily to excuse it. Hannah Arendt scorns the Central and Eastern European pan-movements precisely because they substituted a cooked-up idea for the reality of a nation-state. "If they wanted to match the national pride of Western nations, they had no country, no state, no historic achievement to show but could only point to themselves, and that meant, at best, to their language — as though language by itself were already an achievement — at worst, to their Slavic, or Germanic, or God-knows-what soul."[29] Nairn is light-years away from Arendt here, extending great sympathy to those whose identities are seared by "the fact of not having and the awareness of this intolerable absence."[30]

Third, although nationalism pretends to protect a people's age-old customs and traditions, it actually conjures up the past in order to prepare for a different kind of future. To mobilize against a progress that reaches them in the form of an alien intrusion, the peripheral societies of world capitalism are forced to muster all their resources, "even as they set out to progress themselves." They "try to propel themselves forward . . . *by a certain sort of regression* — by looking inwards, drawing more deeply upon their indigenous resources, resurrecting past folk-heroes and myths about themselves."[31] Nationalism's regressive/progressive character means that it will be prone to chauvinism and democracy, exclusivism and equality, nativism and emancipation. This intrinsic ambiguity eludes not only nationalists who portray the nation as simply good but also scholars who distinguish good varieties of nationalism from bad: patriotic from fascistic, civic from ethnic, anti-imperialist from imperialist. As Nairn writes in *The Break-Up of Britain*, there are no "black cats" and "white cats" here: "The whole family is spotted, without exception." Alluding to Benjamin's famous description of that terrible storm "'we call progress,'" Nairn states that nationalism can be seen as the "pathology" caused by that storm, with its most violent passions resembling the sudden appearance of the id during the breakdown of a personality in a crisis it must weather but does not wittingly author or understand.[32] He uses the psychoanalytic metaphor against critics who fail to decipher the underlying reason for nationalist irrationalities, but the metaphor is bound to irritate nationalists most of all. Can we blame them? In Nairn's eyes, nationalist leaders resemble not warrior heroes but Nietzschean ascetic priests, who reinfect with the germ of nationalist resentment the wounds of inferiority that modernity has inflicted on the weak in order to heal those same wounds.

Is *The Break-Up of Britain* an epitaph for Marxism? Certainly Nairn believes that classical Marxism overlooks—and was doomed to overlook—the most significant feature of our age.[33] As a theory born in Europe, it was primed to see class conflict in the European nation-states as paramount, rather than the regional conflicts caused by Europe's impact on the rest of the world. As a nineteenth-century theory, it could not see those regional conflicts fully in any case, for the whole story of uneven development had yet to unfold. But if nationalism exposes Marxism as "a part of history in a quite uncomplimentary sense, one which has nothing to do with the holy matrimony of theory and practice," Nairn does not repudiate the tradition as a consequence. He seconds in his own analysis Marxism's emphasis on these facets of capitalism: its Western origins, preeminence as the determining force of the modern world, expansive dynamic, and contradictory nature as a system of domination and development. He also looks forward to Marxism's becoming, as he announces it now *can* become (because the historical conditions are ripe for it), "an authentic world-theory . . . founded upon the social development of the whole world."[34]

Is *The Break-Up of Britain* a nationalist manifesto? In that text, Nairn highlights nationalism, explains it, and defends it, but he does not believe it and so cannot coherently believe *in* it. To see nationalism as false but right has tangled logical implications for the seer; the ability to *be* a nationalist is not one of them.[35]

THE BREAKUP OF YUGOSLAVIA

In the years between the publication of *The Break-Up of Britain* and the disintegration of the Soviet empire, Nairn published numerous articles in Great Britain on Thatcherism, North-South disparities in Britain, the Scottish Nationalist Party, and the antirepublicanism of British political culture. He also published his anti-British, anti-empire, and very probably anti-English book, *The Enchanted Glass: Britain and its Monarchy*, on the function of monarchy in an age of Britain's advancing decrepitude. In the early 1990s, he returned to the question of nationalism in general in a series of articles he wrote for *The New Statesman, Dissent, Daedalis, The London Review of Books*, and *New Left Review*, many of which are collected in his 1997 book, *Faces of Nationalism: Janus Revisited*. In these writings, he responds to the emergence of new nationalist movements in Eastern Europe and the former Soviet Union[36] and to the "hysteria" of Western intellectuals in the face of a Balkan conflict that many of them characterized as a "Hobbesian" tribal war.[37] Nairn elects what others would deem a most unpropitious moment — the high point of ethnic cleansing in Bosnia-Herzegovina — not only to underscore nationalism but to come out as a nationalist, too.

In his commentary on the new age of nationalism, Nairn preserves many key themes from his older book. He still claims, very ardently, that regional inequality is "the living marrow of actual development," which begins in certain areas of the world that then become ascendant over other areas. He still understands nationalism as a struggle on the part of the subjected for "modernization on different, less disadvantageous terms."[38] With specific respect to the warring ethnic groups in Eastern Europe and the former Soviet Union, he points to the reasonableness of each group's fears that it will be ruled economically by some other group "in this new free-but-capitalist world" and so to the rationality of each group's attempts to move the others "on, or out of the way."[39] Finally, he still sees capitalism as a globally unifying force that today is pulling even the former

Communist zones into its orbit, precipitating in response to its own expansion and centralization "a previously unimaginable and still escalating number of different ethno-political units."[40]

However, Nairn sets these familiar elements among other ideas that subtly but surely alter his earlier position. History itself, according to Nairn, has forced upon him this first change: the erasure of the socialist alternative to capitalism that had at least a hypothetical existence as a distant vanishing point in his older work. This relatively delicate adjustment in Nairn's theory has indelicate ramifications for his theory and politics. Nairn now tells us that uneven capitalist development "has finally, definitively established itself since 1989 as the sole matrix of future evolution," and he praises nationalism, democracy, *and* capitalism as pillars of modernity "inseparable from progress" in the straightforward, undialectical sense of the term. He also cites the "economic revulsion against the anti-capitalist command economies" as a progressive factor in "the gigantic upheaval against Communism."[41] In only one essay does Nairn allude to socialism with something of his old affection, but even then he does so in a weird hodgepodge of incompatible assertions: "If market-governed development is the only kind there is, then this implies that there will be . . . [only] different kinds of capitalism." Hence, "socialists will have to decide what type of capitalists they will become."[42] So much for the future possibilities of radical difference in the socioeconomic sense.

The second change in Nairn's approach to nationalism is one more of mood than assertion. In *The Break-Up of Britain*, Nairn chides internationalism firmly but not too unkindly for being one part metropolitan ideology and one part socialist fantasy. In his new essays, he launches a scorching assault on internationalism and cosmopolitanism with much uglier undertones.

"There is no doubt about the new spectre haunting Europe." The opening salvo of Nairn's 1990 essay "Beyond Big Brother" announces that this time it is nationalism that is the revolutionary force and intellectuals who are members of the group most threatened by it. With a special animus directed at Eric Hobsbawm and his strongly internationalist *Nations and Nationalism since 1780*, Nairn asserts that internationalism "originated among the Enlightenment elites, and has been transmitted from one intelligentsia to another . . . it has always been the ideology most consonant with their class interests." The prejudice against "inherited diversity" reflects not a humanist ethos but the power of "the big battalions" to define the requisites of humanity.[43]

In a second essay, Nairn traces internationalism not merely to the class interests of metropolitan elites but also to the constitutional antipathy of the European left for ethnic difference — its "desperate will . . . that social progress should not be so much built on ethnic variety as safely divorced from it."[44] But it is in a third essay, "Internationalism and the Second Coming," that Nairn most explicitly exposes all the internationalists who claim to speak "from nowhere in particular." This collection of internationalists includes preindustrial aristocrats, self-proclaimed cosmopolitans who dabble in foreign cultures, and "individuals or families from culturally mixed or transplanted backgrounds who genuinely feel that they could choose to settle anywhere," a "description" that "leaves them open to attack by nativist spokesmen for vices such as rootlessness, lack of allegiance, etc." These early modern figures are joined after 1789 by the "metropolitan schoolteacher" disseminating civilization "out and downwards from the appropriate centers," whose cosmopolitanism is "difficult to distinguish from imperialism," and, finally, the socialist, who hopes to counter both imperialism and nationalism with a universal working class.[45]

Well, not quite finally. Nairn informs us that while post-1789 internationalism lacked "a social basis in the sense of Burke's educated cross-border caste," it did have a "composite and shifting foundation." He lists the three main elements of that foundation as "metropolitan or Atlantic-left cliques," the working-class movement, and, as he puts it, "what George Steiner, in a 1987 television lecture on Vienna, called the 'Judaic intelligentsia.'"[46] One does not need a lesson in semiotics to know why Nairn assumes the voice of a Jew in order to conjure up the image of the Jewish carrier of internationalism, given all that that image has stood for in the modern history of right-wing nationalist and fascist thought. Nairn concludes by denouncing the multinational state as the practical foundation of internationalism, proclaiming the collapse of key overarching states in 1989 to be a harbinger of the good collapse of all the rest. In light of his critique of internationalism, however, this collapse can only be disastrous for the motley crew on the other side of the divide from "the national people": not only the metropolitan elites with their interest in domination but also intellectuals, socialists, foreigners, Jews, all other diasporas groups, and, if we push the logic of his argument all the way, multiethnic local communities, and individuals who are ethnic mixtures in and of themselves.

A third change in Nairn's position is a new fetishism of ethnicity, locality, and nationality, not in the sense of attributing magical powers to them but in the sense of revering them as essential truths. Nairn fetishizes ethnicity partly by modifying the claims that he, Gellner, and Anderson initially made about the modernity of nationalism and the nation as an invented community. In 1990, he introduces the idea that humankind's "arguably most important natural inheritance is . . . [its] own ethno-linguistic variety" and that "Nationalism has always been invention after nature."[47] Two years later, he adds that it is no longer clear that nationalism or regionalism "derives so totally from the circumstances of modernity." There may be something biological, hereditary, and genetic to nationalism and ethnicity after all, which Nairn assures us need not imply a natural hierarchy of peoples but does imply an "internal species diversity" that "through cultural means has always been 'human nature'" in any event.[48] In an essay titled "This Land Is My Land, That Land Is Your Land," Nairn and his coauthor, John Osmond, add a territorial dimension to the equation. "[A]ll land is somebody's," they admonish, and so "Modernity must negotiate with the archaic."[49] With these words Nairn not only affirms the primordial nature of national identity claims but also assimilates land rights to those claims, which allows him to suggest the ancient roots as well as modern causes of ethnic and national animosities in shared territories. Finally, in his introduction to *Faces of Nationalism*, Nairn muses that the modernist theorists of nationalism had attributed too much "generative power" to the modernization process and too little importance to preexisting "clashes and contrasts among particular peoples." He surmises that blood in the sense of "the inherent and irreconcilable diversity of 'human nature'" underlies the "manifest phenomena of nationalism," as well as blood in "the familiar metaphorical sense of transmission or inheritance from the past, in either a biological or a socio-cultural sense." Consequently, he voices the need for a "new paradigm" that can link "biology and kinship" to "political nation-states and resurgent nationality."[50]

The idea of a false internationalism and true ethnic division features prominently in Nairn's account of ethnic conflict in Bosnia-Herzegovina. He holds that the situation there of intimate ethnic "overlay or admixture" is atypical and idiosyncratic, having been "deliberately maintained" by outside imperial powers that artificially enforced the unity of distinct peoples. The real "curse of this old frontier zone is that . . . it was never allowed to unscramble itself along what became the standard lines of European nation-state evolution."[51]

Given Nairn's detailed delineation elsewhere of ethnic multiplicity in the borderlands of Europe and his attacks on big multinational states, one cannot help but protest against his suggestion here that ethnic singularity has been Europe's political "standard line." One also cannot help wondering why he turns an empirical standard that supposedly sums up existing tendencies in modern politics into a normative standard that dictates how modern politics should proceed. Nairn also infers from this so-called standard tendency of peoples the spontaneous and uncoerced preferences of those peoples. Thus he can attribute the demise of ethnic coexistence in Bosnia not to nationalist leaders who, according to Robert Hayden, had to destroy popular ethnic peace because their own ideology proclaimed such peace impossible, and not even to a populism which, in *The Break-Up of Britain*, Nairn is careful to distinguish from democratic politics, but to democracy itself. "Democracy is people power," he remarks in the 1990s. "And in this region people are primarily communities, the democratic impulse is strong but also collective, ethnic rather than individual or abstract." While assuring us that "[n]o endorsement of Great Serb expansionism is implied," Nairn turns to Radovan Karadzic in support of his case. The old ethnic tolerance prevailed " 'before democracy,' " he quotes Karadzic as saying. But " '[n]ow we have democracy. . . . People no longer have to live that way, we have free choice. Why do you wish us punished for that?' " Here Karadzic asserts that the situation in Bosnia is the result of the free choices of all the peoples involved. Nairn seconds him when he declares that regardless of Western metropolitan opinion, a "crude repartition of Bosnia-Herzegovina" already has been effected "on the ground itself," as if all the peoples involved had agreed on that repartition. In this way, he redraws the main battle line in Bosnia into one that divides the West on the internationalist side from the Croats, Serbs, and Muslims on the nationalist. Because he sees Bosnia's "underlying, inherited configuration" as the fundamental problem — rather than a situation that becomes a problem, as Hayden puts it, only " '[o]nce the logic of division was accepted' " — Nairn sees separation as the natural solution. The details of that separation, he declares, necessarily will include the "movement of populations and borders."[52]

Besides purporting that the breakup of large states is democratic for liberating ethnic groups, Nairn believes that breakup democratic for creating numerous local centers of power. His basic argument is that the cold war standoff between the two great empires suppressed "collective and national . . . ferment," with a consequent "narrowing and souring of identity and meaning."[53] The new age of nationalist disorder may have brought with it "dislocation and doubt," but it also released new forms of identity and community that are less rigid and overbearing, more imaginative and diverse than those offered by either the superpowers or the large European-style states. The multiplication of political centers can emancipate the world epistemologically from "the metropolitan virtual reality being pumped out in London, Paris and New York,"[54] while the globalizing economic and cultural force of Big Macs and *L.A. Law* finds its sturdy antidote in "[t]he nonlogical, untidy, refractory, disintegrative, particularistic truth of [little] nation-states."[55] The "whole tendency of the age," Nairn concludes, "seems set against gigantism."[56]

Nairn's fetishization of political smallness or locality is not out of tune with the sensibilities of many "metropolitan intellectuals" today. But a passing glance at political theory should make it plain that while the disintegration of great states may democratize power internationally, internal democracy and cultural independence cannot be deduced from a polity's small size.[57] A passing glance at economic practice should make it equally plain that economic monoliths and political miniatures can go hand in hand, instead of opposing one another as point and counterpoint. And which of the two partners is more likely to dictate the scenes from a marriage between an elephant and an ant?

At this juncture, to say that Nairn fetishizes nationality may seem redundant and hardly a departure from his past work. However, although he can be accused of a single-minded fixation on nations in *The Break-Up of Britain* (although no more single-minded than classical Marxism's fixation on class), Nairn did justice to nationalism's moral-political ambiguity in that text. In his new essays, he is much more entranced, setting nationalism squarely on the side of progress, freedom, diversity, and democracy. He does admit that to say that "nationalism is, very generally, a good thing is not to say that there are no blots, excrescences, or failures." But even this note on the bad exception to a good rule clashes with his older and more complex insight that the whole family of nationalism is spotted, without exception. Nairn explicitly ascribes his new optimism to an uplifting turn in history rather than to a turnaround in his political point of view. "Fifteen years ago, I wrote something about 'The Modern Janus,' likening nationalism to the two-headed Roman deity. . . . Since then the whole world has increasingly come to resemble him. But with an important difference . . . on the whole, the forward-gazing side of the strange visage may be more prominent than it was in 1977 . . . more open and encouraging than it was then."[58]

Against those who demur at the bloody context in which he writes these lines, Nairn harks back to the cold war's threat of species extinction, "under which humanity cowered" for forty years.[59] Compared with *that*, the "new world of liberation-chaos" cannot be anything but a step forward.[60] What most impresses Nairn about the ethnonational turbulence of the period is "how astoundingly, how unbelievably little damage has been done." And indeed, he declares, the consequences of even some "worst-possible-case" nationalist scenario "would not, by the standards of 1948 to 1988, be all that serious. Nobody would have to worry about taking refuge on another planet."[61] In the purely quantitative, body-count sense, Nairn is right: not even genocide can top human annihilation, after all. Still, this line of argument is surely an instance of what Hannah Arendt would call moral stupidity, for human annihilation would not put into perspective but instead put an end to the seriousness of every other human thing. Gazing out on the European landscape as it evolved in the forty years *before* 1948, Arendt is far ahead of Nairn in recognizing the calamities that living human beings can bring on themselves, as soon as they base political membership and exclusion on facts of "sheer being."

BETWEEN PAST AND FUTURE

How might we value Nairn's complicated contributions to the understanding of nationalism thus far, keeping in mind the possibility of new complications in his thought in response to new unpredictabilities in politics? Let us begin with the virtues Nairn inherits from Marxism: a sharp tongue and fighting spirit, so refreshingly at odds with the cultivated irony and world-weariness of our age; a hard-headed defense of nationalism that avoids the more tempting sentiments of mawkishness and moralism; a materialist analysis of collective identity in a period dominated by discourse analysis; and a political antagonism to domination and inequality. Among those virtues, also, he displays a theoretical intelligence that works off the actual world rather than off a world that is ideal in being either a wished-for but nonexistent reality or a conceptual realm where ideas gain their force solely by interlocking with other ideas. Finally, Nairn inherits from Marxism the will to counter claims he believes to be false — even Marxism's own claims — with other claims he believes to be true, rather than solving the problem of competing views by deconstructing everything in sight or, much worse, by celebrating everybody's story. His assertions about modern history may be wrong, but at least they are couched in such a way as to stir up debate rather than crushing it under the rule that to speak with passion on the side of something is to embarrass and to speak with authority against something is to oppress.[62]

What vices does Nairn owe Marxism? If he takes his intellectual obeisance to the objective factor in history from that tradition, he does so in a highly exaggerated form. Revolutionaries from Marx to Lenin, Luxemburg, and Gramsci saw history and capitalism as having an objective logic to them, but they also recognized the importance and open-ended quality of subjective will and intentions, even if they never solved the problem of how the objective and the subjective were to mesh. For Nairn, the objective dynamic of modern capitalism is so dictatorial that subjects can only fall in line. His belief in the necessity of the actual is nowhere more evident than in his theory of development, which he also inherits from Marxism but turns into something newly merciless and fixed. "Capitalist development" at once determines the entire set of possible meanings of "development" and rules like a natural fact over the world. There is no ideational content outside it, no practical escape from it, and no foreseeable end to it: its traumatic unevenness notwithstanding, it is all we can hope for now and in the long run.[63]

There is also a very distant political echo of Marxism in Nairn's peculiar tendency, at least in *The Break-Up of Britain*, to view nationalism in the core countries as a secondary reaction to nationalism in the periphery. Nairn's representation of nationalism as, in its original guise, a politics of the weak against the strong enshrines it as politically left and so as historically "right." And yet, by identifying the initial impulse of nationalism as anti-imperialist, Nairn obscures a point Rosa Luxemburg was able to see years ago: European countries had used the right to national self-determination to justify their colonial adventures in the first place.

What are the most important virtues and vices that Nairn shares with post- and even anti-Marxist thinkers? On the "virtue" side, Nairn trades in an overemphasis on economics for a new appreciation of culture and politics. He reconceives of politics from being a uniform struggle between "a proletariat and a bourgeoisie essentially the same everywhere . . . locked in the same battle from Birmingham to Shanghai,"[64] to being multiple struggles between cores and peripheries, which he also calls fragments and today we call margins. He insists on the significance of ethnic and national fragments more than a decade before nationalism hits the intellectual headlines in the United States, and he is sensitive to the positive as well as negative role of imagination, fantasy, and myth in the making of national community.

On the "vices" side, Nairn's demotion of class as *the* key division in social life comes close to being a demolition of class as *a* key division. Nairn attends to class inequality when he describes England as a core country that seduces its popular classes into social deference and political quiescence, first with imperial material rewards and then by means of what he later will call a royal, antidemocratic and anti-ethnic "familial" nationalism.[65] But more typically, he excises all the right questions that Luxemburg raised long ago about the national unity of classes whose interests are antagonistic, even if, as Nairn shows us, they are not entirely opposed. National unity on whose terms? In whose interests? For what purposes and ends?

Related to his deemphasis on class division is Nairn's evasion of all the unsavory aspects of the division between leaders and led. With respect to the history of nationalism in politics, "elite manipulation" rather than "popular participation" may be the operative reality. Then, too, the fact that nationalist movements draw on the energy of the people does not guarantee that those movements serve the popular classes at the same time that they serve their masters. Nairn treats the proto-fascist possibilities of nationalism as side issues, but are they?[66]

Nairn's most ominous "post-Marxist" flaw, however, is his affirmation of the identity politics principle, "one people, one state." Although he comes to that principle through his empathy for all the "little battalions" in the world, his defense of ethnonationalism has its irremediably unpleasant aspect. To glimpse that aspect, one need only compare Nairn's condemnation of empire as the contrasting political form with Said's much more ambivalent attitude. Said is the master critic of hegemonic centers and imperial oppression but not necessarily of empire-size political unities. Indeed, he occasionally speaks with real regret of their disappearance; although empires may have been politically undemocratic, they allowed for the social intermixture of diverse peoples. Said's nostalgia for the ethnic diversity of empire is reminiscent of Luxemburg's earlier praise for the intermingling of peoples in the old Russian and Austro-Hungarian empires, which she urges Social Democracy to preserve, not destroy, through an international rather than national organization of the working class. In contrast with both thinkers, Nairn calls empire, not ethnonationalism, "the negation of diversity on a deeper plane."[67] He is deafeningly silent about the possibility that ethnic heterogeneity within political unity might be, in and of itself, a positive good.[68]

What are Nairn's most promising new sentiments and ideas? With respect to what we like to think of as the past, Nairn has begun to attribute increased weight to the "enduring pressures of rurality" on the modern age. He muses that he and other modernist theorists may have overstressed "the factors of leading-edge alteration" in the modernizing process, "resulting in understatement of everything left behind the edge." As we have seen, that "everything" for him includes "blood," but it also, more persuasively, includes both the experience of being rooted in and attached to a particular place and the shaping vitality of "rural economy, life and routines." He points to Cambodia, Rwanda, and Serbia to illustrate the potent connection among "rural despair and resentment," a "mobilised peasantry," and nationalist violence against "the spreading tide of 'modernisation,' the market economy and the norms of urban liberalism." Nairn urges his readers to take seriously rural culture and the volatile energies that explode when it comes under assault; in short, to attend to the dynamic impact *on* the modernizing process *of* the agrarian world.[69]

With respect to the present, Nairn challenges, if not in an entirely successful way, two smug prejudices of contemporary liberal thought: its moral dichotomization of ethnic and civic nationalism, and its idealization of civil society. In a 1995 article, Nairn proposes that ethnonationalism stands less as an antithesis to civic nationalism than as a necessary but transitory step on the way, if the appropriate apparatus is put in place, to the practical acknowledgment that, as he quotes Michael Ignatieff, " 'a nation should be a home to all, and that race, colour, religion and creed should be no bar to belonging.' "[70] Alas, as much as it might reassure liberals about the endpoint of Nairn's own politics, this fragmentary proposal mimics as much as it contests the contrast Nairn rightly had buried earlier between an infantile "Eastern" nationalism and a maturely civilized "Western" one. More powerfully, Nairn debunks the glorification of civil society from a different angle than classical Marxism did, by tracing its genealogy within the context of nationalism, not capitalism. He shows us that in the eighteenth century, the concept of civil society functioned as a gloss over Scotland's unique but far from exemplary situation as a nation independent in its civil but subordinate in its political affairs. In the late twentieth century, Western liberals try to impress on the entire world the preeminent importance not of political democracy but of a non-state culture "with the sense of 'decency,' privacy, individual and group or minority rights, freedom of initiative and enterprise, etc." Leery of this new move to impose an Anglo-American social model on all nations and with the old political impotence of Scotland in mind, Nairn defends political self-government over and against "[l]iberal social trust."[71]

With respect to the future, Nairn exhibits an adventurous joy at the new possibilities for political life emerging out of the disintegration of the Soviet Empire and the disintegrative pressures on the great European and American states. While he still most often sees ethnicity as the basis of nascent political units, he has begun to applaud a more eclectic mélange of political forms, including multiethnic cities and city-states. His best anarchist instincts shine through in his vigorous affirmation of political variety, experimentation, and institutional changes that break with all the old rules.

In conclusion, Nairn's original theory of nationalism as a function of the modern dynamic between peripheries and cores can be said to anticipate the end of the Eurocentric and bipolar world order. In a perfect duet of style and substance, the systematic nature of that theory dissolves as that order dissolves. On the one hand, Nairn's jarring, often contradictory new ideas reflect the breathing space for creative political thought and action that "the new world disorder" has opened up. On the other hand, those ideas also are indicative of the "dementia," as Nairn once put it, that can develop in situations of great practical confusion. The Marxist tradition on which Nairn once warily drew had its damning failures, among them an overly airtight conception *of* the world and a consequent inability and unwillingness to grasp new actualities and possibilities *in* the world. But it is worth remembering that tradition's rigorous pursuit of the strands connecting seemingly distinct and separate elements and its belief in the bad impetus but good promise of that connection. The rigor helped preclude an intellectual zigzagging between discordant ideas. The belief helped prevent a political move to divide humanity into self-contained, self-identical ethnic groups.

Nairn's journey from neo-Marxism to neo-nationalism (and perhaps, in the near future, to some third place) is a special variant of the dissolutions and reformulations of critical thought today. Hence, the curious case of Tom Nairn can offer important negative lessons for a more general audience. Nairn's embrace of ethnonationalism should press us to find a way to recognize collective identities and to comprehend political and cultural fragmentation without fetishizing the identities or the fragments. His resignation to capitalism as the fixed economic backdrop for a fluidity and creativity in the political and cultural spheres should jolt us into refusing to *either* reduce politics and culture to economics *or* treat these as disconnected realms. Nor should we treat "capitalist development" as if it were a given, natural process, at odds with all that is mutable and transitory in human affairs.

Finally, Nairn's insights into the promising tumult of the post-1989 world must be tempered by the recognition that the new is never all that new or all that singularly good. At the turn of the twenty-first century, nationalism may resemble a forward-gazing phoenix rising up out of the ashes of the cold war, and it may augur bold innovations in the organization of political life. But nationalism also is part of what Anderson has called "one deep tectonic movement stretching across more than two centuries." As such, it plays out on an end-of-the-twentieth-century stage, a classic nineteenth-century drama of the decomposition of "polyethnic, polyglot, and often polyreligious" empires, with the contradictions of self-determination and separatism, populism and persecution, emancipation and tyranny still very much intact.[72] In the days when he thought on the knife-edge of ambiguity and glared at everything with a half sympathetic, half suspicious eye, wouldn't Nairn have seen that problematic mix?

Chapter Six

Cosmopolitanism in a New Key

V. S. Naipaul and Edward Said

NATIONALISM VERSUS COSMOPOLITANISM

In the final decades of the twentieth century, people with very different political pedigrees come to favor particularistic loyalties, organic traditions, and homogeneous identities over cosmopolitan outlooks, cultural admixtures, and the jostling of diverse peoples inside the same society. American communitarians assert that political societies must be glued together by relations of trust based on familiarity, shared values, and inherited habits of the heart.[1] European conservatives and Hindu communalists protest the integration of aliens, immigrants, and minorities as equal rather than subordinated or assimilated elements within the nation-state. The French New Right calls for the demise of Enlightenment universalism and the preservation of cultural variety through the geographical separation of different ethnic and racial groups.[2] Post–Frankfurt school theorists indict "liberalism as bureaucratic domination over . . . abstract individuals" and "capitalism as the nemesis of local self-determination and traditional cultures."[3] Two of our own thinkers have added their voices to this motley chorus. The liberal pluralist Isaiah Berlin charges cosmopolitanism with being "empty" and "desiccated," insisting that people must "have kith and kin and feel closer to some people than to others."[4] The erstwhile neo-Marxist Tom Nairn attacks cosmopolitanism and internationalism as the self-serving ideology of "big battalion" states, metropolitan managerial and intellectual elites, socialist enemies of ethnic difference, a Jewish international intelligentsia, and diasporic individuals who live as lightly in one country as in another.[5]

Now, "cosmopolitanism" has complex associations and connotations, and admittedly certain of these warrant some of the criticisms that Nairn and others level at the concept as a whole. Even Hannah Arendt, whose thinking displays features of what I am calling a new cosmopolitanism, scoffs at cosmopolitanism in its more typically un-

derstood form. She condemns the general delusion that there can be
a free-floating perspective detached from all concrete locations. She
also condemns the more dangerous delusion particular to individual
members of pariah peoples who had achieved outstanding personal
success (she speaks specifically of Stefan Zweig) that they had been
drawn by the "radiant power of fame" into a "nebulous international society" innocent of "national prejudices."[6]

Even when proponents of cosmopolitanism as a free-floating perspective really mean to stand up for all of humanity, the way they
state their case can leave much to be desired. For example, Martha
Nussbaum surely intends the best for the entire world when she denounces patriotism as the expression of nationalism and ethnocen-
tric particularism alike, opting instead for a Stoic cosmopolitanism
that transcends social divisions by "ask[ing] us to give our first allegiance to what is morally good — and that which, being good, I can
commend as such to all human beings."[7] But Nussbaum is naive in
assuming the uncontestable content of moral goodness and in depicting the "citizen of the world" as a self abstracted from the world's
particulars for the sake of universal right and reason. Kwame Anthony Appiah takes a more promising path when he represents cosmopolitanism as flowing from rather than transcending concrete and
particular ways of life.[8] Appiah fashions his idea of a rooted cosmopolitanism by fastidiously weaving together inherited communal
norms and individual freedom of choice, native populations and diaspora groups, settled peoples and worldly individuals, heterogeneous regional forms and homogeneous market forces, loyalty to
nation and solidarity with humanity. Alas, all these factors Appiah
brings into harmonious relations on the page remain in violent collision in the world. A compelling cosmopolitanism would have to take
that collision into account.

In this chapter I want to examine two writers who fold into their
thought and feeling the antinomies that Nairn, Nussbaum, and Appiah evade: Nairn by standing with nationalism against cosmopolitanism; Nussbaum by standing with cosmopolitanism against nationalism; and Appiah by resolving the antinomies into harmonies. I call
V. S. Naipaul and Edward Said "new cosmopolitans" less to suggest
that their cosmopolitanism is new in the historical sense than to suggest that it breaks with cosmopolitanism as both its friends and its
foes traditionally have understood the term.[9]

History, however, is not unimportant here, for it will be significant to the determination of their mentalities that Naipaul and Said both belong to diasporas shaped by a colonial past. Will it also be significant that they are prominent intellectuals and as such members of an elite social group? Living in Western countries, Naipaul and Said even can be considered members of the "metropolitan elite." This goes to show that Nairn's cover phrase conceals a host of complicating differences within it.[10] It also shows that just as one can never assume an identity between elites and "the people," one cannot assume an identity between the "'optimistic mobility of the intellectual and artist'" and the "mass dislocations endured by economic migrants or expelled refugees."[11] Hence we ultimately will have to ask whether what is true of well-known and well-heeled writers also can be true, if in a less articulate and less happy way, of larger, poorer, more anonymous populations.

Possibly so little joins these two constituencies that a new cosmopolitanism will turn out to characterize privileged intellectuals and a new nationalism the popular classes. Mary Kaldor says as much when she detects a "growing cultural dissonance between those who see themselves as part of an international network, whose identity is shaped within a globally linked and oriented community of people who communicate by e-mail, faxes, telephone, and air travel, and those who still cling to or who have found new types of territorially based identities even though they may not actually live in the territory."[12] In Kaldor's view, the new "defensive" particularisms are the political and cultural expression of populations marginalized, disempowered, and often criminalized in the new global economy. The new cosmopolitanism is the prerogative of wealthy, self-serving, anational agents of capital on the one hand and, on the other, international moralists like Nussbaum who work for human rights, ecology, and world peace. There are shades of Nairn's opposition between popular nationalism and elite internationalism here, although Nairn throws in his cards with the marginalized while Kaldor throws in hers with the moralists.

We must postpone the question of whether the new cosmopolitanism is solely an elite phenomenon until we see just what that cosmopolitanism involves. But a second question of whether the new cosmopolitanism has a specific politics behind it can be answered right away. However strongly both friends and enemies of cosmopolitanism may be tempted to say "yes," Naipaul and Said's juxtaposition will prove that the more accurate answer is "no," if by "politics" we mean a left, center, or right "camp."

To see the political chasm between them, we might note how intensely Naipaul is hated by left-leaning admirers of Said. For example, Caren Kaplan declares that Naipaul is "so powerfully ensconced in the Euro-American world of letters [that] he can serve . . . as the negative nth degree of . . . cosmopolitanism . . . not only privileged but hypocritical."[13] Rob Nixon exposes in Naipaul a host of offending sores: his Brahman ancestry and middle-class background, which separate him from the peasant mainstream of Trinidad society; his "talent for promoting his 'homelessness,'" even while he is not an exile in the "rigorous sense" of being a traumatized and victimized refugee; his closer resemblance to Western tourists than to inhabitants and "[t]rue insiders" in his travels to Zaire, Malaya, and even India, because of his freedom to "terminate his trip as he pleases"; his portrayal of himself as "someone condemned to concentrated alienation," when in fact he stands "among the two or three most lionized writers resident in England"; his self-serving feeling of an "elective affinity" with the celebrated Joseph Conrad; his general "self-intoxication"; and his real position as "a preeminently metropolitan writer."[14]

With a few minor adjustments, however, all these qualities might equally well be ascribed to Said, whose class background even more sharply than Naipaul's separates him from the ordinary masses, who is no less lionized in the United States than Naipaul is in England, who many times has expressed an affinity with Conrad, who is free to leave the countries to which he travels, and so on. The similarities between them show not that Naipaul and Said are mutually sympathetic but that they are divided by their chosen allegiances and ideals rather than by the situations from which their cosmopolitanism largely stems. Said himself recognizes this, berating Naipaul not for what he objectively is but for who he subjectively has decided to become.

More exactly, Said accuses Naipaul of betraying postcolonial societies by highlighting their worst mendacities, venalities, and con-artistries, in contrast with which the old colonial regimes begin to look not so bad and Western civilization, positively good. In a book review published in The Nation, Said describes Naipaul as "a peregrinating writer in the Third World, sending back dispatches to an implied audience of disenchanted Western liberals" — ironically almost the same audience, disenchantment aside, to whom Said is speaking here. These dispatches, Said claims, depict "national liberation movements, revolutionary goals, Third Worldism" as "fraudulent public relations gimmicks, half native impotence, half badly learned 'Western' ideas."[15] In a later essay, he berates Naipaul for having become "a witness for the Western prosecution," reproducing "the tritest, the cheapest and the easiest of colonial mythologies about wogs and darkies, myths that even Lord Cromer and Foster's Turtons and Burtons would have been embarrassed to trade in outside their private clubs."[16] In *Culture and Imperialism*, he reiterates the charge that for Naipaul, to be non-Western is to be "ontologically . . . unfortunate . . . at worst a maniac, and at best a follower, a lazy consumer who . . . can use but could never have invented the telephone."[17]

Nearly as discordant as Said's and Naipaul's politics are the genres in which they most often choose to write. From our vantage point, the most noteworthy formal incongruity between the two men is that Said draws on and indeed helps devise theoretical categories and methodological tools for analyzing the causes and consequences of postcolonial experience that Naipaul as a literary miniaturist does mainly without. But their substantive and stylistic differences should not blind us to key elements of understanding that Naipaul and Said share. Both men focus on the movements of populations across the globe, along with the cultural shocks and strains that ensue from those movements. Both are attuned to the fragility and volatility of inherited identities in the face of modern circumstances and events. Both are strong secularists and intellectual individualists, keeping a sometimes longer and sometimes shorter distance from political parties and institutions for the sake of preserving their critical autonomy. Finally, while each has been known to make an explicit case for the self-determination of his own ethnonational group, both more often imply the need for a pluralistic conception of political membership to suit heterogeneous social realities.

V. S. NAIPAUL

Even amid his complaints, Said describes Naipaul as "too remarkable and gifted a writer to be dismissed."[18] We can assume that Said finds Naipaul remarkable because of the latter's deft way with words, if not also because his highly distorted picture of colonial and postcolonial experience provides an antidote to the opposite distortions of other postcolonial critics.[19] But Naipaul is also remarkable for two of the same reasons that Said is. First, Naipaul grasps the tremendous diversity of peoples in the world, along with the reciprocal aversions and affections, cruelties and generosities that mark their modern interactions. Second, Naipaul grasps the tragic vulnerability, in the modern age, of collective identity and the attachment of people to place. Naipaul's sense of that vulnerability prevents him from reifying origins, homelands, and native cultures, which, against memory's desire, always succumb to the pressures of change. His sense of that tragedy presses him to record the human significance of change as opportunity but also poignant loss.

To account for Naipaul's mentality — a mentality that Said praises elsewhere, without reference to Naipaul, as manifesting true "worldliness" — we might start by noting the places to which he travels: from Trinidad to New York, London, Oxford, Canada, Argentina, Venezuela, Zaire, the Ivory Coast, Uganda, Belize, India, the American South, the English countryside, the Islamic world. We can say, after Oxford, that his travel is chosen to satisfy a personal desire and that it is more and more easily afforded, the "glamorous" perquisite of someone with ample material wealth and an educated understanding of the cultural dimensions of geography. Naipaul also travels as a professional writer, "going about," as he puts it, "one side of his business: traveling, adding to his knowledge of the world, exposing himself to new people and new relationships." But if Naipaul thus seems to belong to a globe-trotting elite, it is not at all with the self-absorbed superficiality of interest that that phrase implies. Naipaul alludes to an enjoyment of "the experience of travel and human discovery for its own sake," but even a deep curiosity about the strange world outside the self is not sufficient to explain his peripatetic inclinations.[20]

For that purpose, Naipaul's retrospective observations on himself are telling. He recalls that he began his travels "to look at various colonial territories in the Caribbean and South America." He says that he was then "still a colonial, traveling to far-off places that were still colonies, in a world still more or less ruled by colonial ideas," but that eventually travel "broadened my world view; it showed me a changing world, and took me out of my own colonial shell."[21] Earlier still, Naipaul traveled from Trinidad to Oxford after having selected and having been selected for an elite education there. Finally, if we look back past those university years, we see two previous, formative journeys. When Naipaul was a boy, his family moved from "the Hindu and Indian countryside [of Trinidad] to the white-negro-mulatto town [of Port of Spain]," where, as Naipaul puts it, he absorbed the multiple influences of an Indian/Hindu background, English literature, and the "negro and G.I. life of its streets."[22] And before Naipaul was born, his ancestors migrated from India as indentured immigrants to work on plantations in this corner of the British Empire. In short, Naipaul's world travel and worldly intelligence cannot be understood simply as a function of an individual's pleasure-seeking and pleasure-affording impulses, or even simply as a function of a writer's search for subject matter. They are determined more fundamentally by the imprint on an astute thinker of the complicated social geography of colonialism and by the fact that colonialism *is* a geography, not just an economy or a history.

In his fiction and nonfiction, Naipaul portrays colonialism as especially precipitating mass migrations and modern capitalist development as especially precipitating the "building over" of familiar landscapes. Both forces disturb the personality and jar inherited identities, and both have their most violent effects in what Nairn would call the peripheries of the capitalist world system. There they take the form of European invasions, massacres of indigenous populations, imports of foreign workers, acquisitions by various ethnic groups of new land and money, nationalist upheavals, dispossessions of diasporic middle classes, and the penetration of native economies by foreign capital as a kind of "second . . . conquest."[23] But colonialism and industrial capitalism also have traumatic effects on the metropolitan regions, where immigrants and refugees from peripheral regions begin to turn up and where modern development makes its inexorable assault on the countryside.

Naipaul can hardly be called a sentimentalist about traditional agrarian societies, given his horror at the remediable but unremedied material poverty of rural people. Nor is he a romantic about diasporic cultures, which he frequently paints as insular, snobbish, living off myths about their countries of origin. He does not fetishize national identity, underscoring its historical contingency and artificiality at least in the context of his own family's experience. Thus he says that "Hindus and Muslims, and people of different castes," isolated in Trinidad from "the people they found themselves among," developed a sense of Indian community that they "would never have known in India," where smaller particularities were and are more intensely felt.[24]

Still, it is his diasporic perspective that enables Naipaul to appreciate not only the unsettling effects of modernization but also the entanglement of diverse ethnic and national peoples through trade, imperial conquest, sexual relations, and the search for economic profit. The scenes in Naipaul's books are always motley: a West Indian and an African in a New York taxicab; a Maltese, Burmese, Kenyan, French Moroccan, northern Englishman, Cockney, and Jew in a London rooming house; Gujars, Afghans, Kaghanis, and Pathans in the Kaghan Valley; Arabs, Persians, Portuguese, and Indians on the East African coast. And Naipaul's global networks, for better or worse, are entirely polyethnic. "All over the world," as a character remarks about the one perhaps truly deracinated social segment, "money is in flight. People have scraped the world clean . . . and now they want to run from the dreadful places where they've made their money and find some nice safe country . . . Koreans, Filipinos, people from Hong Kong and Taiwan, South Africans, Italians, Greeks, South Americans, Argentines, Columbians, Venezuelans, Bolivians, a lot of black people who've cleaned out places you've never heard of, Chinese from everywhere" — typically of Naipaul, not a northern European in that bad lot.[25] If the racial ontology of Naipaul's narrators often replicates colonial ideology — with black Africans at the lowest end of the human species, Arabs and Asians in the ambiguous middle, and great-state Europeans as the superior group — Naipaul is almost always condescending to Europeans, too.[26] This is partly because of their genocidal butcheries in the past,[27] partly because of their ignominious fall from global mastery in the present,[28] and partly, one suspects, because Naipaul knows he has a more thorough and sophisticated knowledge of the world's variety than they do. Ultimately it is Naipaul's view of humanity as a differentiated whole that is bleak — a negative cosmopolitanism, if you like. This bleakness is nowhere more starkly put than in Naipaul's fleeting comment in "Prologue to an Autobiography" that "the conviction that is at the root of so much human anguish and passion, and corrupts so many lives" is that "there [is] justice in the world."[29]

In this sensitivity to the mobility of others, these journeys undertaken by himself, this passing acquaintance with a vast assortment of human types, Naipaul can seem the epitome of the rootless and

alienated soul. He even laments, through an autobiographical protagonist, "the homelessness, the drifting about, I had imposed on
myself."[30] But although Naipaul's "drifting about" never resolves itself in the kind of political project for which the belief in the possibility of justice is a prerequisite, it also never resolves itself into an
obtuse or egotistical or simply consuming attitude toward local settings. Instead, Naipaul approaches every locale with a combination
of irony and empathy, marveling at the peculiarity of the physical
and social landscape but also pressing himself to imagine how that
landscape is connected to a history of peoples, each leaving behind
its sometimes creative and sometimes obliterating mark.

Naipaul concentrates just as intently on the landscape's living
transformation, which he records with extraordinary patience and
painstaking detail in *The Enigma of Arrival*. Here he writes as an
"unanchored and strange" outsider "from another hemisphere, another background," who moves to a cottage in Wiltshire and is
drawn to what he believes is an anciently settled English countryside.
He contrasts himself with "Jack," a local man whose life seems
"genuine, rooted, fitting." Naipaul's lengthy, moving, at times rhap-
sodic descriptions of Jack's garden, a lane, a water meadow, an old
horse, or the look of a mowed strip of grass help make this book one
of the bucolic masterpieces of our time. But Naipaul also charts his
protagonist's slow awakening to infinitesimal changes (the pulling
down of old cowsheds, the replacement of square haystacks with
rolls wrapped in black plastic, the renovation of workers' cottages,
the sale of the manor house) that signal the crumbling of a rural way
of life. Eventually his protagonist realizes that the permanence he
first encountered was only one ephemeral point in an ephemeral
chain, so that "what had caused me delight, when I first came to the
manor, would have caused grief to someone who had been there
before me." The land and the people on it already had been changing long before his arrival; flux and decay had been the true reality
of the scene. Jack himself proves to have been not a "man fitting the
landscape" but a man living "among superseded things." For, after
his death, "[s]o much that had looked traditional, natural, emana-
tions of the landscape, things that country people did . . . now
turned out not to have been traditional or instinctive after all, but to
have been part of Jack's way. When he wasn't there to do these
things, they weren't done; there was only a ruin."[31]

Naipaul can be seen as having "primary affiliations to metro-

politan culture on the London-New York axis," and he can be seen
as seeing himself as having no affiliation at all.[32] At his very worst, he
is capable of representing the world as split into two opposing blocs.
The larger one is prisoner to unchanging rituals, impoverishing customs, rigid political ideologies, and fanatical religious faiths. The
more admirable one manifests a "certain kind of awakened spirit"
and a premium on "ambition, endeavor, individuality . . . responsibility, choice, the life of the intellect, the idea of vocation and per-
fectibility and achievement." Naipaul even is capable of calling the
admirable bloc a "universal" civilization, although it is not obvious
why, since its values apparently flourish only in one tiny portion of
the globe. Perhaps Western culture is universal because of its overwhelming material power to make itself so rather than, as Naipaul
suggests, because of its "extraordinary attempt to accommodate the
rest of the world, and all the currents of that world's thought."[33]

These tendencies of affiliation with metropolitan culture, with nowhere and no place, and with the West all smack of old-style cosmopolitan hubris. But other threads run through Naipaul's fiction and
travel writings that embellish the concept of cosmopolitanism instead of reinforcing its most arrogant details. First, Naipaul casts his
writer's net over a multiplicity of peoples and regions without obscuring either each people's and region's peculiarities or his own particular location in the world, which many of the "I's" of his novels
almost exactly replicate. As he puts it, in a way that accurately con-
veys the spirit of much of his writing, "To me situations and people
are always specific, always of themselves. That is why one travels
and writes: to find out."[34] Thus he illustrates a universalism that is
catholic but not abstract. Second, Naipaul makes extraordinary efforts, distinguishing him even from writers who explicitly speak up
for the oppressed such as Said, to overcome the physical distance
between intellectuals and ordinary people. He determinedly travels
away from metropolitan centers of relative power, wealth, and privi-
lege into their hinterlands to interview remote herdsmen, backwater
teachers and students, lesser officials, crude rednecks, and petty
clerks. Thus he dispels any necessary contradiction between cosmopolitanism and populism and any necessary connection between cosmopolitanism and a haughty disdain for the countryside.

Third, Naipaul provides a graphic account in all of his work of
how modern history itself undermines the possibilities both for
rooted local communities and for large, homogeneous nation-states.

He recognizes the human suffering of which much of that history is made, which gives him a greater depth of feeling than those who treat fragmentation and mobility as unmitigated delights. At the same time, he takes a certain waspish pleasure in the social intermingling afforded by that same suffering history, which saves him from the meanness of spirit of those pressing for a polity in which everyone is ethnically and culturally alike. Fourth, he shows us that transience does not automatically produce a blasé attitude toward locality. More typically in his books, the significance of old locales is heightened as a result either of people's departures from them or of changes in them that people are forced to withstand. The significance of new locales is heightened by the knowledge that they too cannot be counted on to remain intact. Every place, that is, is the site less of indifference and lack of care than of anxiety and anticipated longing. In *A Bend in the River*, one of Naipaul's characters may counsel detachment from all familiar settings on the grounds that "men are in movement, the world is in movement, and the past can only cause pain."[35] But in *The Enigma of Arrival*, Naipaul's protagonist reveals detachment to be only a weak defense against attachment: "I had trained myself to the idea of change, to avoid grief. . . . But philosophy failed me now. . . . Land partakes of what we breathe into it, is touched by our moods and memories."[36]

Fifth, Naipaul captures not only the importance of inherited attachments for people but also their voluntary and coerced breaks from those attachments to a less secure but wider sphere of life. The most local of his fictional and nonfictional figures — Zabeth the bush trader in *A Bend in the River*, Pitton the hired gardener in *The Enigma of Arrival*, Bogart the neighbor in the servant's room in "Prologue to an Autobiography," Rajan the private secretary in *India: A Million Mutinies Now*, Shafi the Malay villager in *Among the Believers* — propel themselves or are propelled outward. Zabeth poles her dugout to foreign regions on the river and sends her son to the "New Domain" for a European education. Pitton is forced to leave the manor estate in the country for a job as laundryman in Salisbury. Bogart sails back and forth between Port of Spain and Venezuela for such mysterious reasons that Naipaul imagines him a bigamist. Rajan, impoverished for much of his life, dreams of joining the creative circles of Calcutta and eventually moves to Bombay, which "had impressed me with its cosmopolitanism and its opportunities."[37] Shafi moves to the capital to work as a Muslim activist even as he grieves for his old way of life, although on a return visit, he sees that "[b]uildings had changed; people had gone away; he no longer knew everybody. The village had ceased to be his, in the way it had been."[38] Even the nationalists in *A Bend in the River* are motivated by both parochial and expansive impulses. In what Nairn would call the classic nationalist script, they mobilize a people to defend its traditional way of life from the intrusions of the modern West but then try to harness the forces of modernity for themselves.

Why are the contradictory desires for home and the world likely to be found in the same breast? As Naipaul implies, it is as embodied creatures that human beings are both prone to a love of the familiar and, because familiar, protective landscape and prey to physical deprivation that can drive them to search elsewhere for relief. Embracing the ideal of "the pursuit of happiness,"[39] Naipaul looks askance at all spiritual passions that demand material sacrifices of poor populations, thereby constricting their already constricted chances for bodily well-being. At the same time, such passions also can drive individuals outward, if only to make the demand for sacrifices more universally. Both material and spiritual needs, therefore, have their world-widening effects.

Naipaul can make crude dualistic distinctions, but at his most nuanced, he shows us that "nationalism" and "cosmopolitanism" connote a split in the twentieth-century personality rather than an opposition between Eastern and Western civilizations, or between illiberal and open-minded individuals, or between popular and elite social groups. In the modern period, all regions are swept up into the maelstrom of shattering and promising change. In turn, individuals and social groups differ from one another not in staying home or moving out into the world but in ranging between home and the world more or less forced by circumstances beyond their control, more or less plagued by misfortune and distress.

EDWARD SAID

Let us now turn to Edward Said, who, by the way, softens considerably toward Naipaul in his 1994 Reith lectures, *Representations of the Intellectual*. Here he praises Naipaul's Salim—the Indian Muslim shopkeeper in *A Bend in the River* who travels into the African interior and then flees to England on the heels of a nationalist upheaval—as "an affecting instance of the modern intellectual in exile." He praises Naipaul himself as an exquisite exile type, "always on the move, revisiting his Caribbean and Indian roots, sifting through the debris of colonialism and post-colonialism, remorselessly judging the illusions and cruelties of independent states and the new true believers."[40]

Said himself is always on the move, having lived or spent time in Jerusalem, Cairo, Beirut, Amman, Alexandria, New York, London, Paris, Tunis, Algiers, and Delhi. Indeed, Said is more cosmopolitan than the classic European cosmopolitan for not being parochially European. He is also more cosmopolitan than Naipaul for being less rural in his origins and interests, more urban and unselfconsciously urbane. Coming from "a prominent Palestinian Christian family"[41] with complicated patterns of residence in Palestine, Egypt, Lebanon, and America,[42] Said was educated early on, like Naipaul, "entirely in British colonial schools"[43] and then sent to boarding school in the United States. He was plucked up by Princeton and Harvard and then hired as a professor of English and comparative literature by Columbia University, visiting the Middle East afterward for vacations and sabbaticals. However unpleasant his experience with the anti-Arab prejudices of Westerners, one does not get the sense here of the material difficulties that Naipaul once had, or of the insecurities of an aspiring young writer setting off by himself into an unknown world.[44]

As in Naipaul's case, however, where Said goes, and why he goes, are determined by the geography of colonialism, or more precisely by the specificities of colonialism in the Middle East. One important specificity is that, as Said puts it, dispossession, not exploitation, is the fundamental injury suffered by the Palestinian people. As a result of Jewish nationalism, Said's extended family leaves Jerusalem. His father — by choice, occupation, and political pressures also a great traveler in his day — is later threatened in Cairo by Nasser's nationalization laws against Egypt's foreign merchant class. A second specificity is that the Jews who come to Palestine are victims of the worst catastrophe of (to borrow Arendt's phrase) continental European imperialism. As a consequence, the Jewish state of Israel acquires the aura of a sacred moral-political imperative, not only to the victims of the West but also to guilty Western eyes. For Palestinians, the formation of Israel, backed by the West, can only be another imperial act, their own exodus another catastrophe of dislocation, their second-class citizenship the policy of another racist state. But to articulate the Palestinian situation is made singularly problematic by the fact that Israel's "Jewish citizens are the remnants of the Nazi Holocaust with a tragic history of genocide and persecution." To fight to change that situation means being cast, "[d]espite our relatively modest actualities as a people," in the role of "inheritors of the Hitlerian legacy."[45]

After 1967, Said's journeys are almost entirely a function of his politicization as a Palestinian, which he describes as occurring as a consequence of the shock of the Six-Day War. He traveled to Lebanon and Jordan to participate in the Palestinian national revival, simultaneously attempting "to make the case for Palestinian presence, to say that there *was* a Palestinian people and that, like all others, it had a history, a society, and most important, a right to self-determination." He flew to North Africa as an independent member of the Palestine National Council but not, he emphasizes, as a member of any party: he is "a partisan, yes, but a joiner . . . no."[46] He returned to Palestine for the first time in twenty-five years. Over this same quarter century, he conferred with Yasir Arafat, spoke with Cyrus Vance, visited C.L.R. James, was on intimate terms with Mahmoud Darwish, Noam Chomsky, and a host of other international luminaries.

If Said is cosmopolitan in the most privileged and elevated sense, he also is made what he is by the politics of territorial loss. His situation certainly does not engender in him any of the anomie or self-indulgence with which nationalists discredit cosmopolitans. To the contrary, he commits himself politically to the cause of Palestinian self-determination and intellectually to representing in speech and writing disinherited and forgotten groups. He does end up in something of a disingenuous position through moving in the most rarified circles of public influence, intellectual honor, and material reward, while speaking up as an outsider, for the outside, at odds with "the chatty, familiar world inhabited by natives."[47] After all, almost the whole human race is more "outside" the chatty world of the powerful and prominent than Said is. This is an embarrassment that Naipaul avoids. Not believing in the possibility of justice, Naipaul never is tempted to take the moral high ground, makes no special claims about himself as an exile, and does not attempt to assimilate his plight to that of the truly wretched of the earth.

Nevertheless, it must be argued that Said is extraordinary in the way he has leapt from a privileged personal position to a vociferous engagement in public debates over crucial questions of his age. Culturally, he has not tried to escape the plight of his own pariah people by identifying himself solely, à la Stefan Zweig, with those basking in the radiance of international fame. Politically, unlike Arendt's Zweig (who was concerned "only with personal dignity and his art" and "kept himself so completely aloof from politics that in retrospect the catastrophe of the last ten years seemed to him like a sudden monstrous and inconceivable earthquake"[48]) and unlike Naipaul, too, Said has intervened in public affairs with militancy, compassion, and popular effect. Theoretically, he has succeeded in conceptualizing many of the great twentieth-century tensions that Naipaul describes in a compelling but different kind of prose.

Many of these tensions stem from paradoxes of nationalism that confound any easy stand for or against it. Said depicts these paradoxes as a chronologically nested set of logics in which practices lead so inexorably to their own negations that they almost can be called "dialectical." In the earliest dialectic, the idea of separate and distinctive national cultures begets ideas of "individual national genius" and a "hierarchy of races" that provide the ideological impetus for imperialism.[49] In turn, imperialism forces different peoples into a cross-fertilizing contact that refutes the original national idea.[50] In the next dialectic, imperialism incites movements for national liberation against itself, which enable "long-deferred and long-denied" identities "to come out into the open and take [their] place among other human identities."[51] National emancipation, however, gives way to new coercions such as statism, in which authoritarian regimes repress their own populations and seek to aggrandize themselves at the expense of other states,[52] and reactionary populism, in which the people turns the nation into a "fetish" and persecutes nonnational minorities.[53]

But it is the latest dialectic of nationalism that is especially germane to cosmopolitanism as an idea and ideal. Nationalism trumpets the elemental importance of "*habitus*, the coherent amalgam of practices linking habit with 'inhabitance,'" when it asserts the right of a people to belong "in and to a place." The condition of belonging somewhere, however, entails the possibility of belonging nowhere, and it is here, in the "perilous territory of not-belonging," that "immense aggregates of humanity [now] loiter." To safeguard its citizens, the nation must stave off the mass of "refugees and displaced persons": staving off no less than belonging to is what the meaning of national citizenship is. Said uses the figure of the exile to stand for all of those who do not immediately belong where they find themselves, including those whose alienation is intellectual rather than geographical. He insists, however, that to be alienated at least in the literal sense of the stateless person is not synonymous with rootlessness. To the contrary, the condition of the literal exile is predicated on a "love for, and bond with, one's native place," a love the exile has not lost but instead associates with loss. The important distinction between the loss of love and the association of love with loss, which Naipaul also makes, allows Said to understand the exile as a heartsick sufferer with cause to envy those who "belong in their surroundings." Out of longing and resentment, exiles can try to "reconstitute their broken lives, usually by choosing to see themselves as part of a triumphant ideology or a restored people." At worst, there is a "drawing of lines" around themselves and their compatriots, an "exaggerated sense of group solidarity, and a passionate hostility to outsiders."[54]

While the exile can gravitate to a kind of shadow nationalism of its own without any of the citizen's material perquisites, it also can be catapulted by its "terrible" situation toward an almost antithetical insight and politics.[55] Cut off from its original habitus, the exile can escape unthinking conformity to inherited beliefs and a life determined by fixed, seemingly essential cultural rules. In its new milieu, the exile can experiment with creative "arrangements of living and eccentric angles of vision." As a "beginner in [its] circumstances," it can indulge in "unending self-discovery" and "the pleasure of being surprised." Then, too, the exile has the benefit of a "double perspective,"[56] for "habits of life, expression or activity in the new environment inevitably occur against the memory of these things in another environment." That the new and the old occur together "contrapuntally"[57] makes "both appear in a sometimes new and unpredictable light"[58] and "gives rise to an awareness of simultaneous dimensions."[59] Less fortunately, perhaps, every exile learns well what Naipaul also has shown us are the following hard lessons of modernity: to become "happy with the idea of unhappiness," "to make do in circumstances of shaky instability,"[60] and to "[r]egard experiences as if they were about to disappear." Finally, the exile can teach others lessons in adventurousness: in its ability to "cross borders, break barriers of thought and experience," it reveals that the borders and barriers that "enclose us within the safety of familiar territory, can also become prisons."[61]

Admittedly, some of the pleasures of exile are the prerogatives of those who enjoy a certain level of material and mental well-being, as well as a certain intellectual sophistication — of exiles like Said himself. Admittedly, too, the bright beam he shines on the exile as cultural maverick shows off Said to radiant advantage. Inversely, Said fails to illuminate the third and most conservative path of the exile: toward an unwavering hyper-loyalty to its adopted nation-state. Moreover, "the exile" obscures crucial differences among those Said implicitly or explicitly treats as exiles of some sort. It glosses over the different opportunities awaiting men and women in exile, men being so much freer than women to indulge in the adventurous pleasures of the exile as maverick. It glosses over typological distinctions among immigrants, refugees, guest workers, expatriates, and voluntary wanderers, although Said does allude to those distinctions periodically. Finally, it glosses over key situational differences in the lives of exiles — between, to take just one example, refugees in camps and refugees accepted by and absorbed into foreign political societies.[62]

These flaws in Said's portrait of the exile must not blind us to the truths it offers us. The first truth Said does not tell us but unwittingly shows us. For years he has lambasted the West and Israel as monolithic imperialist entities, asserting against them the Palestinians' right to national self-determination. Yet he also has insisted that all identities are hybrid and complex, that all national unities contain within them differences that make problematic the idea of national self-determination, and that the best political society is one that welcomes diverse peoples inside its borders. Then, too, in the late 1990s Said reversed his earlier position on the Israeli/Palestinian struggle by endorsing a binational rather than two-state solution to it, supporting equal citizenship inside a multicultural society as opposed to the inequality of peoples inside an ethnonational state. At almost the same time, however, he called for national self-determination for the Albanian Kosovars, albeit with minority rights for resident Serbs.[63] Said's ambivalence here reveals to us that the two paths he says the exile can take are mutually exclusive logically but not phenomenologically. A singular nationalism and a contrapuntal pluralism are contrasting possibilities *for* the self and conflicting tendencies *in* the self. That loyalty to a single people and antagonism toward ethnic

singularity can be felt within a single heart reflects the inevitability of
subjective contradictions in human beings, but also perhaps, a subjective recognition of the objective political limitations of both ethnonationalism (its chauvinistic exclusivity) and cultural pluralism (its
utopianism).

Second, Said effectively counters the nativist's claim that the exile
has no particular commitments, no attachments to people or place.
The care for a people and a place is the great theme of exilic life as
he describes it, whether that theme is made of one long, mournful
note, as it is for the exile as nationalist, or of alternately lonely and
joyful variations, as it is for the exile as maverick. The nativist might
object that the exile as nationalist is not committed to *our* political
community, while the exile as maverick is committed to corroding
the unreflective ties and beliefs on which all organic communities
rest, but in neither case can the exile be dismissed as a disconnected,
deracinated wanderer. Moreover, simply because it has come from
somewhere else, the exile can be an invigorating current for any
shore on which it washes up. Whether it is so will depend on the
shore at least as much as the current. Certainly there have been societies so charmed by strangers that they have clasped them as glitter-
ing additions to a common life. But even if a society tries to close
itself off from the influence of outsiders, the exile is in the position to
complicate the meaning of belonging for it. Naipaul already has
shown us how the exile can approach an alien landscape with
heightened historical intelligence and romantic feeling, while the native can betray, nonchalantly, a landscape it has known all its life.
Natives *do* betray their inherited landscape when they become real
estate speculators, developers, contractors, and other agents of capitalist transformation, but they do so also when they become nationalists, for as Nairn and others have shown us, nationalism no less
surely than capitalism cuts the line of physical continuity between
the future and the past. Said is not as suspicious as Naipaul of the
native's special attachment to place, but he does cast a jaundiced eye
on the native's special attachment to a people. He shows us that a
love of a people that is oceanic and altruistic from the standpoint of
the native is, from the standpoint of the exile, insular and cruel, and
that in a society of natives and exiles, the tale of this love does not
belong to the native alone.

Third, Said's portrait of the exile contests both nationalist and old
cosmopolitan notions of political consciousness. Against the nation-

alist, Said denies that the best kind of consciousness is one with a unified, coherent cultural content and that the best kind of political community is one whose members have identical consciousnesses of this sort. It is more intelligent and imaginative for the individual to look at the world from two angles rather than one and more animating for the political community to include members who see the world from differing perspectives.[64] Against the traditional cosmopolitan, Said attests that a "contrapuntal" perspective on any individual's part does not come from shedding the particular and parochial for a god's-eye point of view. That perspective is the consequence instead of being located in one place and then another and achieving, through that double location, a clarity about home and inherited identity as things that are shaping but not fatally determining.

Said seems much closer to the truth than the old-style cosmopolitan with respect to how one makes one's way out of a parochial mentality. He seems much closer to the good than the nationalist with respect to which mentality is epistemologically preferable,[65] as well as much closer to the thrust of contemporary history, which is fast turning the ideal of homogeneous community into an anachronism.[66] Still, what one thinks of Said's portrait of the exile as a step toward re-conceptualizing membership in political society depends not merely on one's intellectual assessment of it but also on one's visceral response to plurality and intermingling. This raises the vexing question of the psycho-emotional elements that dispose one toward or away from heterogeneity and intermixture in the self and society at large.

Clearly, Said's own celebration of the permeable boundaries between cultures and his will to think "concretely and sympathetically" about others rather than "only about 'us'" are partly reactions to painful aspects of his situation.[67] The most general aspect is his experience of Western imperialism, which he accuses of imposing "a separation between people as members of homogenous races and exclusive nations," a reduction of everyone to "a member of some race or category," and a supremacy of one culture over the rest.[68] Against the imperial ethos, Said declares that humanity is far too multiple to be reduced to the massive, dichotomous categories of "East" and "West" and that "cultures are too intermingled, their contents and histories too interdependent and hybrid," for the "surgical separation" such categories try to effect.[69] The more particular aspect is his experience of Israel and Palestine: on the one side, of a victim that became an executioner through failing to enlarge its stand against its own persecution into a stand against persecution as such; on the other, of a struggle against that former victim that could not shake the world without drawing on universal notions of justice.[70] Both these experiences help explain Said's irritation with identity politics, whose advocates repudiate the false universalism of imperialism only to promote their own identities as uniquely important and their own values as uniquely right for themselves. They thereby reinstate the idea of racial exclusivity and generate, under the sign of difference, "more intolerance."[71]

Nevertheless, others in similarly painful situations have reacted differently than Said has to them: the autism of victims who become executioners and the solipsism of identity politicians testify to that. What seems to play an independent part in stimulating Said's openness to heterogeneity and intermixture is the delight he takes in fluidity and ambiguity as a result of his background and the mysterious contingencies of individual personality. Said expresses this delight sometimes as an enjoyment of ideas that arise in one context and reemerge in another differently inflected and revitalized, sometimes as an enchantment with hybrid identities and sometimes as a fondness for the polyglot milieu of his youth.[72]

No less than the exercise of critical reason, such habits of recoil and delight, with their inevitable element of mystery and idiosyncrasy, animate Said's moral point of view. Isn't some combination of heart and mind at the root of all moral philosophy?

While Said condemns the universalism that once masked European world domination and now is a euphemism for the power of the United States,[73] he affirms the old Enlightenment principles of "peace, reconciliation, abatement of suffering . . . rights and democratic freedoms . . . as a norm for everyone," adding to them a special commitment to "the poor, the disadvantaged, the voiceless."[74] At the same time, he transcends both Western power and the Enlightenment tradition in his articulation of "true worldliness." This is the recognition that "society and culture have been the heterogenous product of heterogenous people in an enormous variety of cultures, traditions, and situations"[75] and the supposition that "one gets a better, perhaps even more universal idea of how to think" about fundamental moral issues through the juxtaposition of different cultural practices and ideals.[76] Summed up in Césaire's phrase, a "'place for all at the rendezvous of victory,'" worldliness demands that no one culture overshadow the rest and that all subordinated or marginalized cultures be brought out of "the neglect and secondariness to which . . . they had previously been condemned." It also demands the restoration of every culture not as "some tiny defensively constituted corner of the world" but as part of "the large, many-windowed house of human culture as a whole,"[77] actively implicated in world history and human community. On individual persons, worldliness imposes the following obligations. They must help demolish "the stereotypes and reductive categories that are so limiting to human thought and communication."[78] They must understand modernity not in terms of "consumerism, or big cars, or lots of television sets" (that is, not in terms of the capitalist interpretation of a universal culture) but in terms of "being an integral part of the world of your time, rather than its fool or slave."[79] Finally, they must combine the care for a particular people with an alertness to the crimes done by that people, supporting "basic human justice . . . for everyone, not just selectively."[80]

THE COSMOPOLITAN AND THE POPULAR

However much Said clashes with Naipaul politically, he joins him in fusing elements that both nationalists and "old" cosmopolitans have assumed to be separate and opposed. Along with Naipaul, he feels the pull of locality, particularity, and nationality; recognizes the instability of the modern experience of home, for which "locality," "particularity," and "nationality" are metaphors; insists on the historical contingency of collective identities; and takes pleasure in the heterogeneity and interminglings of those same collective groups. By undermining the very possibility of absolute rootedness and absolute detachment, Said, with Naipaul, refutes the nationalist claim that absolute rootedness is the condition of belonging to a political community and the traditional cosmopolitan claim that absolute detachment is the condition for a concern for the world at large.

In the precise way in which he complicates political membership and moral obligation, however, Said has less in common with Naipaul than with that master of complication, Hannah Arendt. Notwithstanding her European self-certainty, her pessimism of the will, and her outright dismissal of nationalism *and* universalism, Arendt anticipates certain motifs in Said's work a generation before he begins to write. She underscores the degradations of imperialism and the brutalities of the nation-state, with its expulsions of whole peoples into a zone in which they are denied effective human rights because they have no national rights and so are "received as scum of the earth everywhere."[81] She applauds both those individuals who as a matter of personality "never felt at home in the world" but "still remained committed to it"[82] and the "conscious pariahs"[83] made by social history but "excluded from formal society and with no desire to be embraced within it."[84] These conscious pariahs, with their sense of humanity and "disinterested intelligence,"[85] happily share the "social ostracism" of the common people, joining a fight that is "part and parcel of that which all the down-trodden . . . needs wage to achieve national and social liberation."[86] Finally, she loathes any political order that either crushes or expels social difference to impose on its members a single point of view. She touts instead a plurality of perspectives, a common care for the world "in-between," and an enlarged consciousness that tries to see that world from many angles of vision.

As gratifying as these similarities between Said and Arendt may be, they should prompt us to wonder if Said sometimes valorizes a kind of individual remoteness that Arendt does when she salutes the self not fully at home, who cares for the world from an outsider's position.[87] In Arendt's eyes, such a self stands in courageous isolation from most people: in *The Origins of Totalitarianism*, from the homogeneous mass created by totalitarian regimes; in *The Human Condition*, from the jobholders and consumers of capitalist society; in *Men in Dark Times*, from members of majority groups who turn minority groups into pariahs and from members of pariah groups who either become parvenus in society or huddle together outside society for human warmth. Said's portrait of the exile has an analogously nonpopular tinge to it—not, ironically, in the exile's most tragic moment, when the exile unites with other exiles in an outcast community hostile to those who belong in their surroundings, but in its most ebullient moment, when the exile becomes a rebel who challenges conventions, destabilizes society, and evades the corruptions of power and perversions of gods that fail. This brings us to back to that bedeviling question we postponed at the beginning of this chapter: Is cosmopolitanism the prerogative of the few? We have seen that even sympathizers with certain strands of cosmopolitanism such as Mary Kaldor say "yes." We now can add that cultural Marxists such as Tim Brennan and Aijaz Ahmad level the charge of elitism against postcolonial intellectuals, in Brennan's case from Naipaul to Rushdie and in Ahmad's case from Rushdie to Said. Brennan and Ahmad depict these new cosmopolitans as nomadic celebrities pleasing metropolitan tastes for irony, ambiguity, and exoticism while betraying the national-popular causes of their countries of origin.[88] For most of his career Naipaul has been especially susceptible to this charge, although his recent turn to Hindu nationalism clashes with it, if not on the side of a politics Brennan and Ahmad would like.[89] The same charge is peculiar against Said, in light of his long-standing commitment to the Palestinian movement.[90] At most one can say (and, to be sure, Ahmad says it) that between Said's theoretical cosmopolitanism and practical support for Palestinian nationalism there seems to be a marked incongruity. Or rather, there *would* have seemed to be that incongruity had Said's cosmopolitanism (and Naipaul's) been the old, detached-from-all-concrete-investments type.

Still, there are two ways the exile consciousness is not generalizable in the sense of being recommendable for all members of political society. First, Said frequently uses the figure of the exile as a metaphor for the intellectual who maintains "the outsider's and the skeptic's autonomy" while still "being involved in worldly causes."[91] This formulation requires an "inside" populated by the many, even while it argues for criticizing the conformism, fanaticism, and chauvinism of that same "inside." The intellectual as exile is to challenge all centers of power, including state authority but also mass culture and ideology-driven popular movements such as nationalism and fundamentalism, which means that the intellectual as exile will be often out of joint even with the people in whose interests it performs its gadfly tasks. While Naipaul is personally aloof from the people he travels to meet, he does not get himself into this kind of trouble, and not merely because he reveals all selves to be split between home and the world with no clear pattern of difference between intellectuals and other people. It is also because, traveling to record other people's views but not to try to change them, he refuses to take the political attitude toward human affairs. This is to say not that he has no opinions about those affairs but that he need not exhort intellectuals to do one thing (join a particular political movement) or the other (be a partisan yes, but a joiner, no).

If Naipaul shows us that the critical impulse appears not only in intellectual detachment but also, in inchoate form, in popular dissatisfactions, Said shows us that history can incite whole displaced peoples to think as outsiders, which is why questions of political community are importantly illuminated from that vantage point. Ultimately, the loneliness of intellectuals such as Said may be a function on the one hand of their being literal exiles and on the other hand of a cultural rather than critical gap between intellectual and popular societies. That is, while Said is right by definition to note the strain between critical and conventional consciousness, intellectual and popular societies may not be divided from each other along that particular fault line. They are clearly separated by their different material privileges, paid employment, patterns of consumption and leisure, aesthetic tastes, bodily cultivation, and styles of thought and speech. If one were to list the limitations of the new cosmopolitans, at the top of the list would be their failure as of yet to map out clear political alternatives to the nation-state. But it is in their failure to address the cultural divisions between the intellectual and popular classes that the new cosmopolitans may be at their worst disadvantage vis-à-vis nationalists, who, like Gramsci's Catholic clergy, have always operated to prevent such divisions from becoming apparent.

The second sign that Said's exile consciousness is not generalizable has its most serious implications for regional rather than class difference. This sign can be seen if we turn from metaphorical to literal exiles, those who have been forced by physical violence, expelled by political authority, or pushed by material deprivation into statelessness. I already have noted that the single figure of the exile obscures important differences among and within the literal groups Said means to indicate through that cover term. But, in addition, the existence of the exile entails, as Said has argued in reverse, the existence of the citizen, so that the literal exile logically can be only one kind of member of political society. This is not to say that the citizen itself is simply rooted, unsusceptible to the splinterings of the self that Naipaul traces out. It *is* to say that the splinterings of the self will have, for different kinds of exiles and citizens, different material pressures and constraints, emotional resonances, and political repercussions, requiring distinct categories of analysis and descriptive efforts to capture them. Without exploring the whole panoply of possibilities here, we might mention the world tourist and the world capitalist, both citizens at the opposite end of the spectrum of wanderers from Said's literal exiles. Traveling for the pleasure of relaxing while consuming a variety of geographical and cultural contexts, the world tourist prompts a mammoth effort to reshape places to match its needs, a reshaping that subverts the variety the world tourist supposedly wishes to enjoy. Even more prominent in this respect is the world capitalist, who, as Arendt puts it, is driven across the globe in its pursuit of infinite wealth, destroying private property in the sense of the possession by all people of a niche in the world of their own.[92]

Although this is not the place to pursue the point, the world tourist and the world capitalist together present perhaps the gravest obstacle to the new cosmopolitan ideal. Their effectiveness as, respectively, consumer and producer threatens the "many-windowed house" of human culture at least as much as do the cultural megalomania of the West and the separatist attempts of identity politics to seal off every culture from the rest. At the same time, it is not at all clear whether the new cosmopolitanism will aid or thwart the difference-threatening phase of a world-connecting process that, in its previous, difference-exploiting phase, had provoked anticolonial movements for national liberation. For all his appreciation of heterogeneity, Naipaul can be seen as an oblique ideological accomplice in the molding of diverse regions into a single economic system through his unabashed admiration for Western-style material and intellectual growth. It is a dispiriting note on which to end this essay, but one must wonder if even Said's opposite effort to open the world to the reciprocal recognition of all cultures is doomed to provide, against his intentions, the conceptual accoutrements for a more potent and rapacious kind of world opening. But perhaps all ideas suited to their times can be made to serve contradictory interests and projects. In that case, the struggle for the future may well be a struggle between two types of worldliness, with economic power largely on the side of one kind of world opening and a few intellectuals on the side of the other but with popular power, as always, the great question mark.

Conclusion

No single recipe either can or should be offered in response to the conundrums provoked by nationalism that we have met in this book. No recipe *can* be offered, because there is something so deeply recalcitrant about those conundrums that any attempt to resolve them by means of a simple formula would be doomed to irrelevance and failure. A better plan would be to envision new forms of political community in which the tensions between particular and universal, majority and minority, citizen and exile, home and the world, might play themselves out less cruelly than they have done in the nation-state and less oppressively than they have done under imperial rule. Then again, no single recipe *should* be offered — for "civil society," or "liberal nationalism," or "secularism" — with respect to such community forms. The wish for such a recipe is not only at odds with the idiosyncrasies of local contexts and the unpredictabilities of practical life but also inimical to the principle of variety that both nationalists and cosmopolitans, at their very best, applaud.

As a set, our thinkers have declined to impose on us a mutually agreed-upon answer to modern questions of identity and belonging. This is not to say that they do not offer us flickering candles of political wisdom to brighten our way out of the old century. The most illuminating pair of perceptions they present collectively can be taken equally as an occasion for disappointment or reassurance. No pole of any of the antinomies of nationalism is one on which we should pin all our hopes or fears. And although every antinomy is stubbornly and often explosively real, none is as dichotomous as it first seems to be or as incapable of mutation or metamorphosis.

To illustrate these twin points, let us return to the nationalist and the cosmopolitan to see how they are ambiguous, undiametrical, and unfinished modern types. In this book I have emphasized, against certain prejudices of our times, the enriching and expansive virtues of the cosmopolitan, but many of our authors do not allow us to forget the vices of the cosmopolitan either. These include an impatience with inherited customs and habits, a condescension toward local attachments, an insouciance at the prospect of building over familiar landscapes, a superficiality of social connection, an assumption of the superiority of the metropolis over the hinterland, and an interest in the endless accumulation of wealth without regard for its property-shattering effects. In this book I also have emphasized these disturbing qualities of the nationalist: parochialism, chauvinism, a mythological sense of the past, an overvaluation of one nation's accomplishments, an autistic inability to identify with strangers, and an eagerness to be swallowed up into an overbearing social whole. Once again, however, many of our authors, most dramatically Fanon and Berlin, have tempered this emphasis by insisting that such qualities are not mysterious evils but can be traced to a group's historical experience of humiliation, resentment, and anxiety in the sense of a fear of impending loss. Moreover, they have left us with important clues to the often intertwined sources of that experience, intimating that nationalist disturbances will not disappear until those sources disappear. The economic sources of group humiliation: domination by an imperial power for the purposes of exploitation; the arrival of modernity in the form of a violent incursion from the outside; the uneven development of capitalism, with its greatest injuries for peoples and classes at the losing end of progress; the assault on rural life by the forces and agents of industrialization. The political sources: state conquest, state collapse, and state building, each inciting fears that one group will be stepped on and over by another, or that some groups will be stranded, stateless and rightless, out in the political cold. The social sources: the contempt of a more powerful ethnic, racial, or national group for a less powerful one; minor disparities between peoples living in close proximity, who seem more like than unlike one another to all eyes but their own; a sudden move by one population to tout itself as separate and unique, with boomerang effects on its neighbors. Then there are the misrecognized sources of group humiliation. Among the most dangerous is a dominant majority's experience of its humiliation in the past by some stronger group as humiliation in the present by some weaker group, which the majority then victimizes in retaliation for having been, supposedly, its victim's victim. Among the most common is the outright elite manipulation of identity interpretation so that, for example, religious differences harped on as the essence of identity by nationalist leaders but not popularly experienced as such before eventually are seen as such by everyone, with the less powerful religious group newly resentful of the more powerful one. Finally, there are the various sadomasochistic dances of cultural minorities and majorities. A minority is humiliated by the majority's refusal either to recognize it as different but worthy of respect or to allow it to assimilate into the majority culture. In response to that refusal, the minority retreats to a pariah nationalism that affords it no political rights, no passports, and no military protection. Alternately, a majority is humiliated by the disproportionately successful attempts of a minority to assimilate into the highest reaches of majority society. At the same time, the minority's excessively avid attempts to ingratiate itself with the majority makes the minority all the more visible as a target of nationalist animosity for the majority group.

Two lessons about nationalist humiliation and resentment are crucial yet difficult for even the most sensitive cosmopolitans to take in. One is that feelings of group humiliation must be emotionally assuaged, not merely rationally countered, before the group in question can be expected to take delight in heterogeneity and intermingling. This is true even of the feelings of a group that misrecognizes the true source of its feelings. Thus a dominant majority that attacks some weaker group as its victimizer must be responded to by an intervening third party in ways at once allied with the requirements of justice and soothing to the anxieties generated by the majority's peculiar worldview.

The other, quite different lesson concerns the promise hidden inside the powerful charge of rural resentments against the whole modern development machine. This is a promise that all those invested in that machine are unable and unwilling to see: old industrial communists and new global capitalists, yes, but also cosmopolitan intellectuals — both Western and postcolonial — who despise or are ashamed of the countryside.

Tom Nairn has highlighted rurality under threat as an explosive impetus of nationalist politics, but it is Raymond Williams, the man Said once praised for his sense of place, who can help us pry the fruitful kernel at the center of "the country" from nationalism's hard shell. At the beginning of *The Country and the City*, for us his most pertinent book, Williams describes his grandfather as a farm worker living on the border of England and Wales who, after losing his job and cottage, earned wages in middle age by clearing and cutting roads. Williams's father was a "man in the village, with his gardens and his bees," yet also, in his paid job as a signalman, "part of a network reaching to . . . Newport and Hereford, and beyond them London." After growing up in the same village — that also was not the same as the result of processes of transformation of which his grandfather and father were minor tools — Williams left for school at Cambridge, where he became a literary theorist and a cultural Marxist with deeply felt ties to both agrarian life and metropolitan "centres of settled and often magnificent achievement."[1]

In the main body of *The Country and the City*, Williams looks back over centuries of English literature to chart repeated regrets of the death of the countryside that for each generation of writers seemed to have happened only yesterday. He explains this curious recurrence as, in part, the nostalgia of adults for an inviolate landscape that is really a childhood delusion. Like Naipaul's narrator in *The Enigma of Arrival*, children are always unaware of the changes that were made to their little world before they arrived on the scene. More important, however, Williams explains the recurring sense of the loss of rural life as a misrecognition of a different kind of loss. He finds an analogous misrecognition in the more recently repeated laments of English urban literature for "the delights of corner-shops, gas lamps, horsecabs, trams, piestalls: all gone" and, more recently still, in third world literature mourning the demise, with modern development, of familiar and culturally distinctive milieus. For Williams, the hidden truth in these laments is that the modern transformation of physical surroundings occurs largely behind the backs of most people, as a result of "a series of decisions . . . which were never, in any real sense, socially made, but which were imposed by the priorities of a mode of production."[2] Because they lack agency over the most prodigious things that happen to their villages, towns, and cities, ordinary people assume the role of surprised sufferers of change, not its creative authors or designers. Williams avoids implying that local people are entirely passive in their physical environment; they play their small parts, just as Williams's grandfather and father did, if not by cutting roads or signaling trains, then by laying bricks or selling property or loaning money. A few play larger parts by amassing enough wealth and power to participate in directing change instead of simply being directed by it. Nevertheless, the places to which people are most intimately connected are typically determined not by the intimates but — to borrow a nationalist phrase — by a "foreign master."

Williams implicitly encourages us to disentangle two strands of meaning in nationalism's negative notion of foreignness. One strand is the idea of an outsider who is suspect for belonging to a strange ethnic, racial, or national group. In an age in which, to recall Luxemburg's line about earlier times, different nationalities are "constantly moving about geographically . . . joining, merging, fragmenting and trampling one another,"[3] this idea is fast becoming not only too pernicious but also too anachronistic to animate a worldly politics. The other strand is the idea of someone or some conglomeration of interests and powers that is suspect because it decides the fate of places without the knowledge or will or desire of most of the inhabitants of those spots. This old point of Marx's, new realities of globalization press us to accentuate. By highlighting not the separate identities of peoples but the value to people of the places they inhabit, we can champion not an exclusive care for this people against that one but an effective as opposed to impotent care for place on the part of all people who live *here*.

Nationalism provides a proto-language for defending the right of people to help decide the fate of the places they inhabit, as well as a language for criticizing agents and forces riding roughshod over that right, whether they are the agents and forces of capitalism, of a dictatorial state, or of a power that also is foreign in the ethnic, racial, or national sense. The new cosmopolitanism encourages us to extend the effective care for place in two different directions. First, cosmopolitanism can teach us that what counts as the circumference of any place is a function of the lives seriously affected by changes to that place, which in turn is a function of the nature of those changes. It follows that the limits of a place are not always or even often synonymous with the borders of a country in the "nation-state" sense of the term. Depending on what is at stake — the heating up of a pot of soup, the heating up of an electoral battle, the heating up of the earth's atmosphere — those who have the rights and responsibilities of inhabitants may be the members of a single household, a political society, or the entire world.

Second, the new cosmopolitanism can help us win an effective care for place on behalf of exiles who find themselves living in a strange society. Remember the great gifts that the exile as new cosmopolitan offers native societies: an embellishment of the cultural imagination, through its exhibition of a different sensibility formed in an exotic set of circumstances; a revelation of the contingency of all traditions and the ambiguity of all identities, through its double or "contrapuntal" vision; and a path out of a narrow existence, through its acquaintanceship with the larger world. In addition, there is the material wealth produced by exiles, whether they are cosmopolitan in outlook or not, who labor in countries other than the ones in which they were born. In exchange for both intellectual and material gifts, the rights and obligations of native inhabitants surely should be extended to the exile who has put down roots in a new society. Those rights and obligations will be different in different types of political regimes, but in every case, no immigrant or guest worker or refugee or expatriate from elsewhere (as opposed to a tourist or wandering adventurer or long-distance investor) will be prohibited by political rules from gaining a legitimate and defensible stake in its adopted home.

In sum, worldliness in Said's sense of cultivating a delight in ethnic and racial heterogeneity, joined with worldliness in Arendt's sense of securing a public and private space in the world for human beings, requires that living in a place, not belonging to a people, become the preeminent criterion of citizenship. It also requires that participation in deciding the future of one's place of inhabitance become a basic democratic right. Such worldliness cannot be achieved by homogeneous or homogenizing nation-states, which at best suppress ethnic difference internally to create a single people and at worst drive vulnerable ethnic groups into political homelessness. In a very different way, such worldliness is endangered by the unfettered processes of global capitalism. Those processes jeopardize heterogeneity, for however much they bring the diverse regions of the world into contact, and however much they draw on cultural differences to rationalize production and increase consumption, they more drastically homogenize culture by spreading the civilization of endless production and consumption across national bounds.

Global capitalism also jeopardizes a public and private home in the world for most human beings. The capitalist conviction that freedom and the good are private matters corrodes the legitimacy of a national public sphere where members of political society meet to discuss their common affairs, and where they might agree to inhibit the process of capital accumulation for the sake of some collective good. In turn, it corrodes the legitimacy of an international public sphere whose members might, for example, limit consumption in overdeveloped societies to support ecological sustainability worldwide, or redistribute wealth so that poor countries as well as rich ones can afford to give permanent political homes to the exiles who turn up on their doorsteps. With respect to the private sphere, while the capitalist mode of production works to protect that sphere from state domination and to create such material abundance that it theoretically could provide comfortable and pleasing private shelters for everyone, it makes access to such shelters entirely a function of the individual's position in the market. Private property in the Arendtian sense of a place where humans can attend to intimate bodily needs and desires shielded from the eyes of strangers thus becomes alienable and, for some, profit-generating real estate. For many more — and here class difference is more telling than the difference between natives and exiles — the transformation of private property into a source for the accumulation of wealth means that a private space in the world will be a tenuous, insecure, and often unaffordable possession.

If a "new cosmopolitan" delight in the heterogeneity of peoples and a "new nationalist" care for place require us to transcend the homogeneous nation-state and the unfettered process of capital accumulation, they also require us to transcend the development metaphor with its biologistic and monistic connotations, as well as the variety-destroying, place-destroying, ecology-destroying institutions and organizations in the thrall of that metaphor. This is not to say that the new cosmopolitanism in league with the new nationalism would proscribe efforts to improve the well-being of the hundreds of millions of people who live in physical or mental misery. It is rather that the route to and meaning of well-being would no longer be equated with an objective process of development along Western or American lines. In the absence of that equation, the whole world would be able to embark on a truly open-ended consideration of the classical political philosophical questions: "What is the good life?" and "What is the good society?" But if these questions must no longer be answered by a single country or region for the rest, neither can they any longer be answered by each country or region solely for itself. Given the intensified intermingling of peoples and cultures, in combination with the compelling but incompatible values that have managed to survive on earth thus far, questions of political philosophy are most fertilely addressed by all ways of life in vigorous conversation with each other.[4] How might that conversation become genuinely reciprocal? Abdullahi An-Na'im once remarked that people necessarily approach universalities not from some point of pure abstraction but from their respective relativities. For a reciprocal exchange of views on what are, from the varying vantage points of those relativities, universal aspects of the good life and the good society, the conversationalists must enjoy at least a rough equality of recognition with one another and at best a rough equality of power. In short, a reciprocal conversation about social ideals for the world depends on the world's transcendence of the limits of regional inequality.

In an age that has transcended all of the limitations noted above, dilemmas to do with intervening in a society other than one's own for moral purposes would not fade away, but they would take on a different cast from the thorny dilemmas that confront us now. For a start, there would be no particular idea of justice that could be imposed unilaterally as the universal truth by more powerful societies on less powerful ones. There also would be no presumption dictated by the more powerful societies to the less against fencing in global capital in accordance with particular notions of the collective good. Then again, the old world-dividing principle of national sovereignty would be in other ways significantly curtailed. No sharp distinctions of "blood" or "shared culture" between the "insiders" and "outsiders" of different societies could be used to brand intervention an act of ethnic or racial arrogance. Similarly, international interventions called for by "new universalist" principles of justice would not carry the stigma of imperialist power mongering. Nor would cultural imperialism taint the existential decisions of individual persons, nongovernmental organizations, or social movements to intervene against practices that they find intolerably inhumane.

Our meditations on the national question must end, alas, on a far less utopian note. The reorientations of this question demanded by the social realities of ethnic persecution, mass homelessness, the erosion of distinctive locales, and the various geographical relationships of mastery and servitude hinge on the demise of the enabling conditions of those realities. Yet these enabling conditions—a system of homogenizing nation-states; a politically unfettered process of capital accumulation; a variety-destroying development machine; and inequalities of recognition and power between the literal as well as metaphorical cities and countries of the world—are so fixed a part of modern life as to seem part of the natural order of things. Then again, one of the oldest and truest saws of critical theory is that every existing order mistakes the limits of the actual for the limits of the possible, while every future breaks with the past in ways that would shock every present. This is why, in 1920s Italy, Antonio Gramsci could counsel pessimism of the intellect but optimism of the will. To put the point more cautiously at the dawn of a new century, pessimism might be warranted about prospects for the future but never political indifference and never, or almost never, despair.

Notes

1. This was true even though the group was overwhelmingly male and so, in one sense, as foreign to me and the two other women in it as public political affairs traditionally have been for most women in most nation-states.

2. Honig, "Difference, Dilemmas, and the Politics of Home," 257–77.

3. The phrase comes from Ed Vulliamy's powerful article, "Bosnia: The Crime of Appeasement," 76.

4. See, for example, Woodward, "Diaspora, or the Dangers of Disunification," 159–213. The essay specifically attacks the application of "the model of the Third Reich and Hitler to Serbia and Milosevic" (204), but it is so dauntingly particularistic in its approach that the use of models from any place or time seems impossible. It is fascinating to compare this essay with the very next one in the same volume, Biberaj's "The Albanian National Question," 214–88. Unlike Woodward's relentlessly empirical piece, Biberaj's draws on generalizable principles to make a political argument for the right of Albanian Kosovars to national self-determination.

5. Ignatieff, *The Warrior's Honor*, 34–71. See also Ignatieff, *Blood and Belonging*.

6. Beissinger, "Nationalisms That Bark and Nationalisms That Bite," 169–90.

7. Walker Connor, for example, says that these categories properly do so. See Connor, "Nation-Building or Nation-Destroying," 332–26.

8. Anthony D. Smith makes this argument in *The Ethnic Origins of Nations*. In a different but similarly thought-provoking analysis, Paul Gilbert pinpoints three models of national community grounded, respectively, in the family, civil society, and state. The tribal ethos of the family and the legal-political ethos of the state have the capacity to consolidate a people, but the ethos of economic well-being of civil society is unable to generate the care for national community and sense of social obligation necessary for cultural cohesion. Gilbert, "The Concept of a National Community," 149–66.

9. Benedict Anderson portrays nations as internally unitary and singular above all in his chapter "Patriotism and Racism" in *Imagined Communities*, while Tom Nairn argues in a variety of writings that a unitary national identity can be the result of the conservative co-optation of a working class via ideology and the rewards of imperialism. This, he says, *was* the result in England—but not, according to Nairn, in Scotland. In turn, Anderson accuses Nairn of treating "his 'Scotland'" geographically, genealogically, and ethnically "as an unproblematic, primordial given" (89).

10. This is true even if one party in those wars has been almost entirely eradicated, for every nation that engages in genocidal policies eventually is forced to confront the remaining shards. Elaine Scarry shows us the irony of the attempt to resolve the national question through bloodshed for those who shed their blood. Individuals are national in gait, mannerisms, culinary tastes, intonations, and the like only as long as they are alive. Once slaughtered by the enemy, they become mere flesh and bone, no longer recognizably Kurdish or Irish or Serbian, the bodies on the winning side of war no less radically decultured and denationalized than those on the losing side. Scarry, *The Body in Pain*, esp. 108–18.

11. Almost all contemporary writers on nationalism tell us of this mythic dimension; some have less patience for the myth than do others. For one of the least patient ones, see Hobsbawm, *Nations and Nationalism since 1780*.

12. This is George Lamming's phrase, from *The Pleasures of Exile*.

13. The most positive sense of intellectual cosmopolitanism or "willed homelessness" is defended, as we shall see, by Edward Said in almost all of his writing. Said explicitly probes this sense in "Introduction: Secular Criticism."

14. Thus Simone de Beauvoir remarks, in a different context, "We [Sylvie Le Bon and she] have a much better relationship than what generally exists between mothers and daughters . . . I have always been for chosen relationships as against those that are imposed." Quoted in Kaufmann, "Simone de Beauvoir," 127.

15. But antirationalists often do so with greater literary flair than the rationalists can manage. See, for example, Oakeshott, *Rationalism in Politics and Other Essays*.

16. Indeed, Elie Kedourie sees intellectuals, especially German intellectuals, as responsible for nationalism, because he finds the root cause of nationalism in philosophical ideas. Kedourie, *Nationalism*.

17. See Gellner, *Nations and Nationalism*; Hobsbawm, *Nations and Nationalism since 1780*, 116–18; and Smith, *Theories of Nationalism*.

18. Ignatieff, *The Warrior's Honor*, esp. 6, 15–16, 44.

19. Gellner, *Conditions of Liberty*, esp. chap. 4, "The Marxist Failure."

20. Nairn, "The Modern Janus," in *The Break-Up of Britain*, 332.

21. Or at least to all classical diasporas. See Michael Mandelbaum's introduction to his edited volume, *The New European Diasporas* (1–18), in which he distinguishes between classical diasporas, created when peoples move, and new diasporas, created when borders move. However, Mandelbaum is unpersuasive in claiming that classical diasporas move voluntarily, as opposed to new diasporas, which find themselves, against their will, suddenly under the rule of a foreign state. Surely coercion can precipitate the first move of both classical and new diasporas, while voluntary choice can be the cause of subsequent moves in each case.

CHAPTER 1
KARL MARX UNCOVERS THE TRUTH OF NATIONAL IDENTITY

1. Conceptions of life in terms of center and peripheries, or in terms of regimes of truth and subjects of and against those regimes, are hybrids of these two modalities. In depicting life as structured horizontally, they resemble conceptions of life as the play of appearances across a depthless surface. In depicting that structure as a function of power rather than joyful play, they resemble conceptions of life as surface and depth.

2. This intense captivation is what Nietzsche must have had in mind when he shows that "man" becomes psychologically interesting only when he develops a depth to be plumbed, intellectually interesting only when he investigates himself, and philosophically interesting only when he does not merely pose along with other poseurs but asserts his own substantive value in the world. However, Nietzsche takes depth analysis to the last possible point it can be taken before it self-destructs. He contracts for himself the last great plumbing job by exposing appearance/reality, lies/truth, evil/goodness, and irrationality/reason themselves at once as veils that obscure and as instruments that serve the metamorphosis of a spontaneous, instinctual animal species into a self-torturing, civilized humanity.

3. Thus, for example, Ford Madox Ford's *The Good Soldier* would make a different read altogether if the reinterpretations of a marriage it presents were just one representation and then another rather than repeated accounts of the truth spurred by repeated realizations that the old accounts were based on lies from start to finish.

4. The modern novel once derived its special attraction from providing this kind of voyeurism for its readers through revealing to them the depths of its characters and their relations.

5. Ahmad, *In Theory*, 14.

6. For just a few examples of that dismissal, see Connor, *The National Question*, chap. 1; B. Anderson, *Imagined Communities*, esp. 3–4; Szporluk, *Communism and Nationalism*, esp. 50–56, although Szporluk is a sensitive critic who raises important questions about Marx and nationalism, above all concerning the contradiction between national polity and international economy; and Nimni, *Marxism and Nationalism*.

7. Marx especially likes to lambast social, economic, and political theorists for eternalizing, sanctifying, or naturalizing given social relations; for obscuring the internal relation among elements in a system of production; and for shrouding the historical origins of that system beneath a moralizing myth. See, for example, Marx, *The Communist Manifesto*, 71; Marx, *Grundrisse*, 83–87; Marx, *Capital* 1:713–14.

8. Marx and Engels, *The German Ideology*, 41.

9. Marx, *The Communist Manifesto*, 71.

10. Engels, "1895 Introduction," 560, 561, 562. In turn, this whole discussion forecasts Engels's optimism about the rationality of the working class in what he believes to be, in 1895, the mature capitalist setting. He argues then with precisely the same logic he and Marx had used in 1848 that given the transformation of the franchise by German social democracy "from a means of deception . . . into an instrument of emancipation," it might very well be possible to go the parliamentary route to socialism (566).

11. Marx, preface, 389.

12. This is not to say that I disagree completely with the argument made by Christopher L. Pines in *Ideology and False Consciousness*. Like Pines, I believe that the ideas of mystification, illusion, reification, and so on are central to Marx's concept of ideology and to his critique of the way not only thought but also practices obscure the deep structure of capitalist society. But unlike Pines, I think that the concept of false consciousness a) is far too crude and reductive, especially as it is blithely used by contemporary thinkers, to cover the complexities, variations, and nuances of Marx's critical analysis of appearance and reality; b) is misleading in suggesting that Marx thinks that that consciousness *should* have been "true," when Marx actually believes that the various illusions, mystifications, and inversions of capital are structurally determined; and c) for a similar set of reasons, does not accord, as Pines thinks it does, with Hegel's own notion of actors who do not understand the real forces that move them. Despite my difference with Pines on the category of "false consciousness," I think he does a good job of clarifying not only the historical roots but also the very complexities and structural character of critical theory that make "true" and "false consciousness," with respect to the work of both Hegel and Marx, clumsy and misleading terms.

13. It is when Marxists after Marx witness first, objective crises of capital but no revolutionary response, and next, the entrenchment of capital both objectively and subjectively, that they resort to proletarian false consciousness as a partial explanation. But by that point, given the massive cultural power of capital and the enormous profits made directly from cultural production, the superstructure hardly can be thought to be "merely superstructural." For this reason cultural Marxists in the twentieth century discard the base/superstructure distinction altogether. Eventually they look askance at the concepts of false consciousness and ideology too, not for suggesting the objective dictation of "pressures and limits" on subjects who neither control nor grasp that dictation but for suggesting too heady a conception of those pressures and limits, as if it were merely false ideas that bound subordinate groups to the status quo rather than whole patterns of preoccupations, attachments, achievements, and day-to-day practical routines. See Williams, *Marxism and Literature*.

14. Marx, *Economic and Philosophic Manuscripts of 1844*, 340. Thus,

for Hegelianism, historical change is a function of "pure thoughts . . . that devour one another and are finally swallowed up in 'self-consciousness'." Marx and Engels, *The German Ideology*, 31.

15. Marx and Engels, *The German Ideology*, 15.

16. Ibid., 30–31.

17. True to form, Marx finds the enabling condition of idealism in a feature of practical human existence, and of productive practice at that: the historical division of mental and manual labor, which allows consciousness to "flatter itself that it is something other than consciousness of existing practice" (Marx and Engels, *The German Ideology*, 20).

18. Marx, introduction, 54.

19. Marx and Engels, *The German Ideology*, 30.

20. It is very possible to argue (although it would not be Marx's argument) that nationalism (or, indeed, German idealism) is a form of religious illusion while religion itself is not an illusion. In this case nationalism would be charged with sanctifying the nation and thereby attempting to replace the truly sacred with a false, secular god.

21. B. Anderson, *Imagined Communities*, 6.

22. Ibid., esp. 12–19.

23. Anderson not only avoids the whole question of social inequality inside nations in his depiction of the "horizontal" community of members of the nation. He also avoids the question of regional inequality in his depiction of nationalism's spread throughout the world as a result of a process in which one region "models" its achievement of nationhood on another—all nations except the original thus being culturally equal to one another in their non-originality. This is not to say that theorists of nationalism cannot take Anderson in a more critical direction. See, for example, Romula Thapar's rendition of Anderson's thesis of imagined community in her critique of Hindu communalism, "Imagined Religious Communities," 209–31.

24. To the important question of whether nationalism is an expression of real suffering, as we shall see, contemporary theorists such as Tom Nairn give affirmative answers. Chief among those answers is the claim that nationalism is a response to the suffering caused by the humiliation, marginalization, and economic exploitation of a people ruled and/or despised by a more powerful group.

25. It is this reason for repudiating nationalism that future neo-Marxists will contest by arguing that the worst material antagonisms and exploitations are nation-based, not class-based.

26. In contrast, those who criticize the state do not necessarily appear as enemies of the people. Indeed, such critics often tout themselves as being on the side of the nation against the state.

27. This is precisely Václav Havel's tack when he declares that all collective nouns are deceptive and mythological, that all generalizations must be

distrusted, and that there are in fact no classes or peoples — only individuals. As he puts it, we need to see "the human world as it really is: a complex community of thousands of millions of unique, individual human beings . . . [who] must never be lumped together into homogeneous masses beneath a welter of hollow clichés and sterile words and then en bloc — as 'classes,' 'nations,' or 'political forces' — extolled or denounced, loved or hated, maligned or glorified." Havel, "Words on Words," 8.

28. According to Heinrich Blücher in 1956, "nationalism began when every individual, every small spirit, saw in it his chance to embody something higher than himself and to feel himself, as a German or whatever, to be greater than he could feel alone. What now marks the end of nationalism is that it has become impossible to be both a human being and a German, a Frenchman, or a Jew (in Israel, in any case) . . . as a representative of this and that nationality, one will be forced sooner or later to become an inhuman monster." Blücher, "Letter to Karl Jaspers," 280.

29. Marx, "On the Jewish Question," 3:154.

30. Marx and Engels, *The German Ideology*, 23.

31. Marx, "The Eighteenth Brumaire of Louis Bonaparte," 11:185–86. Thus, as Marx writes with specific reference to the French Legitimist and July monarchies but in a passage relevant to all modern bureaucratic states: "Every *common* interest was straightway severed from society, counterposed to it as a higher, *general* interest, snatched from the activity of society's members themselves and made an object of government activity" (186).

32. Engels, "1891 Introduction," 628.

33. That idea captures spontaneously developing capitalist orders in eighteenth-, nineteenth-, and early twentieth-century Western Europe and the United States. It does not jibe with the state's active orchestration of capitalist development in nineteenth- and twentieth-century Central Europe and Asia, the hybrid economies and states of modern Latin America, or the overt interpenetrations of state and society in advanced capitalist societies today.

34. Habermasians differ among themselves in technical detail as well as in political emphasis. As the differences among individuals are not my concern here, I use Cohen and Arato to stand for the rest. See Cohen and Arato, *Civil Society and Political Theory* for a comprehensive examination of theories of civil society and a defense of their own concept of and hopes for it.

35. At most, only whispered mention is made of the Aryan Nation, the National Rifle Association, Right to Life groups, and other unsavory (to the left) expressions of free individual agency in the West. That is, post-Marxism highlights the left-of-center groups that seek a respectable "respect for difference" in a multicultural national community, not right-of-center and

far right groups. The monocultural conception of the nation of some of those groups, as well as their hatred of the state, professional elites, and minorities, cannot, I suspect, be understood if one does not also understand the resentment of the sinking classes or the flotsam and jetsam, as Marx would put it, of late capitalism.

36. See, for example, Hann, "Nationalism and Civil Society in Central Europe," 243–57. Hann explores the nationalist right in Poland, contrasting liberal theories of civil society with what actually is happening "on the ground" (251).

37. Connolly and Best, *The Politicized Economy*.

38. For a rigorous examination of this schema in "On the Jewish Question" and its lessons for identity politics, see Brown, *States of Injury*.

39. The articles Marx and Engels wrote in the 1850s and 1860s for the *New York Daily Tribune* display the great distance of their mentality from that of contemporary intellectuals, who speak about ethnic, national, and racial groups as if they were walking on eggshells. For example, the two men write that China had existed in "barbarous and hermetic isolation from the civilized world" and that the Chinese emperor and mandarins had to be roused "out of their hereditary stupidity" ("Revolution in China and India," 68); that the English noble families were "scientific barbarians," extending that barbarity in their colonial exploits "to the verge of hell itself" ("Parliamentary Debate on India," 83); that of the different races and nationalities in European Turkey ("Slavonians, Greeks, Wallachians, Arnauts"), "it is hard to say which is the least fit for progress and civilization" ("Turkey," 53). All quotations from Avineri, ed., *Karl Marx on Colonialism and Modernization*. Avineri's introduction to this collection gracefully captures the mixture of strengths and weaknesses in Marx's approach to colonialism and to national and regional "difference." For a compelling, critical defense of Marx's letters on British imperialism in India, see Ahmad, *In Theory*, 221–42.

40. Marx, *The Communist Manifesto*, 59. Marx's analysis of the formation of the nation-state in "The Eighteenth Brumaire of Louis Bonaparte" dovetails with that of *The Communist Manifesto*: "The first French Revolution, with its task of breaking all separate local, territorial, urban and provincial powers in order to create the civil unity of the nation, was bound to develop what the absolute monarchy had begun: the centralisation, but at the same time the extent, the attributes and the agents of governmental power" (185).

41. In Marx's words, these conditions include: the "political unity . . . imposed by the British sword . . . [and] strengthened and perpetuated by the electric telegraph"; the "native army, organized and trained by the British drill-sergeant"; the "free press, introduced for the first time into Asiatic society, and managed . . . by . . . Hindoo and Europeans"; and "a fresh class"

of governors, springing up from "Indian natives, reluctantly and sparingly educated at Calcutta, under English superintendence." Marx, "The Future Results of British Rule in India," 660.

42. Ibid., 663. Given its class agenda no less than its national-cultural one, the English bourgeoisie will "neither emancipate nor materially mend the social condition of the mass of the people" of India, for emancipation depends "not only on the development of the productive powers, but on their appropriation by the people." But frankly, asks Marx, "Has the bourgeoisie ever done more? Has it ever affected a progress without dragging individuals and peoples through blood and dirt, through misery and degradation?" (662).

43. As Marx and Engels put it, "[T]he more the original isolation of the separate nationalities is destroyed by the developed mode of production and intercourse and the division of labour naturally brought forth by these, the more history becomes world history" (*The German Ideology*, 38). Of course, isolation in and of itself is hardly a condition of nationness—indeed, quite the contrary, if one takes to heart Hegel's principle that the determinate thing is always determined by its relation to what it is not. One need not be a Hegelian to rely on this principle. The internal relation of nation to international society is a point James Mayall makes in *Nationalism and International Society* and Tom Nairn in "Internationalism: A Critique," in *The Faces of Nationalism*, 41–42. But national distinctiveness and autonomy, which Marx believes capital also eventually destroys, *are* conditions of nationness, at least in the eyes of nationalists.

44. Marx, *The Communist Manifesto*, 59.

45. Marx and Engels, *The German Ideology*, 27.

46. Marx, "The Future Results of British Rule in India," 663, 664.

47. One finds an analogous puzzle in J. S. Mill's *On Liberty*, a puzzle Mill tacitly recognizes but does not directly confront, when he laments the fact that with the end of traditional status distinctions, all individuals become more and more alike. Can there be a universal enjoyment of real individuality if all inherited cultures confining the individual, as Mill would put it, but also producing in the world vast variations of outlook and style of life, do and should, as Mill argues, disappear? See Mill, *On Liberty*, esp. 90–91.

48. David Held, with worries about democracy in mind, raises the same question in the late twentieth-century context. See his "Democracy, the Nation-State and the Global System," 138–72.

49. Marx, "Critique of the Gotha Program," 533.

50. Marx, *The Communist Manifesto*, 72–73.

51. Ibid., 58, 72, 73, 75.

52. From an economic perspective, it is possible to make sense of national consciousness on the part of forward-looking classes against feudal relations and the absolutist state, on the part of anticolonial movements,

and more generally on the part of subordinate regions in a world capitalist system. But except as an effect of the need for the state to provide economic protection at home or to secure the factors of production abroad, it is difficult to make sense of nationalist consciousness on the part of entrepreneurs, managers, financiers, technical specialists, and professional consultants whose economic horizons are global. As transnational capital depends on nation-states for ensuring social stability and for providing the conditions for the movement and security of the factors of production, there are still pragmatic reasons for the owners of capital to be supporters of state power — but not for such owners to be nationalists. And in the communist world that Marx envisions, it is not possible to make sense of national consciousness at all.

53. Marx, *Capital*, 1:8.

54. The reasons range all the way from the efficiency of authoritarian states in maintaining their political rule and in managing capitalist economic development, to the flattering fit between collectivist cultures and the organizational needs of mature corporate capitalism, to the threat that the prospect of world communism until recently posed to capitalism, which led Western liberal states to prop up non-Western authoritarian ones as long as they were staunchly anticommunist.

55. A point nicely made in conversation by Satyananda Gabriel, professor of economics at Mount Holyoke College.

56. Ernest Gellner suggests that the force of ethnonationalism would be unimaginable in any society steeped in the ethos of what Marx calls bourgeois individualism and what Gellner would call modern mass or interchangeable individualism. Gellner makes the important reservation that such antagonisms are likely to surface in modern civil societies when class is, for historical reasons, mediated by ethnicity or race and to explode there in conditions of recession or depression. But when it is in good health, and (an almost but not quite circular point) to the extent that its market principles prevail over racial and ethnic restrictions on them, modern capitalism seems to sap these collective identities of their felt passion by offering individuals as individuals the chance to succeed by competing against other individuals for occupational position and consumption rewards. Gellner, *Nations and Nationalism*, 94-95.

57. Psychoanalyst Donald Moss once called this, in conversation, a "crisis of identity anxiety," with anxiety clinically understood as being symptomatic of "a fear of impending loss."

CHAPTER 2
IMPERIALISM, SELF-DETERMINATION, AND VIOLENCE

1. Arendt, *Men in Dark Times*, vii. Arendt probably would not protest against being in a common room with her own idea of Luxemburg, which is a different matter.

2. Thus Fanon begins his concluding remarks on anticolonial struggles for national liberation with the line, "Leave this Europe where they are never done talking of Man, yet murder men everywhere they find them," and ends those remarks with the line, "For Europe, for ourselves, and for humanity, comrades, we must turn over a new leaf, we must work out new concepts, and try to set afoot a new man." Fanon, *The Wretched of the Earth*, 311, 316.

3. Or, as Arendt puts it, "This is of course to admit that she was not an orthodox Marxist, so little orthodox indeed that it might be doubted that she was a Marxist at all." Arendt, "Rosa Luxemburg. 1871–1919," 38.

4. Arendt, *On Violence*, 82.

5. Arendt, *On Revolution*, 28, 63.

6. A less kind way to put the point about Arendt is the way Said does when he describes Conrad as "the precursor of the Western views of the Third World which one finds in the work of . . . theoreticians of imperialism like Hannah Arendt": a man "whose *Western* view of the non-Western world is so ingrained as to blind him to other histories, other cultures, other aspirations." Said, *Culture and Imperialism*, xvii–xviii.

7. Fanon, *The Wretched of the Earth*, 156.

8. As Tom Nairn puts it, Luxemburg on nationalism is "heroic" but entirely unrealistic: she strikes a pose of "defiant moral grandeur, in perpetual rebuke of a fallen world." Nairn, *The Break-Up of Britain*, 84.

9. Arendt's involvement in Zionist political affairs and her allegiance to the idea of a Jewish homeland and the growth of Jewish culture are not enough to exempt her from the general association of the European Jewish intellectual with a universalist mentality. Arendt shows a definite antagonism to nationalism in her discussions of Zionism, where she emphasizes "the dangerous tendencies of formerly oppressed peoples to shut themselves off from the rest of the world and develop nationalist superiority complexes of their own." Arendt, "To Save the Jewish Homeland, 186. As we shall see in the next chapter, Arendt counts as one of the worst political costs of the Jewish state "the creation of a new category of homeless people, the Arab refugees" and urges Jewish-Arab cooperation in Palestine, a goal she links to "non-nationalist trends in Jewish tradition — the universality and predominance of learning and the passion for justice." Arendt, "Peace or Armistice in the Near East," 215, 212.

10. The second complaint against Arendt is no longer current in any case.

11. Arendt, *Men in Dark Times*, vii.

12. Luxemburg's own multicultural, multilingual, multinational background, which stands as a lived repudiation of the idea of the kind of singular and coherent identity that nationalism espouses, is taken instead by her most prominent biographer as a sign of a lack that forces Luxemburg to

displace her sense of belonging and patriotism from where they "naturally" should be, with the nation, to a "peer group" of other deracinated Jewish intellectuals and to the international working class. See Nettl's *Rosa Luxemburg*. In her review of Nettl's book, Arendt makes the different argument that Luxemburg, like a minority of other assimilated, middle-class Jews "whose cultural background was German . . . whose political formation was Russian, and whose moral standards . . . were uniquely their own" was "neither cosmopolitan nor international": her "fatherland actually was Europe." Arendt, "Rosa Luxemburg. 1871–1919," 40, 42. Yet surely it is more accurate to say that national-cultural hybrids testify to the conceptual limitations of nationality, which according to nationalism must always be self-identical and singular, and thereby also testify to the political dangers that nationalism poses for those who do not fit within those limitations. As Arendt admits, hybrids like Luxemburg are more likely than anyone else to understand those limitations and to sense those dangers.

13. That is, more obtuse than Lenin, who at least for strategic reasons acknowledges the importance of national identifications, and much more obtuse than Bauer, Renner, and Adler, who, if they condemn the imperialistic logic of bourgeois nationalism, also are sympathetic to the cultural value of nationality in the sense of what Bauer calls a "community of character." See Bauer, "The Concept of the Nation," 107.

14. As Arendt laments, Luxemburg was neglected by non-leftist intellectuals and dismissed by many left intellectuals during her lifetime and after her death. This refusal to consider, as Arendt (echoing Nettl) puts it, ideas that "belong wherever the history of political ideas is seriously taught," is continued with a vengeance through our own day. Arendt, "Rosa Luxemburg. 1871–1919," 56. For a more recent example of the dismissal of Luxemburg from a Leninist perspective, see Blaut, *The National Question*. For a more recent example of her dismissal from a post-structuralist perspective, see Nimni, *Marxism and Nationalism*. For an appreciative perspective on Luxemburg, see Munck, *The Difficult Dialogue*. Munck argues that Nettl perpetuates "the major misinterpretation of Luxemburg's work on the national question" (56–57). And, in fact, Arendt and Nairn as well as other writers (see, for example, Szporluk, *Communism and Nationalism*) rely on Nettl in their comments on Luxemburg and nationalism. Nettl plays down the substantive content of Luxemburg's positions in debates on the national question to play up her bid for power. While chastising Nettl for portraying Luxemburg as merely power hungry, Arendt neglects the content of her positions as well. Like Nairn later on, Arendt stresses Luxemburg's failure to recognize the force of national identification, although Arendt, whose antipathy to this force approaches Luxemburg's own, is more forgiving of that failure than Nairn is.

15. Luxemburg, *The National Question*, 160, 253, 159, 161.

16. Ibid., 259, 260, 251, 252.

17. The relentless disclosure of fracture in a seemingly self-identical whole does become the signature move of postmodernists. But while certain of the modernist theorists of nationalism (that is, the theorists who see nationalism as a modern, not primordial, phenomenon) have affinities with postmodernism, those affinities do not extend to deconstructing the unity of national community.

18. Luxemburg, *The National Question*, 135.

19. However, under certain circumstances, Luxemburg argues, it is the landed aristocracy rather than the bourgeoisie that is actively nationalist.

20. Luxemburg here shows a fondness for the plurality and fluidity of peoples in the old dynastic empires over their separation and fortification in nation-states, a fondness echoed today in the nostalgia of certain political thinkers for the mingling of peoples under imperial rule. As one of our own contemporary authors comments, "I do not want to suggest that the past [in the Arab world, under colonial empire] was better; it wasn't. But it was more healthily interlinked. . . . People actually lived with each other, rather than denying each other from across fortified frontiers. In schools you could encounter Arabs from everywhere, Muslims and Christians, plus Armenians, Jews, Greeks, Italians, Indians and Iranians all mixed up, all under one or another colonial regime, interacting as if it were natural to do so." Said, "Ignorant Armies Clash by Night," 162.

21. Luxemburg, *The National Question*, 138.

22. Luxemburg, *"The Russian Revolution" and "Leninism or Marxism,"* 48.

23. Luxemburg, *The National Question*, 162.

24. Ibid., 161, 134, 162.

25. Ibid., 132–33.

26. Ibid., 124. Luxemburg identifies the most intermixed region as the Caucasus, that "ancient historical trail of the great migrations of peoples between Asia and Europe, strewn with fragments and splinters of those peoples" (274).

27. Marxism can avoid the dominative logic of its own ideal of the self-determination of the proletariat only by representing the proletariat as a universal class.

28. As for Luxemburg, although she rejects the idea of freedom as national self-determination, she does not reject the idea of freedom as self-determination per se. Indeed, her greatest grudge against both capitalism and Bolshevism is that they deny self-determination to most people inside the nation and, in the case of capitalism, outside as well.

29. Luxemburg, *The National Question*, 279–80. Luxemburg makes this argument at the level of the party as well as the national community, warning against the disintegrative logic of dividing the international Social Democratic Party on the basis of ethnonational identity.

30. Ibid., 125, 143, 142, 135–36. The emphasis in the last quotation is mine.

31. For example, see Adler, "The Ideology of the World War," 125–35, esp. 130–32. This essay was written several crucial years after Luxemburg's remarks above.

32. References to power's self-obscuring methods are legion in Luxemburg's work. See her skewering of bourgeois nationalists in the Ukraine, the Social Democratic Party in Germany, and the Bolshevik party in Russia, for hiding ugly motives underneath the lofty principle of the "right of national self-determination" (*"The Russian Revolution" and "Leninism or Marxism,"* 54, 55, 48).

33. Luxemburg, *The Accumulation of Capital*, 387, 358, 385.

34. Compare Luxemburg's bleak final chapters of *The Accumulation of Capital* with Marx's always half bitter but also half triumphant portrayal of the progress the bourgeoisie effects by "dragging individuals and peoples through blood and dirt, through misery and degradation." Marx, "The Future Results of British Rule in India," 662.

35. Thus Tom Nairn errs in insisting on as large a divide as he does between Luxemburg and himself when he discusses her in *The Break-Up of Britain*, 82–84.

36. Arendt, *The Origins of Totalitarianism*, part 2, titled "Imperialism," esp. chap. 8, "Continental Imperialism: The Pan-Movements."

37. Ibid., 269.

38. Ibid., 272.

39. Arendt even congratulates the United States for coming closer than other states to making that phrase into fact.

40. Arendt, *On Revolution*, 9.

41. Arendt, *On Violence*, 82, 67.

42. Arendt defends the limited use of enraged violence: "[U]nder certain circumstances violence — acting without argument or speech and without counting the consequences — is the only way to set the scales of justice right again" (Ibid., 64).

43. Ibid., 79. This is the end of "multiplying natural strength," which she defines in turn as "the property inherent in an object or person," belonging "to its character, which may prove itself in relation to other things or persons, but is essentially independent of them" (46, 44).

44. Ibid., 80.

45. Ibid., 14n. 19. The first and foremost admirer is Sartre, whom she clearly loathes here.

46. Fanon, *The Wretched of the Earth*, 36, 38.

47. Ibid., 38, 37.

48. Ibid., 43.

49. Ibid., 36, 38.

50. Ibid., 37, 51, 52, 45, 53, 94.

51. To get a sense of the difference the different antagonism makes, see Elaine Scarry's *The Body in Pain*.

52. Fanon, *The Wretched of the Earth*, 88.

53. Arendt, *On Revolution*, 89, 90.

54. In the early 1960s, even Arendt succumbs to the temptation to dismiss the twentieth-century significance of nationalism (but also of capitalism and communism), claiming that revolution rather than nationalism and internationalism, capitalism and imperialism, or socialism and communism is central to the age. Arendt, *On Revolution*, 1.

55. Arendt has glimmers of that return in 1969, when she describes — as a reaction against the centralization, anonymity, and monopolization of power (all frustrating "the faculty of action in the modern world") — "the recent rise of a curious new brand of nationalism, usually understood as a swing to the Right, but more probably an indication of a growing, worldwide resentment against 'bigness' as such. While national feelings formerly tended to unite various ethnic groups by focusing their political sentiments on the nation as a whole, we now watch how an ethnic 'nationalism' begins to threaten with dissolution the oldest and best-established nation-states" (*On Violence*, 83, 84–85). This is precisely the line that many critical theorists of nationalism will take by the late 1970s through the early 1990s, although their characteristic defense of the "ethnos" in ethnonationalism as a basis of the polity puts them at an unbridgeable distance from Arendt.

56. Another eminently suitable kind is the opposite, Gandhian response of passive disobedience.

CHAPTER 3
ON THE JEWISH QUESTION

1. In a famous quip, Harold MacMillan noted that that knighthood was to be bestowed on Berlin "for talking." Berger, "Isaiah Berlin," sec. C, p. 24.

2. Collini, "Against Utopia," 3.

3. Annan, foreword, xv.

4. Jahanbegloo, *Conversations with Isaiah Berlin*, xvii.

5. Gray, *Isaiah Berlin*, 1, 2.

6. Hausheer, introduction, xxiv.

7. Ignatieff, *Isaiah Berlin*, 301.

8. Wieseltier, "Isaiah Berlin, 1909–1997," 27.

9. Ignatieff, *Isaiah Berlin*, 283. Ignatieff participates in the taboo when he describes critical commentaries on Berlin as "venom from the left and right," which "confirmed . . . that for all his success, the ground on which

he stood had always been narrower than most people supposed and his liberalism had always been embattled" (300). Who *isn't* embattled in intellectual and political life—and who *shouldn't* be!

10. Jahanbegloo, *Conversations with Isaiah Berlin*, 189.

11. Collini, "Against Utopia," 4.

12. As for the intricacies, Berlin seems unable to enjoy them. Thus, Berlin calls Marx's richly layered essay "On the Jewish Question" "a dull and shallow composition" and the complex *The German Ideology* "a bizarre compilation . . . on the whole . . . a verbose and tedious book." Yet he lavishes praise, still qualified, of course, on Marx and Engels's most dramatic and powerful but least theoretically complicated text, *The Manifesto of the Communist Party*, as "very nearly a work of genius." Berlin, *Karl Marx*, 98, 122, 150. In "successive revisions" to *Karl Marx* published as new editions, Berlin does qualify his earlier "over-bold generalizations," correct "mistakes of fact and emphasis," and make minor changes in his characterization of Marx's three texts. See the 1977 edition, p. x.

13. Jahanbegloo, *Conversations with Isaiah Berlin*, 82, 81, 85.

14. Arendt, *Men in Dark Times*, 158. In a curious way, this little book can be seen as an analogue of *Personal Impressions*, with all the differences of sensibility between Arendt and Berlin manifest in the different approaches to intellectual portraiture of the two texts.

15. Ignatieff, *Isaiah Berlin*, 61.

16. Berlin, *Personal Impressions*, 115.

17. In a talk he gave in the fall of 1998 at Mount Holyoke College, "Neither Disraeli nor Dreyfus: German Jews and Modern Liberalism," historian Fritz Stern at once confirmed and denied Berlin's representation of England as uniquely open-minded by distinguishing liberal and tolerant English *and* French cultures from an illiberal, prejudiced German one.

18. Berlin, "Jewish Slavery and Emancipation," pt. 1, pp. 17, 24. Zygmunt Bauman elaborates on such painful aspects of assimilation in "Exit Visas and Entry Tickets," 45–77. Indeed, this highly stimulating essay can be read as a companion piece that adds to and at points challenges Berlin's work on the Jewish question. For example, Bauman also describes the assimilating Jews' difficulties in fitting into, by copying, the majority that had emancipated them. However, his emphasis is not on the way that the Jews themselves failed by overdoing the copy but on the way that Gentile reactions made Jewish assimilation impossible. He does confirm Berlin's point that the Jews' "conspicuous cultural enthusiasm and obsessive display of cultural nobility" with respect to the majority's national culture gave them away as foreigners, not natives. Thus it was "the rapidly assimilating, reformed and cultivated Jews," distinguished because they were overrepresented in cultural fields and the professions, "who became the butt of new

forms of anti-Semitism," for "[m]odern society found it much easier to absorb traditional Jewish communities" than to come to terms with the "boundary-blurring mobility of 'non-Jewish Jews'" (53–54).

19. Berger, "Isaiah Berlin," 24. The rest of Berger's lines are "that he had been knighted; awarded the Order of Merit, Britain's highest honor for intellectual achievement; that he was a renowned and beloved Oxford scholar, a President of the British Academy. . . ." (24).

20. This is quoted by Berger in ibid., 24. In his turn, Ignatieff quotes Larry Siedentop's comment that Berlin "liked to venture out into the Romantic irrational by day, but always returned to the Enlightenment at nightfall" (*Isaiah Berlin*, 250).

21. Berlin, "Benjamin Disraeli, Karl Marx and the Search for Identity," 254, 255, 257. Bauman describes these new pressures when he writes about "the modern drive toward national self-determination and the concern with boundary-drawing and boundary defense which followed it." Religious conversion as a way of entering the majority society no longer worked. This was in part because of the "general decline of religious beliefs," in part because of the increasing privatism of religion, and in part because the "voluntary, subjective nature of belonging" to which conversion testified clashed with nationalist notions of organic belonging and the racial principle of national segregation. Bauman, "Exit Visas and Entry Tickets," 55.

22. Berlin, "Benjamin Disraeli, Karl Marx and the Search for Identity," 260, 262.

23. Ibid., 264, 268, 260, 274, 265, 271, 273, 275.

24. Christopher Hitchens captures Berlin's contrasting attitudes toward Disraeli and Marx when he says that in Berlin's essay, "every allowance is granted to Disraeli and nary a one to the old incendiary" ("Moderation or Death," 10). Hitchens does this in one of those left-wing assaults on Berlin that Ignatieff despises, which to make matters worse occurs in the form of a review of Ignatieff's biography of Berlin. To be sure, the review is standard Hitchens fare: biting, witty, and merciless in putting Ignatieff to shame for his studied refusal to look critically at Berlin's dubious cold war politics and long bouts of intellectual superficiality. At the same time, Hitchens shows a great deal of affection for Berlin. He also is careful to make it clear that as someone who is very much in-house Oxbridge too, he had his own personal relationship with Berlin, as well as with many of the other stars appearing on Ignatieff's pages.

25. Berlin, "Benjamin Disraeli, Karl Marx and the Search for Identity," 267, 268.

26. Ibid., 279, 276, 277, 278, 280, 260, 283.

27. Berlin, "Chaim Weizmann," 33.

28. Berlin elaborates on how the creation of the state of Israel displays the role of subjective freedom in history in "The Origins of Israel," 204–21.

29. Berlin, "Chaim Weizmann," 42, 43, 46, 49, 62.

30. Jennifer Ring makes an analogous move when she suggests that the Jewish intellectuals in the *Partisan Review* crowd were driven into Marxist politics and an internationalist, cosmopolitan stance by a desire to escape their Jewishness. (Ring almost always puts the word "cosmopolitan" in quotation marks or italics, as if there were something inherently false about it.) Evidently only non-Jews can be Marxists or cosmopolitans for political-intellectual not psychological reasons. It *is* the case, on the other hand, that those intellectuals, by keeping silent about Hitler's anti-Semitism while condemning Germany for its nationalist and imperialist politics, exemplified the kind of Jew Berlin describes as being too focused on capitalism to see the independent dynamic of ethnonationalism at work in Germany. Ring's Jewish intellectuals, unlike Berlin's, were fortunate enough to be living in New York and so did not die as a result of their poor vision. Ring, *The Political Consequences of Thinking*, 96–97.

31. According to Paul Smith, one of Disraeli's more recent biographers, Disraeli's racial fantasies fueled anti-Semitic fantasies directly. Smith writes, "Within five years of his [Disraeli's] death, the foremost French anti-Semite, Edouard Drumont, was using him as an authority for the identification of prominent personalities as Jews; within twenty, Houston Stewart Chamberlain was citing with approval his fetish of racial purity, as a lesson the Teutonic races had better learn if they were to repulse the Jewish challenge" (*Disraeli*, 103).

32. Berlin, "Chaim Weizmann," 60.

33. See George Mosse's *Confronting the Nation*, esp. chaps. 8 and 11. The latter chapter focuses on Max Nordau, a Jew, a liberal, and a nationalist who believed Zionism would cure the "nervousness" and abnormalities of the Jews, which he saw as connected to urban, intellectual life. Ring explores the recent literature on the gender connotations of the distinction between diaspora and Zionist Jew (the first "feminine," the second "masculine") in *The Political Consequences of Thinking*, 73 and chap. 5, "Race, Gender and Judaism."

34. Berlin, "The Origins of Israel," 215–16, 219, 220. Indeed, Berlin expresses positive pleasure at what he sees (erroneously, as it turns out) as the substance of that denominator: a culture "politically liberal," "egalitarian," and "left of centre" (220).

35. Berlin, "Jewish Slavery and Emancipation," pt. 4, p. 8, pt. 3, p. 15.

36. Ibid., pt. 4, p. 8.

37. Ignatieff reports Berlin's eventual misgivings, as well as the fact that he came quietly to favor a two-state solution to the Israeli/Palestinian conflict. Ignatieff, *Isaiah Berlin*, 292–93, 297.

38. Arendt, "The Jewish State," 169.

39. Arendt, "Zionism Reconsidered," 152, 153.

40. Arendt, "Peace or Armistice in the Near East," 215.

41. Arendt, "To Save the Jewish Homeland," 192. For an intelligent explication of Arendt's idiosyncratic approach to Zionism as well as other dimensions of her answer to the Jewish question, see Bernstein, *Hannah Arendt and the Jewish Question*, chap. 5.

42. Arendt, "Peace or Armistice in the Near East," 208. She also chastises nationalism in the Middle East for transforming the region "into a battlefield for the conflicting interests of the great powers to the detriment of all authentic national interests" (217). Zeev Sternhell supports Arendt's suspicion of Herderian nationalism and the putatively pacific nature of Zionism as a form of it over Berlin's defense of both Herzl and Zionism when Sternhell argues that a) the original ideology and purpose of Zionism were national and cultural, an "organic nationalism" that "corresponded to the teachings of tribal nationalism in Europe," a "Herderian, not to say tribal, response to the challenge of emancipation"; b) "the significance of Zionism was the conquest of land and the creation of an independent state through work and settlement, if possible, or by force, if necessary"; and c) until recently, "secular" and religious Zionism were identical at their core, both being bent on a nationalist land conquest. Sternhell, *The Founding Myths of Israel*, 16, 12, 15.

43. Arendt, "Peace or Armistice in the Near East," 222.

44. Jahanbegloo, *Conversations with Isaiah Berlin*, 86.

45. Arendt, "To Save the Jewish Homeland," 187.

46. Arendt, *The Origins of Totalitarianism*, 68–79. Berlin and Arendt's common interests in nationalism, Jewish identity, the deformations of assimilation, and the alternatives to joining a society that despises you are so striking that one is tempted to use the same tools of psychology that Berlin wields on Disraeli and Marx to explain Berlin's refusal to see them. Even though Berlin generally does not refer to secondary sources, it is curious that he never once mentions Arendt's portrait of Disraeli, given the similarity of the purely descriptive elements of the two portraits.

47. Ibid., 68, 69. Arendt correctly charges that Disraeli's concoction of "a full-blown race doctrine out of [the] empty concept of a historic mission" of the Jews as a chosen people, his claim of a secret Jewish organization that ruled the world, and his belief in the power of secret societies in general mirrored convictions "in the more vicious forms of antisemitism" and "could, and did, help transform chimeras into public fears" (73, 71, 78).

48. Ibid., 64.

49. Ibid., 34.

50. Feldman, "Introduction: The Jew as Pariah," 41.

51. Although Feldman captures the spirit of Arendt's argument when he reads her as suggesting that the "unique worldless situation of the Jews

increasingly became the generalized condition of humankind" (ibid., 42), Arendt puts the point more precisely when she writes that worldlessness came to differentiate unfortunate from privileged peoples, with mass propertylessness and nationlessness turning political citizenship, property rights, passports, and birth certificates into "matters of social distinction." Arendt, "We Refugees," 65. See also Bernstein, *Hannah Arendt and the Jewish Question*, 78.

52. In a nightmarish, Arendt-inspired little book, Richard L. Rubenstein links the Jews to modernity's other "surplus populations." See Rubenstein's *The Cunning of History*.

53. Arendt, "The Moral of History," 110.

54. Bauman complicates this dichotomy between Jewish particularism and universalism in his analysis of the Jewish socialism of Eastern European Jews, which joined Jewish particularism and socialist universalism instead of asserting that the first must be sacrificed by assimilating Jews for the cause of the second. See "Exit Visas and Entry Tickets," 76.

55. This form of obtuseness to one's own plight, however, is matched by the obtuseness to the plight of others that the ethnonationalism even of pariah groups almost always fosters. This goes to show that to be a pariah is not necessarily to be one in Arendt's good, "conscious pariah" sense.

56. Ignatieff, *Isaiah Berlin*, 11.

57. Ibid., 66, 156, 283.

58. Notably, Marx drops anti-Semitic remarks especially in his letters to Engels, as if such aspersions were common coin between the two men, with the curious effect of making it seem as though his ethnic origins were the same as those of Engels rather than those of the Jews he seems to despise. See *The Letters of Karl Marx*.

59. Berlin, "L. B. Namier," 66, 72, 70, 69.

60. Ibid., 65.

61. Namier, *Conflicts*, 163, 134–35.

62. Ibid., 163.

CHAPTER 4
ARE LIBERALISM AND NATIONALISM COMPATIBLE?

1. The case for liberal nationalism is actually made in a number of competing ways by a number of different political theorists. My purpose here is simply to trace certain prominent lines of argument in the genre as a whole without differentiating among those different writers.

2. Tamir, *Liberal Nationalism*, 6.

3. Greenfeld, *Nationalism*.

4. Poole, "Freedom, Citizenship, and National Identity," 137. Although not an advocate of liberal nationalism as a recipe for the twenty-first cen-

tury, Poole does argue that liberalism and nationalism have been a close twosome for the past two hundred years.

5. Kymlicka, *Multicultural Citizenship*, 126.

6. Kymlicka, "Misunderstanding Nationalism," 138.

7. Tamir, *Liberal Nationalism*, 71, xii.

8. For example, Taylor writes: "In the case of the politics of difference, we might also say that a universal potential is at its basis, namely, the potential for forming and defining one's own identity, as an individual, and also as a culture" ("The Politics of Recognition," 42).

9. What counts as a deserving nationality? Liberal nationalists tend to stumble over this question because they want to give *some* national minorities cultural autonomy but fear what would happen if *every* minority took advantage of the same right: cultural chaos, social fragmentation, and political disorder. Thus liberal nationalists make deserving a function of relative size (large minorities, yes; small ones, no) and/or of the circumstances under which minorities become minorities (indigenous peoples, yes; immigrants, no), and/or of the degree of their desire for autonomy (a strong desire, yes; a weak one, no), etc.

10. Tamir, *Liberal Nationalism*, 31.

11. Ronald Beiner's *Theorizing Nationalism* and Omar Dahbour's *Philosophical Perspectives on National Identity* are both excellent edited collections that carefully attend to the relationship between liberalism and nationalism.

12. See especially Parekh, "The Incoherence of Nationalism," 295–325.

13. As one astute critic of liberal nationalism puts it, on Kymlicka's grounds that "familiarity with a culture 'provides meaningful options,' determining 'the boundaries of the imaginable' . . . it would seem that familiarity with more than one culture would extend those boundaries, providing a person with a broader range of options." Lichtenberg, "How Liberal Can Nationalism Be," 57.

14. Sanford Levinson makes this argument with specific reference to the Satmar Chassidic Jews in "Is Liberal Nationalism an Oxymoron," 626–45.

15. See Tamir, *Liberal Nationalism*, 161.

16. Kateb, "Can Cultures Be Judged," 1009–38.

17. Jahanbegloo, *Conversations with Isaiah Berlin*, 39.

18. Berlin, "The Origins of Israel," 217.

19. Berlin, "The Decline of Utopian Ideas in the West," 47.

20. Berlin, "Rabindranath Tagore and the Consciousness of Nationality," 254–55.

21. Jahanbegloo, *Conversations with Isaiah Berlin*, 44. For an extended examination of Berlin's views on the relationship between liberalism and pluralism, see Gray, *Isaiah Berlin*, esp. chap. 4, "Nationalism," and chap. 6, "Agonistic Liberalism." For briefer critiques, see Crowder, "Pluralism and

Liberalism," 293–305; and Mack, "Isaiah Berlin and the Quest for Liberal Pluralism," 215–30.

22. Berlin, "Two Concepts of Liberty," 161.

23. Berlin, "Kant as an Unfamiliar Source of Nationalism," 237, 247, 246, 245, 244.

24. Jahanbegloo, *Conversations with Isaiah Berlin*, 99.

25. Berlin, "The Apotheosis of the Romantic Will," 223.

26. Jahanbegloo, *Conversations with Isaiah Berlin*, 100.

27. Ibid., 100, 102.

28. In following this terminology, Berlin differs from Tamir, who uses "political nationalism" to signify the movement for a separate nation-state.

29. Berlin, "Two Concepts of Nationalism," 19.

30. Jahanbegloo, *Conversations with Isaiah Berlin*, 103, 104.

31. Benedict Anderson has argued that the presumed goodness of national community (which he cannot help presuming, too) is grounded in this sense of the simply given, essential, and inevitable character of inherited national group. B. Anderson, *Imagined Communities*, esp. chap. 8, "Patriotism and Racism." Berlin's defense of a good cultural nationalism seems exactly to follow suit.

32. Berlin, "Rabindranath Tagore and the Consciousness of Nationality," 251.

33. Berlin, "Nationalism," 604.

34. Berlin, "European Unity and Its Vicissitudes," 193, 199, 197.

35. Ibid., 197.

36. To take another example, Berlin's deep incision in the concept of liberty sharply distinguishes negative freedom as a private sphere in which the individual can act on his desires without outside interference from positive freedom as either individual or collective self-direction and self-mastery. But while Berlin *tells* us that these are two separate and morally discrete ideas (one good, the other dangerous), he *shows* us how tightly, if tensely, each is related to the other, both logically and genealogically. Political proponents of negative and positive liberty may be divided into right and left camps, but the "two concepts of liberty" overlap with one another, and between both those concepts (and between the various subcategories of positive freedom) there is a strong connecting thread.

37. Berlin, "The Bent Twig," 245, 246.

38. Indeed, the sequence Berlin describes that runs, in nineteenth-century Germany, from cultural inferiority to political nationalism is almost exactly the same as the one Fanon charts in *The Wretched of the Earth* as the stages in the development of national consciousness in Algeria.

39. Berlin, "The Bent Twig," 261, 251, 252.

40. Jahanbegloo, *Conversations with Isaiah Berlin*, 101.

41. Berlin, "The Bent Twig," 246, 258.

42. Berlin, "Two Concepts of Liberty," 156, 158, 157.

43. One might protest that such "freedom" barely deserves the name, being completely dependent on the will or whim of a superior other. Berlin, however, rules out an internal connection between freedom and equality, declaring them different and sometimes incompatible goods.

44. Thus Arendt says, in irony, that nineteenth-century assimilation did not threaten the survival of Jewish existence because whether they were accepted or rejected by the larger society, they were accepted or rejected because they were Jews. Arendt, *The Origins of Totalitarianism*, 64.

45. Berlin, "Nationalism," 600–601. Compare this subjectivist view of the relationship between nationalism and industrialization with Ernest Gellner's objectivist view (explored in the next chapter) that nationalism emerges to satisfy industrial society's own requirement for linguistic and cultural homogeneity within the same political unit.

46. Berlin, "The Bent Twig," 257, 259, 258.

47. Berlin, "European Unity and Its Vicissitudes," 195.

48. Berlin, "Nationalism," 598.

49. Nairn, *The Break-Up of Britain*.

50. Berlin, "European Unity and Its Vicissitudes," 202, 204, 203, 205.

51. Ibid., 205.

52. Berlin thereby exhibits one of the offending attitudes that Arendt wrote *The Origins of Totalitarianism* to counter and condemn.

53. As one commentator writes about the Balkans, "The local mix of ethnic and religious elements" was not combustible because of "'ancient ethnic hatreds'" but "became combustible only in the 19th century or later, when European ideas of state power and national sovereignty spread among the Balkan intelligentsias." Crampton, "The Great Balkan Illusions," 3.

54. Stephen Holmes puts the point about capitalism's discordance with nationalism positively when he argues that the earliest liberals believed that a commercial society could counteract and dilute bloody particularistic passions by fostering the relatively peaceful passions of individual self-interest, greed, and vanity. In their support for limited government, analogously, these liberals aimed in part to de-escalate particularistic passions by privatizing them. Holmes, "Liberalism for a World of Ethnic Passions and Decaying States," 599–610.

55. For an extensive and highly stimulating argument on this point, although not leveled against liberal nationalists alone, see Stevens, *Reproducing the State*.

56. Bernie Yack harpoons the "goodness" of national identity in liberal democracies in the opening to "Reconciling Liberalism and Nationalism," 166. He contests the civic/ethnic distinction in "The Myth of the Civic Nation," 193–211.

57. For other commentators who have criticized liberal nationalism's ide-

alizing tendencies, see Yack, "Reconciling Liberalism and Nationalism," 174; Walker, "Modernity and Cultural Vulnerability, 161n.2; and Lichtenberg, "How Liberal Can Nationalism Be," 60.

CHAPTER 5
IN DEFENSE OF ETHNICITY

1. Gellner, *Nations and Nationalism*, 124–25, 35.

2. Partha Chatterjee impales Gellner for his sociological attitude in *Nationalist Thought and the Colonial World*, 5–6. For other critical commentaries on Gellner, see Hall, *The State of the Nation*.

3. B. Anderson, *Imagined Communities*, 36.

4. Ibid., 7, 123.

5. Ibid., 43, chap. 6. We can see both Anderson's stylistic elegance and capacity for ironic suspicion at work in his depiction of the inheritance by even "the most determinedly radical revolutionaries" of state capitals: "In fact, there are very few, if any, socialist leaderships which have *not* clambered up into such worn, warm seats. . . . Like the complex electrical system in any large mansion when the owner has fled, the state awaits the new owner's hand at the switch to be very much its old brilliant self again" (159–60).

6. Ibid., chap. 8. In *The Origins of Totalitarianism*, Arendt also argues that racial ideologies are aristocratic, not nationalist, in origin, but she does this as a prelude to analyzing rather than denying the complex ties among racism, nationalism, and the pan-movements.

7. B. Anderson, *Imagined Communities*, chap. 8. Elaine Scarry makes this point in *The Body in Pain* to impress upon her readers the opposite lesson: nationalism in politics obscures its own realities from soldiers in war by couching its demands on them in terms of dying for the nation, not killing for it—and soldiers in war do *both* those things, without a doubt.

8. Nairn's prominence is such that one Australian theorist of nationalism can write that "Nairn has become a figure of almost compulsory citation." James, *Nation Formation*, 108.

9. Nairn, *The Break-Up of Britain*, 72, 338.

10. Nairn actually says that he is defending neo-nationalism, which he describes as "comparable to elemental nationalism in being a forced byproduct of the grotesquely uneven nature of capitalist development," but a by-product that "occurs at a far more advanced stage of general development, in areas . . . on the fringe of the new metropolitan growth zones" (*The Break-Up of Britain*, 128).

11. Ibid., 129.

12. Nairn does believe that the prospects for Scottish nationalism brighten considerably in the late twentieth century, but he thinks they do so

because Scotland then finds itself in a stronger, not weaker, position vis-à-vis its metropolitan center. Especially with the benefits of North Sea oil, why should a dynamic Scotland continue to be chained to a sickly English economy, a premodern English polity, and an almost entirely degenerated empire? Thus, as Nairn puts it, "Ever more clearly, the outlook of the previously rather quiescent Scottish bourgeoisie is one of restive impatience with English 'backwardness,' London muddle, economic incompetence, state parasitism, and so forth" (ibid., 204). It is also why, "[i]n relation to *this* specific 'metropolis' (or ex-metropolis)" and its "moribund" state, the smaller countries "have good reason to want out, and good cause for claiming that their exit is a progressive action" (89).

13. Said, "Narrative, Geography and Interpretation," 83.

14. Nairn, *The Break-Up of Britain*, 125.

15. Lamming, *The Pleasures of Exile*.

16. In his acknowledgments to *The Break-Up of Britain*, Nairn explicitly notes that he wrote part of the book in London and none of it in Scotland.

17. For an especially hotheaded concentration on Great Britain, see Nairn's runaway attack on the British monarchy and its "[a]rchaism, trash, quaintness and a burdensome family *Schmalz*" in *The Enchanted Glass* (371). Nairn's attack seems too bitter to be motivated merely by his political hatred of empire, or by his economic irritation with England for remaining stalled at an early stage of capitalist development, or by his pro-nationalist annoyance that England still refuses to " 'modernize' into the standard nation-state form — [to become] a 'Little England' to match the mainstream of modern nation-building imposed on most peoples by 19th and 20th century history" (257). A combination of all three motivations is probably at work, but an ethnic hostility to the English might play its part, too. Nairn's signature populism, of course, always puts him on the side of democracy against royalty — above all, *this* royalty. Nairn stands with "the people" at least as an idea, even when he scorns the "instincts" of most actual people in Great Britain for being "channelled upwards into an adoration of the Crown" (370).

18. Nairn, *The Break-Up of Britain*, 317.

19. Here, Nairn explicitly follows Immanuel Wallerstein, writing that capitalism's impact "was invariably uneven . . . on the world scale, establishing and re-establishing that hierarchy of core and peripheric regions Wallerstein describes. . . . One area, one nationality, one well-situated urban region always obtained the upper hand. . . . The others found themselves, by the same token, 'deprived.' . . . Hence, the new developments forced open fissures between those cultures which had previously lain together peaceably" (ibid., 318–19).

20. Ibid., 354.

21. The resemblance is there even though world systems theorists define

the periphery as being inside the world capitalist system, not outside it and so "noncapitalist."

22. Nairn, *The Break-Up of Britain*, 338.

23. Eric Hobsbawm sums up the reasons for this postponement in a nutshell: "[T]here is no way of turning the formation of 'national communities' (i.e., the multiplication of nation-states as *such*) into a historic engine for generating socialism either to replace or to supplement the Marxian historic mechanism" ("Some Reflections on 'The Break-Up of Britain,'" 12).

24. Nairn, *The Break-Up of Britain*, 85. Nairn also asserts that in other underdeveloped regions, Marxism drops its internationalist guise altogether, becoming outright an ideology of national liberation and modernization.

25. Ibid., 319.

26. Scholars and of course proponents of nationalism who dislike the book usually dislike it for this reason. See, for example, Beveridge and Turnbull's *Eclipse of Scottish Culture*. In their chapter "Scottish Nationalist, British Marxist: The Strange Case of Tom Nairn" (which I came across after I had titled this chapter), Beveridge and Turnbull respond to early essays of Nairn's that culminated in *The Break-Up of Britain*. They see him as a "strange case" because of his mixture of nationalism and Marxism, but their complaint against him, almost the opposite of mine, is that he defends nationalism for Marxist purposes. See also the Scottish nationalist John Herdman's objections to Nairn for treating the "'sweeping away of archaic or predatory social forms'" and the "'mobilising of populations for socio-economic development'" as the purpose of nationalism, when that purpose is really "the mobilising of populations for *spiritual* development." Herdman, "Politics," 109. Herdman quotes Nairn's "Essay on Scottish Nationalism," in *Memoirs of a Modern Scotland*, ed. Karl Miller (London: Faber and Faber, 1920).

27. Nairn, *The Break-Up of Britain*, 332, 335.

28. Ibid., 323.

29. Arendt, *The Origins of Totalitarianism*, 231–32.

30. Nairn, *The Break-Up of Britain*, 343–44.

31. Ibid., 339, 348. Hence the title of Nairn's famous final chapter, "The Modern Janus," and its poignant lines: "Thus does nationalism stand over the passage to modernity. . . . As human kind is forced through its strait doorway, it must look desperately back into the past, to gather strength wherever it can be found for the ordeal of 'development'" (348–49).

32. Ibid., 348, 360. Nairn's most infamous words are that this "pathology" is "as inescapable as 'neurosis' in the individual, with much the same essential ambiguity . . . a similar built-in capacity for descent into dementia, rooted in the dilemmas of helplessness thrust upon most of the world . . . and largely incurable" (359).

33. However, on this subject, Nairn declares, "[O]ther traditions of Western thought have not done better" (ibid., 329).

34. Ibid., 329, 360.

35. Whether Nairn is, by the end of the 1970s, a nationalist or a Marxist or some curious amalgam of the two was the subject of some debate in Britain. The answer of course depends not just on the theoretical position that is this chapter's focus but also on Nairn's actions and his relations with Scottish nationalists and British Marxists at the time.

36. All of these essays dwell on Europe, but Africa clearly is on Nairn's mind, too.

37. Nairn, "All Bosnians Now," 404, 403.

38. Nairn, "Beyond Big Brother," 30.

39. Nairn, "All Bosnians Now," 407, 408.

40. Nairn, "Demonizing Nationalism," 5.

41. Ibid., 6, 3. The other progressive factors were the "democratic rebellion against one-party autocracy and state terror," and the "national mould into which these revolts were somehow inevitably flowing" (3).

42. Nairn, "Internationalism and the Second Coming," 163, 164. Another example: "Socialism has to find new, post-1989 bearings, although some may find this a charitable description of its plight. . . . The alternative lies within what used to be called the enemy" (163).

43. Nairn, "Beyond Big Brother," 30. Nairn argues here that the only alternative to nationalism is not internationalism or cosmopolitanism but empire. As for Germany in the 1930s, which seems to have joined nationalism and empire together, Nairn makes an argument diametrically opposed to that of Hannah Arendt. Arendt sees Nazism as originating as a transnational and antinational racial ideology but becoming an ideology of national aggrandizement. Nairn asserts that Nazism was founded on a nationalism of defeat and revenge that became a nonnational, "universalist crusade" (31).

44. Nairn, "Does Tomorrow Belong to the Bullets or the Bouquets," 30.

45. Nairn, "Internationalism and the Second Coming," 156, 160.

46. Ibid., 161.

47. Nairn, "Beyond Big Brother," 32.

48. Nairn, "Does Tomorrow Belong to the Bullets or the Bouquets," 30, 31.

49. Nairn and Osmond, "This Land Is My Land, That Land Is Your Land," 3.

50. Nairn, *Faces of Nationalism*, 8, 11, 14, 9, 13.

51. Nairn, "All Bosnians Now," 404, 406.

52. Ibid., 407, 409, 408.

53. Nairn, "Breakwaters of 2000," 94.

54. Nairn, "Demonizing Nationalism," 6.

55. Nairn, "Internationalism and the Second Coming," 158.

56. Nairn, "Breakwaters of 2000," 98. Nairn actually uses this phrase while scoffing at those who are horrified by the tendency "against gigantism, and in favour of identity delusions" (98).

57. Nairn admits to the possibility of an agenda of decentralization and localism that is right wing instead of left wing (in the anarchist, not socialist, sense of "left wing"), but he does so only in a qualification of his main point, which is to equate "small battalions" with democracy. See his "Does Tomorrow Belong to the Bullets or the Bouquets," 31.

58. Nairn, "Demonizing Nationalism," 5, 6.

59. Ibid., 3.

60. Nairn, "Beyond Big Brother," 32.

61. Nairn, "Demonizing Nationalism," 3.

62. The delicate balance between intellectual rigor and angry sarcasm is not easy to maintain — Nairn's *Enchanted Glass* is an example of what happens when sarcasm wins out.

63. It is ironic but not surprising that the conceptual conflation of capitalism and development, the development metaphor itself, and the conviction that the limits of the actual are the limits of the possible are even more entrenched today than they were before Marxism died. What deconstruction can do not just for Nairn but for us is to turn the beam of its corrosive intelligence in this direction.

64. Nairn, *The Break-Up of Britain*, 341.

65. Nairn, *The Enchanted Glass*, 231–38.

66. For an analysis of nationalism that argues, very differently, that democratization gives rise to nationalism and that it does so "because it serves the interests of powerful groups within the nation who seek to harness popular energies to the tasks of war and economic development without surrendering real political authority to the average citizen," see Snyder, *From Voting to Violence*, quote on p. 36.

67. Nairn, *Faces of Nationalism*, 23.

68. To put the point negatively, he is deafeningly silent about what Eric Hobsbawm describes as "the enormous difficulties and cruelties to which the attempt to divide Europe [and by extension, every other part of the world] into homogeneous nation-states has led in this century (including separation, partition, mass expulsion and genocide)" ("Some Reflections on 'The Break-Up of Britain,'" 4).

69. Nairn, *Faces of Nationalism*, 111, 16, 106, 108.

70. Nairn, "Breakwaters of 2000," 101. Nairn quotes from Ignatieff's *Blood and Belonging*.

71. Nairn, *Faces of Nationalism*, 87, 84.

72. B. Anderson, "The New World Disorder," 3.

CHAPTER 6
COSMOPOLITANISM IN A NEW KEY

1. See Etzioni, *Rights and the Common Good*.

2. As distasteful as such "heterophile racism" might seem (Pierre-Andre

Taguieff's term in his essay "From Race to Culture," 34–53), the antirationalism and anti-universalism supporting it have been mainstays of postmodernism and multiculturalism too, even though postmodernists scoff at identity fetishism and multiculturalists encourage political intercourse between different cultural groups.

3. Piccone, "Confronting the French New Right," 7. Piccone admires that New Right for standing against "the bureaucratic centralism of the former Soviet Union and the liberal technocracy in the West . . . [as] variations of the same basic Enlightenment model" (8).

4. Berlin, "Two Concepts of Nationalism," 22.

5. For Nairn's critique of internationalism, see especially "Internationalism and the Second Coming," 155–70. For more recent reservations about ethnonationalism, see his "Cleaning Up," 11–14.

6. Arendt, "Portrait of a Period," 119–20.

7. Nussbaum, "Patriotism and Cosmopolitanism," 5.

8. Appiah, "Cosmopolitan Patriots," 617–39.

9. For a nuanced discussion of the "new cosmopolitans" today, see Robbins, "Introduction: Part I," 1–19. Here Robbins aptly notes that "Like nations, cosmopolitanisms are now plural and particular" (2); that they signify not "an ideal of detachment" but "a reality of (re)attachment, multiple attachment, or attachment at a distance" (3); and that "Habitation that is complex and multiple is already shot through with unavoidable distances and indifferences, with comparison and critique; yet it does not thereby cease to be a mode of belonging" (3). See also A. Anderson, "Cosmopolitanism, Universalism, and the Divided Legacies of Modernity," 265–89, which situates the debate over cosmopolitanism and universalism within poststructural social theory, neo-Kantian philosophy, and critical anthropology.

10. Some thinkers elide the postcolonial component of "metropolitan theory" far more purposefully than Nairn does. See, for example, Radhakrishnan, *Diasporic Mediations*, esp. chap. 8, "Postcoloniality and the Boundaries of Identity," where Radhakrishnan equates postcolonial theory with first world or Western theory.

11. Parry, "Overlapping Territories and Intertwined Histories," 20. Parry partly quotes Said here: the first phrase is Said's, the second, Parry's.

12. Kaldor, "Cosmopolitanism versus Nationalism," 43. Kaldor notes that the new particularism is both more particularistic than earlier forms of nationalism and more transnational.

13. Kaplan, *Questions of Travel*, 126.

14. Nixon, "London Calling," 5, 7, 14, 12, 11, 27.

15. Said, "Bitter Dispatches from the Third World," 523.

16. Said, "Intellectuals in the Post-Colonial World," 53.

17. Said, *Culture and Imperialism* 304. Said's attacks on Naipaul are fierce but not far off the mark or based on a false representation of him.

Naipaul often portrays civilized order as collapsing after colonialism's end, and he often sounds like a shocked outside observer of the third world, most obviously when he refers to African primitivism and Islamic fundamentalism but also when he writes about his own country of distant origin, lamenting India's overcrowded housing, poverty, and unemployment, the half-finished quality of its goods, its sorry efforts at industrialization, and its spiritual preoccupations that both overshadow and justify extreme material distress. See Naipaul, *India*. The gravest difference of opinion between Said and Naipaul, at least from Said's point of view, concerns Naipaul's recent depiction of Islam as a universalist, imperializing religion that has worked to stamp out a variety of indigenous cultural forms as well as to stamp out intellectual curiosity and open-mindedness in Asia. Naipaul presents his depiction as a courageous critique of a dominative power about which other critics of domination have been silent. Said calls it a hostile prejudice disguised as a moral principle to justify Hindu supremacy over Muslims and other minorities in India. But the difference in human spirit between the two men is graver still. If one indication of that difference is Naipaul's contemptuous representation of Africans, another is his contemptuous treatment of women of all races not only in representation but also, if Paul Theroux's account in *Sir Vidia's Shadow* is to be trusted, in actual life. Prejudice that appears in the form of a fastidious distaste separates Naipaul in the most deeply personal terms from Said and possibly from everyone else mentioned between the covers of this book.

18. Said, "Bitter Dispatches from the Third World," 524.

19. As Salman Rushdie suggests in his introduction to a collection of Indian fiction edited by Rushdie and Elizabeth West (from which Naipaul "is regrettably absent . . . not by our choice, but by his own"), Naipaul is, in the "harshness of his responses" to postcolonial societies, partly right and partly wrong. Thus, as "one leading South Indian novelist" told Rushdie, " 'I'm anti-Naipaul when I visit the West . . . but I'm often pro-Naipaul back home' " (xix).

20. Naipaul, *Finding the Center*, x, viii, xi.

21. Ibid., ix, x.

22. Naipaul, "Prologue to an Autobiography," 4, 18.

23. Ibid., 50, 38.

24. Naipaul, *India*, 7.

25. Naipaul, *A Bend in the River*, 242.

26. Perhaps many North Americans are in the middle, too. See, for example, Naipaul, "Rednecks," 8–12.

27. See Naipaul's remarks on the extermination of the Indians in his *Return of Eva Peron*.

28. See, for example, Naipaul's embarrassingly astute portrayal of Raymond in *A Bend in the River*.

29. Naipaul, "Prologue to an Autobiography," 31. Naipaul actually makes his point more subtly, in the middle of noting his boyhood ideals: "From the earliest stories and bits of stories my father had read to me . . . I had arrived at the conviction — the conviction that is at the root of so much human anguish and passion, and corrupts so many lives — that there was justice in the world" (31).

30. Naipaul, *The Enigma of Arrival*, 166. More than many of his other novels, this one so ambiguously crosses the border between autobiography and fiction that it is equally problematic to say that Naipaul's narrator is Naipaul or Naipaul's protagonist.

31. Ibid., 15, 278, 47.

32. Nixon, "London Calling," 3. For an analysis of different complexities to do with the assessment of Naipaul, see Robbins, *Secular Vocations*, esp. chap. 6, "Comparative Cosmopolitans."

33. Naipaul, "Our Universal Civilization," 25.

34. Ibid., 22. Ironically, Naipaul makes this comment on the same occasion in which he splits the world into two monolithic parts.

35. Naipaul, *A Bend in the River*, 148.

36. Naipaul, *The Enigma of Arrival*, 335.

37. Naipaul, *India*, 130.

38. Naipaul, *Among the Believers*, 246.

39. Naipaul, "Our Universal Civilization," 25.

40. Said, *Representations of the Intellectual*, 49, 54. Or rather, he praises the early Naipaul, but in fact Naipaul continues to do this throughout his literary career. The remark about Naipaul, by the way, is more accurate than the remark about Salim, who is an exile but not an intellectual.

41. Glass, "A Passionate Reading," 15.

42. A controversy over this complicated pattern exploded a few years ago, summarized in Eakin's "Look Homeward, Edward," 49–52. Critics accused Said of misrepresenting, up until the publication of his memoir, his early childhood years, which were spent mainly in Cairo, not Jerusalem. It was not his own family, his critics charged, but his aunt's, that left its Jerusalem home in fearful anticipation of Jewish sovereignty over Palestine. Those critics also accused Said of taking personal advantage of the Palestinian tragedy by making himself a subject of righteous indignation and an object of pity. With respect to the first charge, Said often *had* intimated that he spent his early years in Palestine and that the Jerusalem house was his family's. Middle Eastern autobiographies and memoirs suggest, however, that assumptions about American middle-class nuclear family property use cannot be exported to regions of the world in which extended families in the upper classes move regularly among houses that various members of those families own. In a period and place in which the fixed borders of a nation-state system were only beginning to emerge, moreover, it is a mistake

to call for such fixity in the geographical imagination of a young boy, or even in the memories that an adult man has of his experience of place as a child. With respect to the second charge, my interpretation of Said's identification of himself with impoverished Palestinian refugees is the opposite of the interpretation of his critics. I see Said as emphasizing his own situation as a Palestinian exile for pedagogical purposes, in order to move members of a Western audience who are able to sympathize with him because he is cosmopolitan enough to be familiar to them, to extend their sympathy to a people most of them, until fairly recently, either knew or cared little about or condemned as fanatical fundamentalists.

43. Said, "Identity, Authority, and Freedom," 218.

44. This is true not only in Said's *Out of Place* but also in other written and spoken comments he has made about his life.

45. Said, *The Politics of Dispossession*, xviii, xx. As Said points out on another occasion, "To be the victim of a victim does present quite unusual difficulties" ("On Palestinian Identity," 74).

46. Said, *The Politics of Dispossession*, xvi, xxiv.

47. Said, *Representations of the Intellectual*, 53.

48. Arendt, "Portrait of a Period," 112.

49. Said, "Nationalism, Human Rights, and Interpretation," 28.

50. Said, "Third World Intellectuals and Metropolitan Culture," 49. At the same time, Said writes in the knowledge that the refusal to accept that contact and cross-fertilization is very powerful. Witness the ideology of reduction and dichotomous opposition in that same imperial history and witness, today, the political explosiveness in metropolitan countries of "the largely unaccommodated exiles, like Palestinians or the new Muslim immigrants in continental Europe, or the West Indian and African blacks in England, whose presence complicates the presumed homogeneity of the new societies in which they live." Said, *Representations of the Intellectual*, 50.

51. Said, "Identity, Authority, and Freedom," 226.

52. Thus we see "struggles for dominance between states, nationalism, ethnic groups, regions and cultural entities . . . amplified as well as conducted to a very large degree by the manipulation of opinion and discourse . . . the simplification . . . of vast complexities, the easier to deploy and exploit in the interest of state policy." Said, "Intellectuals in the Post-Colonial World," 59–60.

53. "Interview with Edward Said," 231, 232. Said specifically mentions Palestinians, Jews, Armenians, Kurds, Christians, and Egyptian Copts as minorities whose status today is "extraordinarily inflamed" (232). In *Culture and Imperialism*, Said notes that the state's "inculcation of new authority" can incite against it a counter-identity equally authoritarian, if also popular rather than, for the moment, official (267). The double aspect of nationalism — its initial ethos of emancipation and its eventual end in mysti-

fication and coercion — accounts for Said's otherwise curious remark that it is "the tragedy . . . of all anti-imperial or decolonizing struggles that independence is the stage through which you must try to pass" ("Interview with Edward Said," 236–37).

54. Said, "Reflections on Exile," 162, 171, 166, 163, 164.

55. Ibid., 159. To ward off any tendency to romanticize that situation, Said warns us to think not of exiled poets and writers associated with the literature of adventure but of the "millions of people [torn] from the nourishment of tradition, family and geography"; the "refugee-peasants . . . armed only with a ration card and an agency number"; and the "unknown men and women" in foreign cities, who "have spent years of miserable loneliness" (160, 161). See Kaplan's *Questions of Travel*, especially her chapter "Traveling Theorists: Cosmopolitan Diasporas," on the ways Said's "exile" is used to signify "both cataclysmic loss and critical possibility" (117).

56. Said, *Representations of the Intellectual*, 59, 62, 63, 60.

57. Said, "Reflections on Exile," 172.

58. Said, *Representations of the Intellectual*, 60.

59. Said, "Reflections on Exile," 172.

60. Said, *Representations of the Intellectual*, 53, 59.

61. Said, "Reflections on Exile," 171, 170.

62. Ulf Hannerz's way of dealing with such conceptual problems is sharply to distinquish the exile from the cosmopolitan, citing in support of that move Said's description of the exile who becomes a diasporic nationalist. But Said in fact describes the exile who becomes a maverick in some of the same terms that Hannerz uses to describe the cosmopolitan as opposed to the exile. Said is much more loath than Hannerz to draw a stark dividing line between the cosmopolitan and other mobile types. See Hannerz, "Cosmopolitans and Locals in World Culture," 237–51.

63. For his position on Israel, see Said's thought-provoking article "The One-State Solution," 36–39. He circulated his position on Kosovo through an electronic discussion list (*saga-owner@jrn.columbia.edu*), in an article bitterly denouncing NATO's bombing of Kosovo titled "Protecting the Kosovars."

64. Heterogeneity does produce certain problems for political community, but these are merely different from rather than more serious than the problems that homogeneity produces. The one threatens a community's political unity, the other a community's political vitality.

65. This is not to say that one mentality is closer to moral virtue than the other.

66. "No country on earth," Said declares, "is made up of homogeneous natives," so that there is a fundamental "discrepancy between the heterogeneous reality and the concept of national identity" ("Identity, Authority, and Freedom," 222). Said does not take up the task of conceiving of alter-

native political arrangements for uniting heterogeneity and national identity in the way that, for example, Michael Walzer does in *On Toleration*. On another note, there is a gap or "slippage" in Said's analysis, as Kaplan is right to point out (*Questions of Travel*, 140), between what Said himself describes as the great difference between "the optimistic mobility, the intellectual liveliness, and the 'logic of daring'" of the exile as critical outsider and "the massive dislocations, waste, misery, and horrors endured in our century's migrations and mutilated lives." Said only partly closes this gap by regarding the intellectual exile as "first distilling then articulating the predicaments . . . [of] mass deportation, imprisonment, population transfer, collective dispossession, and forced immigrations" (*Culture and Imperialism*, 332–33).

67. Said, *Culture and Imperialism*, 336.

68. Said, "The Politics of Knowledge," 21–22.

69. Said, *Representations of the Intellectual*, xii.

70. That is, it must be able to be argued that Israel and the Palestinians are not "just a matter of two stories contesting with each other. . . . For there is a truly profound, irreducible injustice for which the injured side needs to get institutional recognition." Said, "On Palestinian Identity," 78. Still, Said admits to the possibility of "certain irreconcilables between cultures" — in this case, the convictions of two peoples in conflict that each of them is just, when relations between them are such that both convictions cannot be simultaneously true. He also hopes that coexistence can be achieved if each people distances itself enough from itself to recognize the experience and history of the other. The phrase quoted above is from a talk Said gave at Mount Holyoke College in October 1997.

71. Said, *Representations of the Intellectual*, 91. Richard Rorty and conservative communitarians show us that the overt substitution of "our truths" for universal truth is not always a subordinate identity move.

72. Thus, in "Traveling Theory" Said charts the geographical mobility of ideas. In "On Palestinian Identity," he notes that the "whole notion of crossing over, of moving from one identity to another, is extremely important to me" (74). In *Representations of the Intellectual*, he writes: "I have long been deeply drawn to those large expatriate or exile communities who peopled the landscape of my youth in Palestine and Egypt . . . Armenians . . . Jews, Italians and Greeks who . . . settled in the Levant" (48). The rest of the point is that these peoples were forced out after the establishment of Israel, the Suez War, and the rise of nationalist governments of Egypt and Iraq.

73. Said, "Nationalism, Human Rights, and Interpretation," 45.

74. Said, *Representations of the Intellectual*, 99–100, 113.

75. Said, "The Politics of Knowledge," 25.

76. Said, *Representations of the Intellectual*, 60.

77. Said, "The Politics of Knowledge," 24, 28.

78. Said, *Representations of the Intellectual*, xi.

79. Said, *Peace and Its Discontents*, 98–99.

80. Said, *Representations of the Intellectual*, 93.

81. Arendt, *The Origins of Totalitarianism*, 269.

82. Arendt, *Men in Dark Times*, 5.

83. Arendt, "We Refugees," 66.

84. Arendt, "The Jew as Pariah," 71.

85. Arendt, "We Refugees," 66.

86. Arendt, "The Jew as Pariah," 71, 76.

87. This is the case especially but not solely in Said's *Representations of the Intellectual*.

88. Brennan, "Cosmopolitans and Celebrities," 1–19; Ahmad, *In Theory*.

89. Naipaul has become involved with the worst possible kind of national-popular cause, from Brennan and Ahmad's point of view. See Naipaul, "A Million Mutinies."

90. Thus from opposite political directions (one on the side of a dominant ethnic group, the other on the side of a group dispossessed and displaced), both Naipaul and Said illustrate my point that the new cosmopolitanism is not opposed to national belonging but incorporates within itself the tension between home and the world. The question of whether Naipaul's defense of Hindu nationalism is, as he depicts it, a reaction against Islam's imperial conquest of India in the past and its fundamentalist politics in Pakistan in the present, or is instead Hindu chauvinism and anti-Muslim racism pure and simple, is all-important with respect to assessing Naipaul's integrity. Either answer, however, would indicate particularistic, national-popular prejudices and loyalties on Naipaul's part.

91. Said, *Representations of the Intellectual*, 108–9.

92. Arendt, *The Human Condition*, 58–67. According to Arendt, whose telling distinction between wealth and private property is in modern thought entirely unique, "[T]he enormous and still proceeding accumulation of wealth in modern society, which was started by expropriation . . . has never shown much consideration for private property but has sacrificed it whenever it came into conflict with the accumulation of wealth" (66–67).

CONCLUSION

1. Williams, *The Country and the City*, 4, 5.

2. Ibid., 297, 296.

3. Luxemburg, *The National Question*, 124.

4. For a more extended argument on behalf of a comparative political philosophy as the scholarly variant of that conversation, see Dallmayr, *Beyond Orientalism*; and Euben, *Enemy in the Mirror*.

Bibliography

Adler, Max. "The Ideology of the World War." (1915.) In *Austro-Marxism*, ed. Tom Bottomore and Patrick Goode, 125–35. Oxford: Oxford University Press, 1978.

Ahmad, Aijaz. *In Theory: Classes, Nations, Literatures*. London: Verso, 1992.

———. "Public Histories, Private Memories: The Partition and After." Public lecture, Smith College, March 2000.

Anderson, Amanda. "Cosmopolitanism, Universalism, and the Divided Legacies of Modernity." In *Cosmopolitics: Thinking and Feeling beyond the Nation*, ed. Pheng Cheah and Bruce Robbins, 265–89. Minneapolis: University of Minnesota Press, 1998.

Anderson, Benedict. *Imagined Communities: Reflections on the Origin and Spread of Nationalism*. 2d ed. London: Verso, 1991 (1983).

———. "The New World Disorder." *New Left Review*, no. 193 (May/June 1992): 3–13.

Annan, Noel. Foreword to *The Proper Study of Mankind*, ed. Henry Hardy and Roger Hausheer, ix–xv. London: Chatto and Windus, 1997.

Appiah, Kwame Anthony. "Cosmopolitan Patriots." *Critical Inquiry* 23 (Spring 1997): 617–39.

Arendt, Hannah. *The Human Condition*. Chicago: University of Chicago Press, 1958.

———. "The Jew as Pariah: A Hidden Tradition." (April 1944.) In *The Jew as Pariah: Jewish Identity and Politics in the Modern Age*, ed. Ron H. Feldman, 67–90. New York: Grove, 1978.

———. *The Jew as Pariah: Jewish Identity and Politics in the Modern Age*. Ed. Ron H. Feldman. New York: Grove, 1978.

———. "The Jewish State: Fifty Years After. Where Have Herzl's Politics Led?" (May 1946.) In *The Jew as Pariah: Jewish Identity and Politics in the Modern Age*, ed. Ron H. Feldman, 164–77. New York: Grove, 1978.

———. *Men in Dark Times*. New York: Harcourt Brace Jovanovich, 1983 (1955).

———. "The Moral of History." (January 1946.) In *The Jew as Pariah: Jewish Identity and Politics in the Modern Age*, ed. Ron H. Feldman, 106–11. New York: Grove, 1978.

———. *On Revolution*. New York: Viking, 1965.

———. *On Violence*. New York: Harcourt Brace Jovanovich, 1970 (1969).

———. *The Origins of Totalitarianism*. 2d ed. New York: Harcourt Brace Jovanovich, 1973 (1951).

———. "Peace or Armistice in the Near East?" (January 1950.) In *The Jew as Pariah: Jewish Identity and Politics in the Modern Age*, ed. Ron H. Feldman, 193–222. New York: Grove, 1978.

———. "Portrait of a Period." (October 1943.) In *The Jew as Pariah: Jewish Identity and Politics in the Modern Age*, ed. Ron H. Feldman, 112–21. New York: Grove, 1978.

———. "Rosa Luxemburg. 1871–1919." In *Men in Dark Times*, 33–56. New York: Harcourt Brace Jovanovich, 1983.

———. "To Save the Jewish Homeland: *There Is Still Time*." (May 1948.) In *The Jew as Pariah: Jewish Identity and Politics in the Modern Age*, ed. Ron H. Feldman, 178–92. New York: Grove, 1978.

———. "We Refugees." (January 1943.) In *The Jew as Pariah: Jewish Identity and Politics in the Modern Age*, ed. Ron H. Feldman, 55–66. New York: Grove, 1978.

———. "Zionism Reconsidered." (October 1945.) In *The Jew as Pariah: Jewish Identity and Politics in the Modern Age*, ed. Ron H. Feldman, 131–63. New York: Grove, 1978.

Avineri, Shlomo, ed. *Karl Marx on Colonialism and Modernization*. New York: Anchor Books, 1969.

Bauer, Otto. "The Concept of the 'Nation.'" (1907.) In *Austro-Marxism*, ed. Tom Bottomore and Patrick Goode, 102–9. Oxford: Oxford University Press, 1978.

Bauman, Zygmunt. "Exit Visas and Entry Tickets: Paradoxes of Jewish Assimilation." *Telos*, no. 77 (Fall 1988): 45–77.

Beiner, Ronald, ed. *Theorizing Nationalism*. Albany: State University of New York Press, 1999.

Beissinger, Mark. "Nationalisms That Bark and Nationalisms That Bite: Ernest Gellner and the Substantiation of Nations." In *The State of the Nation: Ernest Gellner and the Theory of Nationalism*, ed. John A. Hall, 169–90. Cambridge: Cambridge University Press, 1998.

Berger, Marilyn. "Isaiah Berlin, Philosopher and Pluralist, Is Dead at 88." *New York Times*, 7 November 1997, sec. A, p. 1, and sec. C, p. 24.

Berlin, Isaiah. "The Apotheosis of the Romantic Will." (1975.) In *The Crooked Timber of Humanity*, ed. Henry Hardy, 207–37. New York: Vintage, 1992.

———. "Benjamin Disraeli, Karl Marx and the Search for Identity." (1970.) In *Against the Current*, ed. Henry Hardy, 252–86. New York: Viking, 1980.

———. "The Bent Twig: On the Rise of Nationalism." (1972.) In *The Crooked Timber of Humanity*, ed. Henry Hardy, 238–61. New York: Vintage, 1992.

———. "Chaim Weizmann." (1958.) In *Personal Impressions*, ed. Henry Hardy, 32–62. New York: Viking, 1981.

———. *The Crooked Timber of Humanity*. Ed. Henry Hardy. New York: Vintage, 1992.

———. "The Decline of Utopian Ideas in the West." (1978.) In *The Crooked Timber of Humanity*, ed. Henry Hardy, 20–48. New York: Vintage, 1992.

———. "European Unity and Its Vicissitudes." (1959.) In *The Crooked Timber of Humanity*, ed. Henry Hardy, 175–206. New York: Vintage, 1992.

———. "Jewish Slavery and Emancipation." Parts 1–4. *The Jewish Chronicle*, 21 September, 28 September, 5 October, 12 October 1951.

———. "Kant as an Unfamiliar Source of Nationalism." (Original lecture, 1972.) In *The Sense of Reality*, ed. Henry Hardy, 232–48. New York: Farrar, Straus, and Giroux, 1996.

———. *Karl Marx: His Life and Environment*. 2d ed. New York: Oxford University Press, 1959 (1939).

———. "L.B. Namier." (1966.) In *Personal Impressions*, ed. Henry Hardy, 63–82. New York: Viking, 1981.

———. "Nationalism: Past Neglect and Present Power." (1978.) In *The Proper Study of Mankind*, ed. Henry Hardy and Roger Hausheer, 581–604. London: Chatto and Windus, 1997.

———. "The Origins of Israel." (Original lecture, 1953.) In *The Middle East in Transition: Studies in Contemporary History*, ed. Walter Z. Laqueur, 204–21. New York: Praeger, 1958.

———. *Personal Impressions*. Ed. Henry Hardy. New York: Viking, 1981.

———. *The Proper Study of Mankind*. Ed. Henry Hardy and Roger Hausheer. London: Chatto and Windus, 1997.

———. "Rabindranath Tagore and the Consciousness of Nationality." (Original lecture, 1961.) In *The Sense of Reality*, ed. Henry Hardy, 249–66. New York: Farrar, Straus, and Giroux, 1996.

———. *The Sense of Reality*. Ed. Henry Hardy. New York: Farrar, Straus, and Giroux, 1996.

———. "Two Concepts of Liberty." (1958.) In *Four Essays on Liberty*, 118–72. Oxford: Oxford University Press, 1984.

———. "Two Concepts of Nationalism: An Interview with Isaiah Berlin." By Nathan Gardels. *New York Review of Books*, 21 November 1991, pp. 19–23.

Bernstein, Richard J. *Hannah Arendt and the Jewish Question*. Cambridge, MA: MIT Press, 1996.

Beveridge, Craig, and Ronald Turnbull. *The Eclipse of Scottish Culture*. Edinburgh: Polygon, 1989.

Biberaj, Elez. "The Albanian National Question: The Challenges of Autonomy, Independence, and Separatism." In *The New European Diasporas*, ed. Michael Mandelbaum, 214–88. New York: The Council on Foreign Relations Press, 2000.

Blaut, J. M. *The National Question: Decolonising the Theory of Nationalism*. London: Zed Books, 1987.

Blücher, Heinrich. "Letter to Karl Jaspers." (February 14, 1956.) In *Hannah Arendt/Karl Jaspers Correspondence 1926–1969*, ed. Lotte Kohler and Hans Saner, 276–80. New York: Harcourt Brace, 1992.

Bottomore, Tom, and Patrick Goode, eds. *Austro-Marxism*. Oxford: Oxford University Press, 1978.

Brennan, Tim. "Cosmopolitans and Celebrities." *Race and Class* 31, no. 1 (1989): 1–19.

Brown, Wendy. *States of Injury: Power and Freedom in Late Modernity*. Princeton: Princeton University Press, 1995.

Chatterjee, Partha. *Nationalist Thought and the Colonial World: A Derivative Discourse*. Minneapolis: University of Minnesota Press, 1993 (1986).

Cheah, Pheng, and Bruce Robbins, eds. *Cosmopolitics: Thinking and Feeling beyond the Nation*. Minneapolis: University of Minnesota Press, 1998.

Cohen, Jean L., and Andrew Arato. *Civil Society and Political Theory*. Cambridge, MA: MIT Press, 1992.

Collini, Stefan. "Against Utopia." Review of *The Proper Study of Mankind*, by Isaiah Berlin. *Times Literary Supplement*, 22 August 1997, pp. 3–5.

Connolly, William E., and Michael H. Best. *The Politicized Economy*, 2d. ed. Lexington, MA: D. C. Heath, 1982 (1976).

Connor, Walker. "Nation-Building or Nation-Destroying?" *World Politics* 24, no. 3 (April 1972): 319–55.

———. *The National Question in Marxist-Leninist Theory and Strategy*. Princeton: Princeton University Press, 1984.

Crampton, Richard. "The Great Balkan Illusions." Review of *Kosovo: A Short History*, by Noel Malcolm. *Times Literary Supplement*, 24 April 1998, pp. 3–4.

Crowder, George. "Pluralism and Liberalism." *Political Studies* 42 (1994): 293–305.

Dahbour, Omar, ed. *The Philosophical Forum: Philosophical Perspectives on National Identity* 28, nos. 1–2 (Fall/Winter 1996–97).

Dallmayr, Fred. *Beyond Orientalism: Essays on Cross-Cultural Encounter*. Albany: State University of New York Press, 1996.

Eakin, Emily. "Look Homeward, Edward." *New York Times Sunday Magazine*, 27 September 1999, pp. 49–52.

Engels, Frederick. Introduction (1891) to "The Civil War in France," by Karl Marx. In *The Marx-Engels Reader*, 2d ed., ed. Robert Tucker, 618–29. New York: W. W. Norton, 1978.

———. Introduction (1895) to *The Class Struggles in France, 1848–1850*, by Karl Marx. In *The Marx-Engels Reader*, 2d ed., ed. Robert Tucker, 556–73. New York: W. W. Norton, 1978.

Etzioni, Amitai, ed. *Rights and the Common Good: The Communitarian Perspective*. New York: St. Martin's Press, 1995.

Euben, Roxanne. *Enemy in the Mirror: Islamic Fundamentalism and the Limits of Modern Rationalism*. Princeton: Princeton University Press, 1999.

Fanon, Frantz. *The Wretched of the Earth*. New York: Grove, 1963.

Feldman, Ron H. "Introduction: The Jew as Pariah: The Case of Hannah Arendt (1906–1975)." In *The Jew as Pariah: Jewish Identity and Politics in the Modern Age*, ed. Ron H. Feldman, 15–52. New York: Grove, 1978.

Ford, Ford Madox. *The Good Soldier*. New York: Knopf, 1991.

Gellner, Ernest. *Conditions of Liberty: Civil Society and Its Rivals*. London: Penguin Books, 1996 (1994).

———. *Nations and Nationalism*. Ithaca: Cornell University Press, 1983.

Gilbert, Paul. "The Concept of a National Community." *The Philosophical Forum: Philosophical Perspectives on National Identity* 28, nos. 1–2 (Fall/Winter 1996–97): 149–66.

Glass, Charles. "A Passionate Reading." *Times Literary Supplement*, 16 February 1996, p. 15.

Gray, John. *Isaiah Berlin*. Princeton: Princeton University Press, 1996.

Greenfeld, Liah. *Nationalism: Five Roads to Modernity*. Cambridge, MA: Harvard University Press, 1992.

Hall, John A., ed. *The State of the Nation: Ernest Gellner and the Theory of Nationalism*. Cambridge: Cambridge University Press, 1998.

Hann, Chris. "Nationalism and Civil Society in Central Europe: From Ruritania to the Carpathian Euroregion." In *The State of the Nation: Ernest Gellner and the Theory of Nationalism*, ed. John A. Hall, 243–57. Cambridge: Cambridge University Press, 1998.

Hannerz, Ulf. "Cosmopolitans and Locals in World Culture." In *Global Culture: Nationalism, Globalization and Modernity*, ed. Mike Featherstone, 237–51. London: Sage, 1997.

Hausheer, Roger. Introduction to *The Proper Study of Mankind*, ed. Henry Hardy and Roger Hausheer, xxiii–xxxvi. London: Chatto and Windus, 1997.

Havel, Václav. "Words on Words." *New York Review of Books*, 18 January 1990, p. 80.

Held, David. "Democracy, the Nation-State and the Global System." *Economy and Society* 20, no. 2 (May 1991): 138–72.

Herdman, John. "Politics." In *Whither Scotland: A Prejudiced Look at the Future of a Nation*, ed. Duncan Glen, 103–11. London: Victor Gollancz, 1971.

Hitchens, Christopher. "Moderation or Death." *London Review of Books*, 26 November 1998, pp. 3–11.

Hobsbawm, E. J. *Nations and Nationalism since 1780*. Cambridge: Cambridge University Press, 1991.

Hobsbawm, E. J. "Some Reflections on 'The Break-Up of Britain'." *New Left Review*, no. 105 (September/October 1977): 3–23.

Holmes, Stephen. "Liberalism for a World of Ethnic Passions and Decaying States." *Social Research* 61, no. 3 (Fall 1994): 599–610.

Honig, Bonnie. "Difference, Dilemmas, and the Politics of Home." In *Democracy and Difference*, ed. Seyla Benhabib, 257–77. Princeton: Princeton University Press, 1996.

Ignatieff, Michael. *Blood and Belonging: Journeys into the New Nationalism*. New York: Farrar, Straus, and Giroux, 1993.

———. *Isaiah Berlin: A Life*. New York: Henry Holt, 1998.

———. *The Warrior's Honor: Ethnic War and the Modern Conscience*. New York: Henry Holt, 1997.

Jahanbegloo, Ramin. *Conversations with Isaiah Berlin*. New York: Scribner, 1991.

James, Paul. *Nation Formation: Towards a Theory of Abstract Community*. London: Sage, 1996.

Kaldor, Mary. "Cosmopolitanism versus Nationalism: The New Divide?" In *Europe's New Nationalism*, ed. Richard Caplan and John Feffer, 42–58. Oxford: Oxford University Press, 1996.

Kaplan, Caren. *Questions of Travel: Postmodern Discourses of Displacement*. Durham: Duke University Press, 1996.

Kateb, George. "Can Cultures Be Judged? Two Defenses of Cultural Pluralism in Isaiah Berlin's Work." *Social Research* 66, no. 4 (Winter 1999): 1009–38.

Kaufmann, Dorothy. "Simone de Beauvoir: Questions of Difference and Generation." In *Simone de Beauvoir: Witness to a Century*, ed. Hélène Vivienne Wenzel, 121–31. Yale French Studies, no. 72. New Haven: Yale University Press, 1986.

Kedourie, Elie. *Nationalism*. 4th ed. Oxford: Blackwell, 1993 (1960).

Kymlicka, Will. "Misunderstanding Nationalism." In *Theorizing Nationalism*, ed. Ronald Beiner, 131–40. Albany: State University of New York Press, 1999.

———. *Multicultural Citizenship*. Oxford: Oxford University Press, 1996 (1995).

Lamming, George. *The Pleasures of Exile*. New York: Allison and Busby, 1984.

Levinson, Sanford. "Is Liberal Nationalism an Oxymoron? An Essay for Judith Shklar." *Ethics* 105 (April 1995): 626–45.

Lichtenberg, Judith. "How Liberal Can Nationalism Be?" *The Philosophical Forum: Philosophical Perspectives on National Identity* 28, nos. 1–2 (Fall/Winter 1996–97): 53–72.

Luxemburg, Rosa. *The Accumulation of Capital*. (1913.) London: Routledge, 1963.

————. *The National Question: Selected Writings by Rosa Luxemburg.* Ed. Horace B. Davis. New York: Monthly Review Press, 1976.

————. *"The Russian Revolution" and "Leninism or Marxism?"* Ann Arbor: University of Michigan Press, 1961.

Mack, Eric. "Isaiah Berlin and the Quest for Liberal Pluralism." *Public Affairs Quarterly* 7, no. 3 (July 1993): 215–30.

Mandelbaum, Michael, ed. *The New European Diasporas.* New York: The Council on Foreign Relations Press, 2000.

Marx, Karl. *Capital.* Vol. 1. (1867.) New York: International Publishers, 1974.

————. *The Communist Manifesto.* (1848.) New York: W. W. Norton, 1988.

————. "Critique of the Gotha Program." (Written, 1875; first published, 1891.) In *The Marx-Engels Reader*, 2d ed., ed. Robert Tucker, 525–41. New York: W. W. Norton, 1978.

————. *Economic and Philosophic Manuscripts of 1844.* In *Karl Marx Frederick Engels Collected Works.* Vol. 3, "1843–1844," 229–346. New York: International Publishers, 1975.

————. "The Eighteenth Brumaire of Louis Bonaparte." In *Karl Marx Frederick Engels Collected Works.* Vol. 11, "1851–1853," 99–197. New York: International Publishers, 1979.

————. "The Future Results of British Rule in India." (1853.) In *The Marx-Engels Reader*, 2d ed., ed. Robert Tucker, 659–64. New York: W. W. Norton, 1978.

————. *Grundrisse.* (Written, 1857–58; first published, 1939–41.) New York: Vintage, 1973.

————. Introduction to *Contribution to the Critique of Hegel's "Philosophy of Right."* (1844.) In *The Marx-Engels Reader*, 2d ed., ed. Robert Tucker, 53–65. New York: W. W. Norton, 1978.

————. *The Letters of Karl Marx.* Ed. Saul K. Padover. Englewood Cliffs, NJ: Prentice-Hall, 1979.

————. "On the Jewish Question." In *Karl Marx Frederick Engels Collected Works.* Vol. 3, "1843–1844," 146–74. New York: International Publishers, 1975.

————. Preface to *A Contribution to the Critique of Political Economy.* (1859.) In *Karl Marx: Selected Writings*, ed. David McLellan. Oxford: Oxford University Press, 1977.

Marx, Karl, and Frederich Engels. *The German Ideology.* (Written 1845–46; first published, 1932.) New York: International Publishers, 1969.

————. *The Marx-Engels Reader.* 2d ed. Ed. Robert Tucker. New York: W. W. Norton, 1978.

Mayall, James. *Nationalism and International Society.* Cambridge: Cambridge University Press, 1990.

Mazower, Mark. *Dark Continent: Europe's Twentieth Century.* New York: Knopf, 1999.

Mill, John Stuart. *On Liberty.* In *Three Essays*, 5–141. Oxford: Oxford University Press, 1975 (1859).

Mosse, George. *Confronting the Nation: Jewish and Western Nationalism.* Hanover, NH: Brandeis University Press, 1993.

Munck, Ronaldo. *The Difficult Dialogue: Marxism and Nationalism.* London: Zed Books, 1986.

Naipaul, V. S. *Among the Believers.* New York: Knopf, 1981.

———. *A Bend in the River.* New York: Penguin, 1980.

———. *The Enigma of Arrival.* New York: Knopf, 1987.

———. *Finding the Center.* New York: Knopf, 1984.

———. *India: A Million Mutinies Now.* New York: Viking, 1990.

———. "A Million Mutinies." *India Today*, 16 August 1997, pp. 20–22.

———. "Our Universal Civilization." *New York Review of Books*, 31 January 1991, pp. 22–24.

———. "Prologue to an Autobiography." In *Finding the Center*, 1–72. New York: Knopf, 1984.

———. "Rednecks." *New York Review of Books*, 22 December 1988, pp. 8–12.

———. *The Return of Eva Peron.* New York: Knopf, 1980.

Nairn, Tom. "All Bosnians Now?" *Dissent* 40 (Fall 1993): 403–10.

———. "Beyond Big Brother." *New Statesman & Society*, 15 June 1990, pp. 29–32.

———. *The Break-Up of Britain: Crisis and Neo-Nationalism.* London: New Left Books, 1977.

———. "Breakwaters of 2000: From Ethnic to Civic Nationalism." *New Left Review*, no. 214 (November/December 1995): 91–103.

———. "Cleaning Up." Review of *The Pol Pot Regime: Race, Power and Genocide in Cambodia*, by Ben Kiernan. *London Review of Books*, 3 October 1996, pp. 11–14.

———. "Demonizing Nationalism." *London Review of Books*, 5 February 1993, pp. 3–6.

———. "Does Tomorrow Belong to the Bullets or the Bouquets?" *Borderlands: Nations and Nationalism, Culture and Community in the New Europe.* Special supplement to *New Statesman & Society*, 19 June 1992, pp. 30–31.

———. *The Enchanted Glass: Britain and Its Monarchy.* London: Radius, 1988.

———. *Faces of Nationalism: Janus Revisited.* London: Verso, 1997.

———. "Internationalism and the Second Coming." *Daedalus* 122, no. 3 (Summer 1993): 155–70.

Nairn, Tom, and John Osmond. "This Land Is My Land, That Land Is Your land." *Borderlands: Nations and Nationalism, Culture and Community in the New Europe.* Special supplement to *New Statesman & Society,* 19 June 1992, pp. 3–5.

Namier, L. B. *Conflicts: Studies in Contemporary History.* London: Macmillan, 1942.

Nettl, Peter. *Rosa Luxemburg.* Oxford: Oxford University Press, 1966.

Nimni, Ephraim. *Marxism and Nationalism: Theoretical Origins of a Political Crisis.* London: Pluto Press, 1991.

Nixon, Rob. "London Calling: V. S. Naipaul and the License of Exile." *South Atlanta Quarterly* 87, no. 1 (Winter 1988): 1–37.

Nussbaum, Martha. "Patriotism and Cosmopolitanism." In *For Love of Country,* ed. Joshua Cohen, 2–17. Boston: Beacon Press, 1996.

Oakeshott, Michael. *Rationalism in Politics and Other Essays.* London: Methuen, 1984.

Parekh, Bhikhu. "The Incoherence of Nationalism." In *Theorizing Nationalism,* ed. Ronald Beiner, 295–325. Albany: State University of New York Press, 1999.

Parry, Benita. "Overlapping Territories and Intertwined Histories: Edward Said's Postcolonial Cosmopolitanism." In *Edward Said: A Critical Reader,* ed. Michael Sprinkler, 19–47. Oxford: Blackwell, 1992.

Piccone, Paul. "Confronting the French New Right: Old Prejudices or a New Political Paradigm?" *Telos,* nos. 98–99 (Winter/Spring 1993–94): 3–22.

Pines, Christopher. *Ideology and False Consciousness: Marx and His Historical Progenitors.* Albany: State University of New York Press, 1993.

Poole, Ross. "Freedom, Citizenship, and National Identity." *The Philosophical Forum: Perspectives on National Identity* 28, nos. 1–2 (Fall/Winter 1996–97): 125–48.

Radhakrishnan, R. *Diasporic Mediations: Between Home and Location.* Minneapolis: University of Minnesota Press, 1996.

Ring, Jennifer. *The Political Consequences of Thinking: Gender and Judaism in the Work of Hannah Arendt.* Albany: State University of New York Press, 1997.

Robbins, Bruce. "Introduction: Part I." In *Cosmopolitics: Thinking and Feeling beyond the Nation,* ed. Pheng Cheah and Bruce Robbins, 1–19. Minneapolis: University of Minnesota Press, 1998.

———. *Secular Vocations: Intellectuals, Professionalism, Culture.* London: Verso, 1993.

Rubenstein, Richard L. *The Cunning of History: The Holocaust and the American Future.* New York: Harper and Row, 1987 (1975).

Rushdie, Salman. Introduction to *The Vintage Book of Indian Writing 1947–1997,* ed. Salman Rushdie and Elizabeth West, ix–xxii. London: Vintage, 1997.

Said, Edward. "Bitter Dispatches from the Third World." Review of *The Return of Eva Peron* with *The Killings in Trinidad*, by V. S. Naipaul. *The Nation*, 3 May 1980, pp. 522–25.

———. *Culture and Imperialism*. New York: Knopf, 1993.

———. "Identity, Authority, and Freedom: The Potentate and the Traveler." In *The Future of Academic Freedom*, ed. Louis Menand, 214–28. Chicago: University of Chicago Press, 1996.

———. "Ignorant Armies Clash by Night." *The Nation*, 11 February 1991, front cover and pp. 160–63.

———. "Intellectuals in the Post-Colonial World." *Salmagundi: The Post-Colonial Intellectual* 70–71 (Spring/Summer 1986): 44–64.

———. "Interview with Edward Said." By Jennifer Wicke and Michael Sprinkler. In *Edward Said: A Critical Reader*, ed. Michael Sprinkler, 221–64. Oxford: Blackwell, 1992.

———. "Introduction: Secular Criticism." In *The World, the Text, and the Critic*, 1–30. Cambridge, MA: Harvard University Press, 1983.

———. "Narrative, Geography and Interpretation." *New Left Review*, no. 180 (March/April 1990): 81–97.

———. "Nationalism, Human Rights, and Interpretation." *Raritan* 12, no. 3 (Winter 1993): 26–51.

———. "On Palestinian Identity: A Conversation with Salman Rushdie." *New Left Review*, no. 160 (November/December 1986): 63–80.

———. "The One-State Solution." *New York Times Sunday Magazine*, 10 January 1999, pp. 36–39.

———. *Out of Place: A Memoir*. New York: Knopf, 1999.

———. *Peace and Its Discontents: Essays on Palestine in the Middle East Peace Process*. New York: Vintage, 1995.

———. *The Politics of Dispossession*. New York: Pantheon, 1994.

———. "The Politics of Knowledge." *Raritan* 11 (Summer 1991): 17–31.

———. "Protecting the Kosovars." *saga-owner@jrn.columbia.edu*.

———. "Reflections on Exile." *Granta* 13 (Autumn 1984): 159–72.

———. *Representations of the Intellectual*. New York: Pantheon, 1994.

———. "Third World Intellectuals and Metropolitan Culture." *Raritan* 9, no. 3 (Winter 1990): 27–50.

———. "Traveling Theory." In *The World, the Text and the Critic*, 226–47. Cambridge, MA: Harvard University Press, 1983.

———. *The World, the Text, and the Critic*. Cambridge, MA: Harvard University Press, 1983.

Scarry, Elaine. *The Body in Pain: The Making and Unmaking of the World*. Oxford: Oxford University Press, 1985.

Smith, Anthony D. *The Ethnic Origins of Nations*. Oxford: Blackwell, 1986.

———. *Theories of Nationalism*. London: Duckworth, 1971.

Smith, Paul. *Disraeli: A Brief Life*. Cambridge: Cambridge University Press, 1966.

Snyder, Jack. *From Voting to Violence: Democratization and Nationalist Conflict*. New York: W. W. Norton, 2000.

Sprinkler, Michael, ed. *Edward Said: A Critical Reader*. Oxford: Basil Blackwell, 1992.

Sternhell, Zeev. *The Founding Myths of Israel*. Princeton: Princeton University Press, 1998.

Stevens, Jacqueline. *Reproducing the State*. Princeton: Princeton University Press, 1999.

Szporluk, Roman. *Communism and Nationalism: Karl Marx versus Friedrich List*. Oxford: Oxford University Press, 1988.

Taguieff, Pierre-Andre. "From Race to Culture: The New Right's View of European Identity." *Telos*, nos. 98–99 (Winter/Spring 1993–94): 34–53.

Tamir, Yael. *Liberal Nationalism*. Princeton: Princeton University Press, 1993.

Taylor, Charles. "The Politics of Recognition." In *Multiculturalism*, ed. Amy Gutmann, 25–73. Princeton: Princeton University Press, 1994.

Thapar, Romula. "Imagined Religious Communities." *Modern Asian Studies* 23, no. 2 (1989): 209–31.

Theroux, Paul. *Sir Vidia's Shadow: A Friendship Across Five Continents*. New York: Houghton Mifflin, 1998.

Vulliamy, Ed. "Bosnia: The Crime of Appeasement." *International Affairs* 74, no. 1 (January 1998): 73–91.

Walker, Brian. "Modernity and Cultural Vulnerability: Should Ethnicity Be Privileged?" In *Theorizing Nationalism*, ed. Ronald Beiner, 141–65. Albany: State University of New York Press, 1999.

Walzer, Michael. *On Toleration*. New Haven: Yale University Press, 1997.

Wieseltier, Leon. "Isaiah Berlin, 1909–1997: When a Sage Dies, All Are His Kin." *The New Republic*, 1 December 1997, 27–31.

Williams, Raymond. *The Country and the City*. New York: Oxford University Press, 1973.

——. *Marxism and Literature*. Oxford: Oxford University Press, 1977.

Woodward, Susan. "Diaspora, or the Dangers of Disunification? Putting the 'Serbian Model' into Perspective." In *The New European Diasporas*, ed. Michael Mandelbaum, 159–213. New York: The Council on Foreign Relations Press, 2000.

Yack, Bernie. "The Myth of the Civic Nation." *Critical Review* 10, no. 2 (Spring 1996): 193–211.

——. "Reconciling Liberalism and Nationalism." Review of *Nationalism: Five Roads to Modernity*, by Liah Greenfeld; *Nations without Nationalism*, by Julia Kristeva; and *Liberal Nationalism*, by Yael Tamir. *Political Theory* 23, no. 1 (February 1995): 166–82.

Index